THE UK AND EIRE Internet
starter kit

2001 edition

THE UK AND EIRE
Internet
starter kit

2001 edition

ROB YOUNG

An imprint of Pearson Education
London ■ New York ■ Toronto ■ Sydney ■ Tokyo ■ Singapore
Madrid ■ Mexico City ■ Munich ■ Paris

PEARSON EDUCATION LIMITED

Head Office:
Edinburgh Gate
Harlow CM20 2JE
Tel: +44 (0)1279 623623
Fax: +44 (0)1279 431059

London Office:
128 Long Acre
London WC2E 9AN
Tel: +44 (0)20 7447 2000
Fax: +44 (0)20 7240 5771

First published in Great Britain in 2001

Pearson Education has made every effort to seek permission to reproduce the screenshots used in this book. The Publishers
wish to thank the following for permission to reproduce material: Allaire Corporation, BBC Online, Big Save UK Ltd,
Bonus.com, Emap Online, The Flash Team, Ginger Media Group, Ipswitch, JobSearch UK, Live Update, Look.net, LLC,
Maps.com, Microsoft Corporation, Mirago, mirc.com, MoneyWorld UK Ltd, Movie Web, Naturenet, Neosoft, NetBanx Ltd,
New Scientist, One Look Dictionaries, The Paris Pages, Purple Interactive, a division of Purple Trading Ltd, QXL.com plc,
Qualcomm, Inc, SFA State University, Kevin Savetz, Surf.To, Peter Tanis, Tesco, Thawte.com, UK Online, UK Politics, UK
Plus, Visualization Group, Yahoo!, Yellow Pages, WSGopher, WS Ping Propack, Yorkdale Ltd (The UK Shopping City), The
Zone Ltd and Mania and the United States Department of Energy, Idaho National Engineering Engineering and
Environmental Laboratory.

'My Rules for Online Safety' on page 203 are from *Child Safety on the Information Highway* by Lawrence J. Magid. It is
reprinted with kind permission of the National Center for Missing and Exploited Children (NCMEC). Copyright ©
NCMEC 1994. All rights reserved. The screenshot on page 298 is reproduced with permission of CyberDiet. © 1999
CyberDiet. The screenshots on pages 88, 171 and 242 are reproduced by permission of Lycos. © 2000 Lycos, Inc. Lycos® is a
registered trademark of Carnegie Mellon University. All rights reserved. © Gamesville, Inc, a Lycos Network site. All rights
reserved. The screenshot on page 61 is reproduced by permission of The Natural History Museum © The Natural History
Museum, London, 2000. The WinZip screen image on page 194 is reproduced with permission of WinZip Computing, Inc.
Copyright 1991-2000, WinZip Computing, Inc. WinZip is available from *www.winzip.com*. WinZip® is a registered trademark
of WinZip Computing, Inc. The Top 50 UK Web Sites screenshot on page 93 is from Zebra Communications.

British Library Cataloguing in Publication Data
A catalogue record for this book is available from the British Library.

ISBN 0-13-033987-3 (pbk)

1 2 3 4 5   03 02 01 00 99

Typeset by Pantek Arts Ltd, Maidstone, Kent.
Printed and bound by Biddles of Guildford and King's Lynn.

The publishers' policy is to use paper manufactured from sustainable forests.

CONTENTS

Contents ▶

INTRODUCTION

The Internet really hit the headlines in 1994. People started talking about it, newspapers started writing articles about it, and those weird-looking addresses full of dots and dashes started popping up at the end of TV shows and adverts. *Ah yes*, everyone said, knowingly. *Hype. It'll be something different next year*. But something unexpected happened…

Unlike most other objects of media hype in recent years, after the dust has settled, millions of people are still using the Internet every day – for entertainment, for business, for leisure, to communicate with others, to learn or research, to buy goods, the list is almost endless. And every day the number of people using the Internet grows by thousands. If these people weren't finding it useful or enjoyable, that number would instead be getting smaller.

These people can't all be computer whiz-kids either, can they? In fact, you don't have to be a technical genius to use the Internet. As long as you're reasonably comfortable with using a PC and Windows, it's no more tricky than anything else you use your computer for. That's the thing that really happened in 1994: although the Internet has been around since the 1960s, in 1994 software that made it friendly and easy to use started to appear.

But that's history, and I'm not going to bore you with lengthy history lessons, or throw a lot of impressive but unnecessary jargon at you. The aim of this book is twofold – first, to help you connect your computer to the Internet and find your way around it, and second, to point you towards the practical, useful, or just plain fun things that the Internet has to offer. To that end, any technical detail that you won't need straight away has been banished to the back of the book. In fact, you may never need all that technical detail at all!

Why Do I Need A *UK* and *Eire* Guide To The Internet?

In the UK and Eire we use the Internet differently from our American counterparts: different companies provide the services we need, charge different prices for them, and give us different options to choose from. And once we're connected, we want to find the information that matters to us, so we need to look in different places to find it. In addition, because we're not from the USA (or France, or Italy, etc.), our interests, habits, laws, environment, and whole way of life differ enormously. These affect both the way we use the Internet, and what we use it for.

▶ Most American users have access to free local phone calls, which means that they can stay connected to the Internet all day long for no extra charge. In the UK, where most of us still pay by the minute, to follow some of the suggestions given in an American guide could end up costing a small fortune! Throughout this book, it's assumed that you want your time on the Internet to have as little impact as possible on the size of your phone bill.

▶ As a local user, you want to find local information. For example, you want to read local newspapers and magazines; see local weather forecasts; check local TV listings and sports results; find out what's showing at your nearest cinema; use local travel agents, hotels, airlines and trains, plan days out at local theme parks and museums, and so on.

▶ Many Internet sites give support, help and advice on any subject you can imagine. Although some American Internet books can point you towards valuable information, they won't tell you where to get the best UK and Eire legal or consumer advice, find a job, or discuss financial matters with other UK and Eire investors.

▶ You can now buy almost anything from 'cyberstores' on the Internet. But do you really want to do your shopping in dollars and wait for the goods to be shipped from America when there are plenty of UK and Eire shopping sites just a couple of mouse clicks away? In fact, if you want to use the Internet to arrange car insurance, manage your bank account, or book theatre tickets, among other things, you'll have to find the right sites in the UK and Eire!

How Is This Book Organised?

This book is split into six major parts to help you find the answers you want quickly and easily.

Part 1, *Getting Online*, introduces all the basic concepts and services of the Internet, helps you choose the type of Internet account that suits you best, and tells you what you need to know to get online.

Part 2, *Finding Your Way Around*, shows you the main services you can use on the Internet, and the software you'll need to access them. All of this software can be found on the CD-ROM in the back of this book (as well as on the Internet itself), and these chapters explain how to set it up and how to use it.

Part 3, *Using The Internet*, gives an in-depth guide to using your connection and software to accomplish something on the Internet, such as reading online newspapers and magazines, doing research, shopping, planning days out, finding computer software, managing your bank account, or just having heaps of fun.

Part 4, *The Web – Active & Interactive*, introduces you to multimedia on the Internet, and leads you to some of the weird, wonderful and exotic locations on the World Wide Web. You'll also learn how to design your own World Wide Web pages and publish them for the rest of the world to see.

The *Appendices* section includes handy references, lists and glossaries, and a 'JargonBuster Super Reference' to help you decipher what everyone's talking about!

The *Directory* is a useful collection of contact details for companies that provide access to the Internet, sell computer software and hardware, or offer other computer-related services.

How Should I Use It?

This book is organised in such a way that you can read it from cover to cover if you want to, but you certainly don't have to. I like books that you can dip into and learn something new from by reading just a couple of paragraphs, so don't feel guilty if you like to do that too! You'll find plenty of cross-references to tempt you towards other parts of the book. However, I do have a few suggestions:

▶ If you haven't yet connected to the Internet and you don't have an Internet account, I recommend that you read the first two parts of the book which will help you get online and give you all the basic information in a sensible order.

▶ If you already have an Internet connection, you can cheerfully skip Part 1 and begin with Part 2, which will get you started on the road to mastering the Internet's services and software.

▶ If you've been using the Internet's tools and services for a while and you know the basics, skip about the book all you like. You might still find some things you didn't know in Part 2, but I suggest taking a look at Parts 3 and 4 – you'll find plenty of great sites to visit, together with information and tips to help you get the most out of the Internet, design and publish your own Web pages, explore virtual worlds online, and lots more.

Icons & Conventions

Throughout the book I've used a few special features and conventions that make it easier to find your way around. In particular you'll notice that chapters are split up into bite-sized chunks with subheadings. If something looks a bit complicated or dull, just skip to the next heading.

You'll also find some icons and text in boxes containing extra information that you may find useful:

 A question-and-answer format highlighting questions or problems that might present themselves while you're reading about something or trying it out yourself.

 A selection of handy hints, tips and incidental notes that might save you some time, point you in a new direction, or help you avoid a few pitfalls.

 Explains any technical terms that couldn't be avoided, or any related jargon that you may encounter when dealing with a particular area of the Internet.

Indicates that the software program being mentioned is included on the free CD-ROM attached to the inside back cover of this book.

I've also used different type-styles and keyboard conventions to make particular meanings clear, as shown below.

Convention	Description
bold type	Indicates a new term being encountered, an Internet address, or text that you'll type yourself.
bold-italic type	Means that you'll type this text yourself, but I don't know exactly what it will be. For example, if you have to type the location of a file you want to open, you'll see something like ***open directory/filename***.
Ctrl+C	A key-combination, saving frequent mouse excursions to pull-down menus. The keys to press will be separated by '+' signs. This example means press and hold the 'Ctrl' key while pressing 'C' once.
**File	Open**	Means that you should open the software's 'File' menu, and select its 'Open' option. You might see something longer, such as View	Options	General: in this case you'll open the 'View' menu, select the 'Options' entry and then click on something that says 'General' – it may be a button or a tabbed page, but it will always be obvious when you get there!
Enter	Although I've referred to the 'Enter' key throughout, on your keyboard this key might be labelled 'Return' instead.
Directories	To users of Windows 95 and later, these are better known as 'folders'. On the Internet (just as in MS-DOS and Windows 3.x) they're known as 'directories', but the meaning is the same.

A Few Basic Assumptions

Finally, I'm assuming that you know how to use a computer and you're reasonably familiar with the different parts of Windows. By that, I mean that you know how to use the mouse, you understand what directories and files are, you're comfortable with using menus and dialogs, and you know how to start programs and switch between windows. If you get stuck, you can usually find the answers in Windows' Help files, but for a solid grounding in how to use your computer and Windows, grab a copy of my book, *The UK PC Starter Kit*, also published by Prentice Hall.

1

GETTING ONLINE

▶ **IN THIS PART**

MEET THE INTERNET

Before you can really get excited at the prospect of 'getting on the Internet', it helps to have some idea of what it really is, what you can use it for, and (I hate to say it) how it works. So let's kick off by looking at how the Internet is organised, and at some of the ways you can use it. I'm also going to introduce most of the technical-sounding stuff you'll need to know in this chapter. It's all quite painless, though, and hopefully this appetiser will leave you hungry for the main course.

What Is The Internet?

This is the obvious first question, but let's try and skip through its literal answer as quickly as possible. The technical explanation is that it's a giant, worldwide computer network made up of lots of smaller computer networks. As with any network, these computers are connected to one another so that they can share information. Unlike most networks, though, the vastness of the Internet means that this information has to be passed around using modems and telephone lines rather than an office full of cables.

But all that's just hardware, and it's probably not making your mouth water. Instead, let's zoom in on that word 'information', the key to the *real* Internet. The types of information these computers can share covers a huge (and expanding) range – pictures, sounds, text, video, applications, music, and much more – making the Internet a true multimedia experience. Anyone can connect their computer to the Internet and gain instant access to millions of files, browse around, or search for some specific item, and grab as much as they want while they're there.

GOOD QUESTION!

How big is the Internet?

When it comes to numbers, no one knows. A lot of informed guesswork goes on, but it doesn't look terribly well informed when you compare results. It's safest just to say that millions of computers are serving several hundred million people, and leave it at that. To be honest, even if I could give you the exact numbers right now, they'd be wrong by lunchtime and wildly inaccurate before *EastEnders* started.

People Power

The other aspect of the real Internet is people. All the information you'll find is put there by real people, often simply because they want to share their knowledge, skills, interests or creations with anyone who's interested. The people themselves may be companies keen to promote their products; organisations such as universities, charities and governments; or individual users like you and me.

Along with people, of course, comes communication, and the Internet is a great communications system. You can exchange messages (email) with other users, as you'll see in Chapter 8, hold conversations or online meetings by typing messages back and forth, or actually send your voice over the Internet using a microphone instead of a telephone (which we'll investigate in Chapter 10). You can take part in any of fifty thousand discussion groups on any subject you'd care to mention (and quite a few more you wouldn't!), and you'll find out how in Chapter 9. Add to this the wealth of human knowledge and experience that lies at its heart, and the Internet is, quite simply, a very big place that makes the world seem much smaller.

What Can I Use It For?

Once you're armed with a connection to the Internet, the possibilities for using it could fill a book. (Well okay, they do fill a book – that's why you picked it up!) Here's just a tiny sample of the things you can do on the Net, all of which you'll be learning about later:

▶ Control robots and movie cameras on other continents while the live camera footage is beamed straight to your desktop.

▶ Book a skiing holiday online, and check the snow conditions in your chosen resort with up-to-the-minute pictures.

▶ Hold conversations with people on the other side of the world by typing on your keyboard, talking into a microphone, or adopting the role of a cartoon character.

▶ Chat one-to-one with friends and colleagues anywhere in the world and see, at a glance, which friends are online at the same time as you are.

▶ Manage your bank account, transfer money, and pay bills at any time of the day or night, or do all your shopping in online supermarkets and stores.

▶ Read magazines and newspapers online, along with books, dictionaries, encyclopaedias, thesauri, and every type of reference you could dream of.

▶ Download the latest versions and updates of your software long before they hit the shops, or be among the first to use brand new 'test editions' of major software titles (known as **beta releases**).

JARGON BUSTER

Download

The act of copying a file from one distant computer across a network of computers and telephone lines to your own hard disk. The opposite term is 'upload' – copying a file from your own disk to a remote computer.

▶ *And a microscopic taste of the rest*: Do you need legal advice or a map of the Cotswolds? Are you looking for a new job or an old master? Do you want a picture of your favourite rock star or the price of the latest Jaguar? Do you need a car-insurance quote or a change of diet? You get the idea…

The Magnificent Seven – Popular Internet Services

What you've just read is a general taste of what's on offer on the Net, but all the things you want to do (or get, or see) will be scattered around the world on different computers. In other words, these computers offer the *services* you want to use. The Internet is made up of a bundle of different services, but here's a quick look at the seven most popular:

▶ **email.** email is the oldest and most used of the Internet services with millions of messages whizzing around it every day. Most email messages are just ordinary text, but you can attach almost any type of computer file you want to send along with it (such as a spreadsheet or a small program), and encrypt the message so that no one except the intended recipient will be able to read it.

▶ **The World Wide Web.** This service, often known simply as the Web, has had so much publicity and acclaim that you may think it *is* the Internet. In fact it's just one area of the Internet, but it's the one that gave the Net mass appeal when it appeared in the early 1990s, packed with pictures, text, video, music, and information about every subject under the sun. All the pages on the Web are linked together, so that a page you're viewing from a computer in Bristol might lead you to a page in Tokyo, Brisbane or Oslo with a single mouse click. Many individual users have their own pages on the Web, along with multinational companies, political parties, universities and colleges, football teams, local councils, and so on.

▶ **Newsgroups.** A newsgroup is a discussion group that focuses on one particular subject. The discussion itself takes place through a form of email, but the big difference is that these messages are posted for the whole group to read and respond to. You can join any group you like from a choice of over 50 000, with subjects ranging from spina bifida support to alien landings, James Bond films to Turkish culture.

▶ **Chat.** This isn't chat as in 'yakety-yak', more 'clickety-click'. You can hold conversations with one or more people by typing messages back and forth which instantly appear on the screens of everyone involved. Some recent chat programs allow 'whiteboarding' (drawing pictures and diagrams in collaboration), private online conferences, and control of programs running on someone else's computer.

▶ **Internet telephony.** This *is* chat as in 'yakety-yak'. As long as you've got a soundcard in your computer, and a microphone plugged into it, you can talk to anyone in the world just as you do with the telephone. Add a web-camera to that setup and you can make video phone calls (albeit with rather jerky video). Best of all, an Internet phone call to Australia will cost you little more than an ordinary phone call to your next-door neighbour.

▶ **FTP.** The computers that make up the Internet hold a combined library of millions upon millions of files. The FTP system lets you look inside directories on some of these computers and copy files straight to your hard disk just as if you were copying files around between your own directories.

▶ **Archie.** (Yes, really, Archie!). Copying files from some distant computer to your own using FTP really is as straightforward as I just made it sound. But first you've got to track down the file you want which, if it exists at all, may exist on only one computer in the whole world. Don't even try – ask Archie instead, he'll usually find it in seconds.

Although other services exist, these are almost certainly the ones you'll be using most (and you may use nothing but email and the World Wide Web – the services are there if you want them, but you don't have to use them).

Understanding Internet Addresses

So the Internet is big, the computers that form the Internet are counted in millions, and yet somehow all that information manages to get to wherever it's supposed to go. But how does that tiny, helpless file find its way from deepest Ohio to your own computer all by itself?

The answer is in much the same way that an ordinary letter manages to arrive at your house: it has an address attached to it that identifies one single house in the whole world. Every single computer on the Internet has a unique address, called its IP address, which consists of four numbers separated by dots, such as 132.185.132.204.

JARGON BUSTER

IP address

'IP' stands for Internet Protocol. IP works with its best friend, TCP, to handle the tricky job of sending computer files down telephone lines, and part of this job is knowing which computer is asking for the file and which is sending it. Is it really as exciting as it sounds? Yes, almost exactly. But if you still want to know more about TCP, IP, and protocols in general, skip ahead to the glossary on page 389.

Domain Names – The Easier Way

Of course, if you need to connect to one of these computers you'll need to know its address. But don't panic! You don't have to remember streams of meaningless numbers: there's an easy way. As well as this numerical IP address, each computer is given a much friendlier domain name. Going back to that IP address I mentioned, the domain name of that computer is the much more memorable *bbc.co.uk*. Best of all, most of the Internet programs you'll be using will store these addresses for you so that you can just recall them with a couple of mouse clicks.

Talking in dots

If you're ever in that awkward situation where you have to say a domain name out loud, use the word 'dot' to replace the dot itself (as in 'bbc dot co dot uk' for *bbc.co.uk*). This has even led to the invention of a new word: a *dotcom* is one of a new breed of Web-based companies whose name is the same as its Internet address, so invariably ends with a **.com**.

The function of the domain name is just to make life less complicated for Internet users. The computers themselves still use that numerical IP address. Whenever you want to connect to a computer somewhere on the Internet, you'll type its domain name into your software (or perhaps select it from a list of your favourites). The domain name is sent to another computer called a **domain name server** (DNS). The job of the DNS is to find the 'numbers and dots' IP address of the computer that uses that nickname and send it back to your computer. It might sound cumbersome, but this conversation between computers should happen very quickly. You probably won't be aware that it's happening, but you'd certainly be aware it it stopped happening!

Dissecting Domain Names

Apart from being a lot easier to remember than numbers, domain names can also tell you whose computer you're connected to, what type of organisation they are, and where the computer is located. The 'who' part is usually easy: given an address like **www.bbc.co.uk**, the computer almost certainly belongs to the BBC TV company. It's the bits that come after the easily recognisable part of the name (known as **top-level domains**) that can be interesting, so here's a few to look out for:

Domain	Used by
.co	a commercial company
.com	until recently, an American company; now also used for companies outside the States
.ac	an academic establishment (college, university, etc.)
.edu	another college or university domain
.gov	a government agency
.mil	a military establishment
.net	a company specialising in Internet-related services
.org	an organisation (as opposed to a commercial company)

Room for more on top

Back in 1997 it was announced that a few more top-level domains were to be added. Although they've been a long time coming, we should eventually see businesses using **.firm**, information services using **.info**, consumer retailers using **.store**, and individuals using **.nom**, among others.

American domain names stop at this point (that's one way to tell they *are* American). Domain names in other countries have an added country code after the **.co** (or instead of it), so you'll see **.uk** for United Kingdom, **. se** for Sweden, **.fr** for France, **. jp** for Japan, and **.de** for Germany. Sometimes the country code gives an indication of the origin of the company or organisation, but not always: domain names have become as valuable as trademarks, and many companies try to register domain names in all the countries they trade in.

Getting Everything To Work Together

At this point you've jumped the last fence on the technical background course, and you're blazing down the final straight. There are just three more elements that should be mentioned – **clients**, **servers** and **protocols**. These are the vital ingredients that, when mixed together, give you access to all the Internet's services.

▶ The client is a software program that you run on your own computer to access a particular service. For example, if you want to send and receive email messages you'll need an email client; if you want to browse the World Wide Web you'll need a web client. These all look and work in much the same way as any other program you already use on your computer, and you can pick, choose and swap programs until you find the ones you're most comfortable using.

▶ The server is a computer owned by whoever provides your Internet access, but servers work in a similar way to clients. When you're dealing with email, your email client will contact the mail server; when you want to look at a page on the World Wide Web, your web client will ask the web server to fetch it from wherever it is in the world and send it down the line to you.

▶ The word 'protocols' popped up a couple of pages back – to mere mortals they're dull as ditchwater, but they're the vital link in the chain that makes everything work. These protocols (you won't be surprised to hear) are known by bunches of initial letters like HTTP, SMTP and NNTP.

Protocol

JARGON BUSTER

When two computers need to communicate but don't speak the same language, they follow a set of rules called a 'protocol', just as a Czech and a Frenchman who don't speak each other's language may still be able to communicate in Spanish. For example, your email program will talk to the mail server in a language called SMTP (Simple Mail Transport Protocol) whenever you want to send an email message.

IT'S ON THE CD

You may need to know which protocol is which when you're setting up your Internet connection or installing new client programs, but the rest of the time it's all just technical drivel. If you do need to know, you'll find it all explained in the 'JargonBuster Super Reference' in Appendix D and on the CD-ROM.

2

HOW CAN I
GET ONLINE?

Congratulations – you've waded through all the technical stuff and emerged unscathed! In this chapter you'll find out about the different ways you can go online and surf the Net, the decisions you'll need to make about how you want to do it, and the pros and cons of the two connection options.

Where Can I Get Internet Access?

There are several ways to get access to the Internet, and at least one of them is available to you immediately:

▶ **Set up your own Internet connection.** This is the option you probably want to take, and the rest of this part of the book is devoted to making it happen. With your own computer connected to the Internet, you can use all its services whenever you want to.

▶ **Visit a cyber café.** These cafés and converted pubs have been springing up all over the place in the last couple of years, offering coffee, beer, Twiglets and Internet access. If you're not convinced that the Internet is for you, cyber cafés offer valuable hands-on experience. Expect to pay around £6 per hour, and try to book time in advance (especially at lunchtimes, evenings and weekends). Turn to page 436 for a list of UK cyber cafés.

▶ **Use your account at work.** Some companies have an Internet connection to their own internal network to take advantage of its email, research, and long-distance collaboration opportunities. Be warned, though – if you spend your working hours surfing the Net for pleasure, your boss can still find out exactly where you've been, regardless of the care you've taken to cover your tracks!

▶ **Use your college account.** Many universities and colleges provide use of computers with Internet connections for their students. As long as you can avoid doing something as rash as graduating you'll enjoy unlimited free access.

What Do I Need?

That's the first decision taken care of – you want your own private Internet connection. The next step is to consult the checklist and see which of the required bits and pieces you're missing. Actually, it's a very short list: you'll need a telephone line, a computer, a modem, and an Internet access account. Let's look at each one in a little more detail.

Telephone Line

Just an ordinary phone line, with a socket fairly close to your computer so that you can plug your modem into it. For a pound or two you can buy an adapter to let you plug a phone and a modem into the same socket which is a worthwhile investment. If you find yourself spending a lot of time online, you may want to consider installing a second phone line just for Internet access so that people can still telephone you while you're surfing (or upgrade to BT's Home Highway service, which we'll come to in a moment) but that's a decision for later. In the meantime, a cheaper alternative for British Telecom subscribers is the Call Minder service, which can take messages from callers when your line is engaged.

Turn off Call Waiting!

If you have the Call Waiting service on your phone line, make sure you turn if off (by dialling **# 43 #**) every time you go online and back on again (*** 43 #**) when you've finished. Otherwise, an incoming call at the wrong moment could disconnect you and cancel anything you were doing (particularly irritating if you were waiting for a huge file to download and were just seconds from completion!).

Computer

Yes, you knew you needed a computer! But a common misconception is that you've got to have a fast, powerful computer to surf the Net. In fact, almost any computer will be up to the task. I do have a few suggestions that will enrich your online time though:

▶ Windows 95 and later have built-in support for Internet connections that make all the setting-up and connecting happen smoothly and simply.

- ▶ To hear the Internet's musical offerings and use Internet telephony software (see Chapter 10) you'll need a soundcard.

- ▶ To enjoy the World Wide Web at its graphical, vibrant best, you'll be happiest with at least a high-colour, 800×600 display. On modern computers that's a standard setup, so don't worry if that's all Greek to you!

- ▶ Finally, a large hard disk. It's not vital – you'll have to install a few new programs but they won't take more than a few megabytes – but you'll find it hard to resist downloading some of the free or inexpensive software you'll find on the Net!

Modem

The modem is the device that converts the information on a computer into sound that can be sent down a phone line, and converts it back to meaningful information again when it gets to the other end. The most important thing to look at when buying a modem is its speed – how much information it can move around per second. The faster your modem (in theory, at least), the quicker you'll get everything done that you planned to do, cutting your phone bill and any online charges as a result.

GOOD QUESTION!

Is fast Internet access really worth the extra money?

Generally speaking, yes it is. But you've heard the term 'superhighway' used to describe the Internet. Like any highway, there's a lot of people all trying to get to the same place and things can get jammed solid, so while the user with slow access is gazing at his screen for some sign of information arriving, the user with fast access is doing just the same. But, when everything's running smoothly, a 56Kbps modem is streets ahead of a 33.6, and digital access is far better than analogue. You just have to decide how much the increased speed and reliability is worth to you as a Net user.

At the moment, the fastest modems shift data around at a maximum speed of 56Kbps (56 thousand bits per second). There have been slower models available in the past (28.8Kbps and 33.6Kbps could still be bought until recently) but the price of the 56K modem has fallen to rock bottom, so no one's building the slower models any more, other than as PC Card devices for notebook computers. Slower modems really are a false economy: if you connect to the Net for more than a few minutes a week at these speeds you'll be miserable. Most new desktop computers come with a built-in modem (some notebook and handheld computers do too), but if you do have to buy one, avoid anything slower than a 56Kbps model.

You'll also get a choice between an internal and an external model. Although the external modem is slightly more expensive I'd go for it every time. It's much easier to install (just plug in the phone cable, serial cable and main plug), and the lights on the front make it easier to tell what's going on.

Turbo-charge your modem

Data passing into and out of your computer through the modem is compressed, so make sure you squeeze the most out of it. Find the settings for the serial (COM) port that your modem is plugged into, and change the port speed to at least double your modem's rated speed (e.g. 115 200 for a 56Kbps modem).

Internet Access Account

With all the necessary hardware bits and bobs in place, the final thing you need is a way to connect to a computer that's a part of the Internet. There are hundreds of UK companies who specialise in selling dial-up connections to the Internet (in fact, since late 1998 a number of companies have even started providing *free* connections), so the next step is to choose one of these companies and set up an account with them.

This leads to the final decision you have to make: do you want an account with an **Internet service provider** (often just called an ISP) or with an **online service?**

Online Services & Internet Service Providers – What's the Difference?

The most important thing that service providers and the major online services have in common is that they both let you connect to the Internet. It's the way they do it and what else they have to offer that makes them different, along with their methods of deciding how much you should pay. To round off this chapter, and to help you decide which path to follow, let's take a look at the two options and the pros and cons of each.

Online Services

You may have heard of the two biggest online services, **America Online** (AOL) and **CompuServe** (CSi). In fact, if you buy computer magazines, you're probably snowed under with floppy disks and CD-ROMs inviting you to sign up to one or other of these. One of the main plus points about these online services is the speed and ease with which you can sign up: just this one disk and a credit or debit card number is all you need.

But it's important not to confuse online services with the Internet itself. An online service is rather like an exclusive club: once you subscribe you'll have access to a range of members only areas such as discussion forums, chat rooms and file libraries. Although you can 'escape' to the Internet from here, non-members can't get in. You won't find much in the members-only areas that you can't find on the Internet itself, but online services do have the combined benefits of ease of use, online help if you get lost, and a friendly all-in-one program from which you can reach everything you need. Although the Internet certainly isn't the chamber of horrors that some newspapers would have you believe, there's little control over what gets published there; online services carefully filter and control their members only content, making them the preferred choice for getting the whole family online.

How easy is it to connect to an online service?

I knew you'd ask, so I've just signed up with a major online service (I won't say which). It took 12 minutes from inserting the CD-ROM to officially 'arriving online'. Yes, I know, I've done it before; the point is that the most difficult thing I had to do was read those shiny numbers on my credit card.

So online services give you the Internet, plus a bit more. In the past, what counted against online services was the monthly charge, but with the arrival of free Internet service providers the online services have had to run to keep up. At the time of writing, America Online is charging a fixed £9.99 per month and subsidises the cost of your connection phone calls, leaving you with a flat rate of 1p per minute. By the time you read this, it should be possible to sign up for unmetered access through AOL (and perhaps other online services) at a fixed monthly rate with no call charges.

Finally, online services tend to offer Internet access as an 'extra' – when you step out onto the Net itself you may find that the information doesn't travel as quickly as it does on a direct Internet connection.

▶ *If an online service sounds like your preferred method of getting online, you might like to skip ahead to Chapter 4 to find out how to go about choosing one and connecting.*

Internet Service Providers

An Internet service provider (ISP) gives you access to the Internet, plain and simple. When you dial in to your access provider's computer, you'll see some sort of message on the screen that tells you you're connected, but you won't feel the earth move. Instead, you'll start your email program or your web software and start doing whatever it is you want to do.

The ISP account has several valuable points in its favour. The first is pricing: the competition among companies to gain subscribers means that you can now access the Internet without paying a penny (apart from your telephone bill, of course, although that's starting to change too. If you prefer to pay – and there may be reasons why you would, as we'll see in Chapter 3 – a single low monthly charge will give you unrestricted Internet access with extra charges for the time you spend online. Second, you'll have far greater flexibility in your choice of software. Most service providers will give you a bundle of programs when you sign up, but you don't have to use them – try some of the programs on the free CD-ROM accompanying this book, or others mentioned in later chapters, until you find the ones that you're most comfortable with.

GOOD QUESTION!

Free Internet access? What's the catch?

The main catch is that you'll be paying upwards of 50p per minute for calls to the company's help line if you get stuck. It's a pretty small catch though: you're not going to get stuck very often, and you may never need to phone the help line at all. Turn to Chapter 3 for a more detailed look at these free services.

ISPs have their negative side too, of course. Until quite recently, as soon as you'd signed up your ISP would be vanishing into the distance, clutching your money and giggling insanely at the mess he'd left you in. (My first account took 14 hours of slaving over a hot keyboard before I finally managed to connect!). However, most ISPs now send out *pre-configured* software (all the complicated settings are made for you) so that you can just install it and connect.

▶ *If you like the sound of an ISP account, keep reading! In Chapter 3 you'll learn some of the finer points of choosing a service provider and setting up your Internet connection.*

Any Suggestions?

If you can't decide whether to go for an ISP account or an online service, let me make a suggestion: start by setting up an account with one of the free ISPs. You can subscribe to one of the best-known free service providers, Virgin Net, using the CD-ROM that accompanies this book and be online in a few minutes. If you decide later that you want to switch to an online service or start paying for an ISP account, you won't have the palaver of cancelling your Virgin Net account since they're not charging you anything.

What's the most popular way to get online?

UK users have traditionally favoured online services, with the top companies being America Online and CompuServe. But the recent introduction of free accounts from companies like Freeserve and Virgin Net has been attracting huge numbers of new and existing Internet users, so this question may have a different answer by next year.

Phone Calls & Connections

Whether you've chosen to hook up with an ISP or an online service, you'll have to dial in to that company's computer every time you want to go online. This means that if you connect for 20 minutes you'll pay for a 20-minute phone call (although it's your modem using the line, not your phone). So how much are these phone calls going to cost?

It may be free!

Service providers are starting to offer premium-rate services (at around £10 per month) which give you free Internet calls during evenings and weekends. Some service providers offer a BT package called SurfTime which gives completely free Internet calls all day long for around a fixed fee of £20 per month, or evenings and weekends only at about £6, and other companies are trying to outdo each other with similar offers. If you have one of these packages, you can probably ignore this section!

The good news is that you should always be able to connect through a local phone number. At the time of writing, British Telecom's local call rate (per minute) is 4p peak, 1.7p cheap, and 1p at weekends. Add your access number to your 'Friends & Family' list and you'll save at least ten per cent. And if your phone bill is high enough to qualify for the PremierLine scheme you'll be able to knock off another 15 per cent.

Are There Any Other Options?

Yes indeed. Although there's no escaping the cost of the phone calls, you can find faster ways to connect to the Internet. These tend to be the domain of companies and individuals who work extensively on the Net, and they replace the humble modem. Not surprisingly, they're also more expensive than a modem connection so you'll probably want to ignore them for the time being, but here's a brief description of each:

▶ **Home Highway.** This service from British Telecom converts your phone line from analogue to digital (putting a larger phone socket junction box on your wall in the process) and uses a digital device called a terminal adapter or ISDN card instead of a modem. This gives you two phone lines with speeds of 64Kbps, so you can make phone calls or send faxes on one line while you surf the Net on the other. In theory you can link the two lines together to give yourself a 128Kbps connection, but there are currently few ISPs who allow you to connect this way and you'll be paying double the price for the call. Other benefits of Home Highway are that connections are made in around 5 seconds, and silently (better than the modem's 30 seconds of whistling and screeching!), and the connection speed of 64Kbps is fixed and won't drop by 25% when your ISP is having a busy time. If you already have Internet access, you can find out more about Home Highway and its sister service, Business Highway, at **http://www.bt.com/homehighway**

▶ **ISDN line.** The details and benefits of an ISDN line are similar to those of Home Highway, but this option requires the installation of a digital phone line which, together with a few other subtle differences, results in higher costs. ISDN may be the best connection method for some businesses, but home users will usually ignore this one.

Dig deeper

If you're seriously considering an ISDN line or Home Highway, make sure you check your service provider's charges too. Many ISPs charge a higher monthly subscription for high-speed connections like this, and some may not allow them at all.

▶ **Leased line.** This is a mind-bogglingly fast direct connection to the Internet. A leased line will set you back anything from £2000 to £200 000 annually (so don't buy one until you're sure you need it!), and gives you permanent connection to the Net with instant high-speed access.

▶ **ADSL.** This long-promised digital service from BT is finally starting to become available in some parts of the country. ADSL gives you a permanent connection to the Internet and a download speed of between 500Kbps and 2Mbps (10 to 40 times the maximum speed of a modem), with prices starting at £40 per month. The catch is that you'll probably have to wait a while: ADSL should be available to half the UK population by mid-2001. You can learn more (and find out if your local exchange has been upgraded to support ADSL yet) online at **http://www.bt.com/adsl**

▶ **Cable connection.** If you can get one, you'll probably want one! Cable connections are very fast, and may be permanent, similar to a leased line. Like ADSL connections, the drawback is that they're more expensive than an ordinary modem connection, but the speed makes it a price worth paying for many users with cable-connected homes.

3

CONNECTING TO A SERVICE PROVIDER

▶ **IN THIS CHAPTER**

How to pick the best ISP for your needs

Pros and cons of free services

The six essential questions to ask before subscribing

Choose what you want your email address to be

Make sense of all the technical info your ISP gives you

Now that you've made the all-important decisions, this is where things start to happen – after following the instructions in this chapter you'll be online and ready to start exploring the Internet. Right now you're just two steps away from connecting: you need to choose and subscribe to a service provider (ISP), and configure your version of Windows to make the connection. It may look a bit involved on first sight, but remember – you should only have to do it once!

Choosing A Service Provider

Okay, it's decision time again! There are countless ISPs in the UK, and more are starting up all the time. You'll find a list of several dozen UK service providers on pages 430–5, and the first step is to whittle this lot down to just one (or pick one that doesn't appear on the list if you've heard good things about them).

Since late 1998, UK Internet users have had to make one extra decision at this stage: *do you want to pay for Internet access or not?* It may seem a silly question at first, but let's look at it in a bit more detail.

Free Access Pros & Cons

Although it's a recent innovation in the UK, the free-access bandwagon has gained immense speed with all manner of companies jumping on board. Well-known names like Dixons, Tesco and the Mirror now offer free Internet access; telecommunications companies are trying to steal us away from BT by providing free access combined with lower call charges; and established ISPs like Virgin Net and BT Internet have introduced free accounts to cling on to their existing users.

GOOD QUESTION!

What does 'free' actually mean?

For the last couple of years, 'free access' has meant that you don't pay any subscription fees to the service providing your Internet service, but you still have to pay the cost of the connection phone calls. After some recent court cases, though, it looks as if 'free' will soon have to mean what it says: no subscription, no call charges, and no time-related fees.

The obvious benefit of using a free ISP is that you don't pay, thereby saving yourself £6 to £15 per month. That leads to a couple more benefits:

▶ If you find the service poor or unreliable you can stop using it and pick another without the aggravation of cancelling your subscription and stopping payments.

▶ You can sign up with several ISPs – still at no cost – as an increasing number of Internet users choose to do (see Chapter 15).

The negative side of free service providers is that they're heavily geared towards the home user – if you want to get your company online or set up a business website, a free ISP probably won't be flexible enough for you. The result is that the folk who subscribe to free ISPs are home users who all pile on to the Net at the same time: evenings and weekends. If your chosen ISP hasn't invested enough in its service to cope with these sudden rushes, you may find things a bit slow or unreliable.

Don't let the paragraph above put you off though! I have accounts with several ISPs – some free, some not – and I don't find much to choose between them in terms of reliability and speed. Unless you have a good reason not to, free access is still the route to take.

Asking Questions – Six Of The Best

It never hurts to ask a few questions, and if you've opted for a subscription service you want to know what you're going to get for your money! When you've picked a promising candidate, give them a ring and ask a few questions.

First, check any details from the list of ISPs at the back of this book, and any that were given to you by another subscriber, to make sure they're accurate and up-to-date. Then work your way down this list:

1 **What is your monthly subscription fee?** A common price is about £12 including VAT. If an ISP charges more, it's worth asking what else they provide that other companies don't. Although this question doesn't usually apply to free ISPs, a few offer a two-tier service with which you can opt to pay a low monthly fee instead of paying a premium rate for calls to their support line.

2 **Do you charge extra for the time I spend online?** The correct answer to this is 'No we don't'. If they get this one wrong, go no further!

3 **Do you support my connection method?** Any ISP will now support your 56Kbps modem, but if you're using something different (such as Home Highway) it's worth checking that they support it and that they won't charge extra for the faster connection.

4 **Do you have a local access number for my area?** You need to know the location of the computer you're dialling in to (usually called a PoP or Point of Presence) – you must be able to dial in using a local phone number. Many providers have PoPs all over the UK, or provide a single local-rate 0845 number. Others might be smaller companies with, perhaps, a single computer in Blackpool. This could be ideal if you live in the Blackpool area, but if you're in Torquay forget it.

5 **When is telephone support available and is it free?** These days getting online is as quick and simple as installing a new piece of software, and you may never need to call a support line for help. In case you do, though, make sure it'll be available when you're most likely to need it (for example, during evenings and weekends) and find out how much you'll be paying for support calls.

6 **Do you provide pre-configured connection software for my computer?** The answer should be 'yes', but if you're not using Windows 95/98/Me you may get a 'no'. (The software will usually be on CD-ROM – very few companies use floppy disks these days.) You should be able to pop the CD into the drive, follow some simple instructions and be online in a few minutes.

When you've found the service provider of your dreams, you're almost ready to subscribe. But first…

Choosing Your Username

When you start a subscription with a service provider, you'll be identified by your choice of username (some companies refer to it as a user ID, logon name or member name). You'll need to quote this when you call the support line with a question, and when you log on to the provider's computer to surf the Internet. More importantly, it forms the unique part of your email address. If you were to start an account with **mycompany.co.uk**, your email address would be *username*@**mycompany.co.uk** or *anything@username*.**mycompany.co.uk** (where everyone in the family could have their own name in place of the *anything*). ISPs who offer unlimited email addresses usually give you the second type of address.

Do I have to use my own name?

No, you can use just about anything you want. It'll be easier for you (and other people) to remember if it doesn't contain numbers, but there's nothing to stop you having a username like **jellyfish** or **zapdoodle**, as long as your ISP doesn't already have a zapdoodle on its subscriber list.

The rules on usernames vary a little between providers. In general, they can't contain spaces (in common with any Internet address), but dots, dashes and underscores are usually okay. Most importantly, it must be a username that hasn't already been scooped by another subscriber to your chosen service provider, so it's worth putting a bit of thought into a second and third choice in case your first is unavailable.

And Now... Subscribe!

It's time to get your hands on the software you need to set up your account. Depending which ISP you chose, you may already have the software on the cover disk of a computing magazine, or you may have to go to a high street store such as Dixons (for Freeserve) or Tesco (for Tesco Net) and ask for a CD-ROM. (If you already have an Internet connection and you're looking for another, you may be able to sign up online at the ISP's website.) More often than not, though, you'll have to call your chosen ISP and ask them to send you the disk. What happens next will depend on the individual service provider, but it will usually be one of the following:

▶ Following the instructions on the CD-ROM will install the software you need and then dial the ISP's central computer to create your subscription. At some point during this process you should be told the **username** and **password** you've been assigned. Make a note of these somewhere safe before continuing. At the end of this short process your computer will be ready to connect to the Internet.

▶ You may receive a disk of software and some documentation that tells you how to install it and how to configure your computer yourself.

You may also receive a wonderfully technical-looking list of IP addresses, domain names and so on, to accompany the software package. Even if your software is pre-configured for quick and easy installation, make sure you hang on to this list for reference – you'll need to enter some of these settings into other software you use in the future. Included on the list will be most (though not necessarily all) of the following items:

▶ **Local dial-up phone number.** The number your modem will dial to connect to the provider's computer.

▶ **Username and password.** Confirmation of your chosen username, and a personal password. You'll enter both of these into your dial-up software so that you can log on to the provider's computer.

▶ **email address.** As mentioned above, this will consist of your username and your provider's domain name, looking something like **username@accessprovider.co.uk**

▶ **email account username and password.** If you have a POP3 email account, you'll use these to retrieve your email messages. An SMTP email account will use your normal logon details. (We'll look at these two types of account in Chapter 8.)

▶ **Mail server address.** The domain name of the computer you'll connect to when you want to send and receive email. You'll probably have addresses for **SMTP mail server** and **POP3 mail server** – I'll explain these in Chapter 8, but they'll usually both be something like **mail.accessprovider.co.uk**

▶ **News server address.** The domain name of the computer that handles newsgroup messages, which is usually **news.accessprovider.co.uk**

▶ **Domain name server (DNS).** This will be an IP address (you remember those four numbers separated by dots?) for the computer that translates friendly domain names into something that computers can understand and mere mortals can't. You may also be given an **alternative DNS** that your computer will try to connect to if the first one fails.

▶ **Other bits and pieces.** The address of your company's website in case you want to take a look at it (**www.accessprovider.co.uk**); the address of your provider's FTP server if it has one (**ftp.accessprovider.co.uk**); and the telephone number and email address of the provider's technical support services.

Now that your account has been set up, and you're the proud owner of a list of technical gobbledegook and a disk of software from your access provider, it's time to get that connection working. Your provider should have included instructions telling you how to install the software, so this should be a pretty painless step. All the same, keep that support line number handy, just in case! If you need a bit more help, you can head for the back of this book where all the technical stuff is gathered together. If you're using Windows 95 or later, turn to Appendix A; if you're using Windows 3.1, go to Appendix B.

No list of technical stuff?

BY THE WAY

If you don't get a list of technical bits and pieces, don't worry. Nowadays the sign-up procedure should get everything working for you automatically and you'll find any other information you need on the ISP's website once you're connected. The vital things to keep track of (preferably on paper or in a file on a floppy disk) are your username and password.

CONNECTING TO AN ONLINE SERVICE

▶ **IN THIS CHAPTER**

Discover the differences between three popular online services

Follow the simple sign-up routines to get connected

Start exploring the member areas and the Internet

Choosing An Online Service

This should be an easy choice to make – not only is the list of online services fairly short, but most offer a free 30-day trial, so you've got nothing to lose by picking one at random. All the same, it's better to make an informed choice if you can, so let's take a slightly closer look at the most popular online services, **CompuServe**, **America Online** and **The Microsoft Network**.

CompuServe

CompuServe has over 1000 different areas covering just about every conceivable subject including finance, news, TV listings, articles from popular magazines, travel information, movie and music previews, along with interactive chat rooms. Many retail companies have their own forums offering advice and product support, and business users will probably find more to interest them on CompuServe than the other services. The program used to move around this lot (shown on page 105) is smart and fairly formal, although not quite as easy to get to grips with as America Online. UK-specific content is sparse for a company with so many UK users, but CompuServe are trying to improve things in this area. Parents can download a program called Cyber Patrol to restrict kids' access to areas of CompuServe itself or the Internet, and limit the time they can spend online.

Do I have to use an online service to control my kids' access to the Internet?

Not at all. There are many good programs available that you can use with an Internet Service Provider account to restrict access to different areas of the Net, or to particular types of information. You'll learn about those programs in Chapter 14.

America Online

In comparison with CompuServe, America Online (AOL) has a very sunny, friendly and informal feel to it (as you can see from the picture on page 38), making it a good choice for children and inexperienced computer-users. The content provided is very similar to that of CompuServe, with a couple of differences: business content, although growing, is still far from comprehensive, but you will find plenty of UK content. Parental controls are very good, although there's currently no way to restrict how long your kids stay online. One major bonus is that AOL allows an account-holder to have up to five different member-names (AOL calls them Screen Names), which means that you can have five email addresses; for families or small businesses, this allows everyone to receive their own personal email. More importantly perhaps for families, you can set different restrictions for the different Screen Names, allowing you to bar access to areas of the service by your children without affecting your own access to the same areas.

The Microsoft Network

The Microsoft Network (or MSN) has a very stylish and modern appearance, contrasting massively with CompuServe's formality and AOL's friendliness. It also requires Windows 95 or later in order to run, and a reasonably fast computer. MSN is 'cool', and unashamedly American in style, and this follows through to its content which is geared more towards entertainment than information. The service is primarily split into four main areas, OnStage, Essentials, Communicate, and Find. The first of these splits into sub-areas called 'channels', with each channel aimed at users with particular types of interest. Parental controls do exist, but they don't match those of CompuServe or AOL – you'll have to grab Junior by the ear and drag him away. Also in contrast with those two services, MSN is an Internet-based service: when you decide to explore the rest of the Net's offerings you'll generally find that the information travels much more speedily than with AOL and CompuServe.

How Do I Sign Up?

The first job is to get your hands on the free connection software. These disks are regularly glued to the covers of computer magazines so you may have dozens of them already. If you have, make sure you pick the most recent. If you haven't, either take a trip to your newsagent or phone the services and ask them to send you the correct software for your computer and operating system. You'll find their telephone numbers on pages 435–6.

GOOD QUESTION!

What's to stop me using free 30-day trials forever?

Don't think that online services haven't thought of this one! The setup routines for most online services will recognise your personal details. They'll still allow you to sign up a second time of course, but you're unlikely to get another free trial.

That was the tricky part! Somewhere on the disk you'll be told how to start the program that signs you up, and the whole process will advance in simple steps. The exact routine will vary from one service to another, so I can't tell you exactly what to expect, but here are a few tips to bear in mind:

▶ Somewhere on the disk packaging you'll find a reference number (perhaps on a small label, or perhaps on the disk itself). Don't lose it – you'll have to enter this into the software to start the sign-up procedure.

▶ Make sure you've got your credit card or debit card handy. Although you won't be charged for the first 30 days' access, you'll have to enter the card number and its expiry date when you sign up.

▶ You may be asked to choose a dial-in phone number from a list covering the whole country. If so, make sure you choose a local number. (In some cases, the software will work out the best dial-in point for you, based on your own phone number, or it may use a local-rate 0845 number.)

▶ After you've entered all the necessary personal details, the program will dial up the service's computer and set up your subscription automatically. Within a minute or two you'll receive a username and password. These are your entry-ticket, so write them down and keep them safe.

Don't pass on your password

Keep your password private. Never include it in an email message, don't type it in front of anyone, and make sure you change it at least once a month (you'll find instructions for this online). If possible, use a combination of letters and numbers at least five characters in length. And don't even consider using the word 'password' as your password!

How Do I Use An Online Service?

When you dial-in to your online service and log on using your username and password (which should happen automatically), you won't actually be on the Internet. At the click of a few buttons you can enter chat rooms or join in with other activities and forums, and you'll find plenty of assistance if you get lost, both in help files and online support areas.

Access to the Internet itself will be marked as one of the areas you can visit, and you'll probably see a big friendly button marked 'Internet' that will take you there. In most cases any extra software needed for Internet access was installed when you signed up, but you might be told that you need to download it yourself. If so, another friendly button will probably appear in front of you and all the spadework will be done for you while you sit back and wait.

Because this is a book about the Internet I'm not going to dwell on the members only areas of online services. But once you've clicked that big friendly button you're surfing the same Internet as everyone else, so the rest of the book is just as relevant to you.

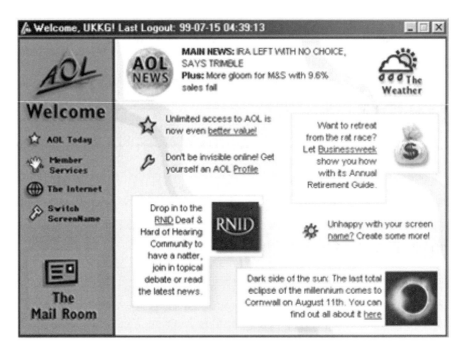

▶ The main AOL desktop lets you click on a button to access the Internet or to use one of its own private services.

2

FINDING YOUR WAY AROUND

▶ **IN THIS PART**

EXPLORING THE WORLD WIDE WEB

A First Look At The Wonders Of The Web

How would you describe television to someone who's never seen it? Somehow you've got to convey its variety, its entertainment value, and its potential as a learning tool. You've got to explain that some of the content is staggeringly good, and some is mindless twaddle, but sometimes the mindless twaddle can be more entertaining than the 'good' stuff. How do you describe a whole amazing new experience?

You wouldn't even *try* to describe it – you'd switch on the TV and say 'Just watch!' To describe the World Wide Web experience on paper isn't as easy – I can't show you the colour or the animation, and although it's interactive, you won't be able to interact with it. Nevertheless, a picture paints a thousand words, so here's the Web equivalent of a few photos of your TV screen.

Pepsi World
http://www.pepsiworld.com

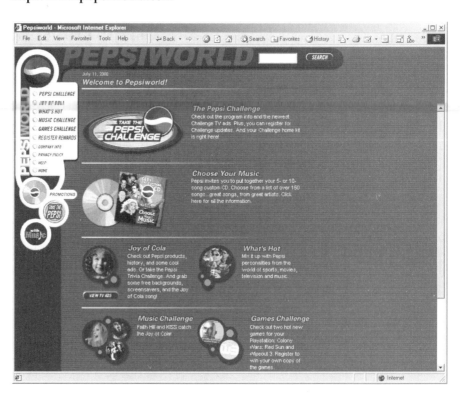

▶ All of the fizz, none of the stickiness. Pepsi's state-of-the-art site bristles with sounds, animations and interactive games. Plus the odd mention of soft drinks, but that's probably to be expected.

The Virtual Frog Dissection Kit
http://george.lbl.gov/ITG.hm.pg.docs/dissect/dissect.html

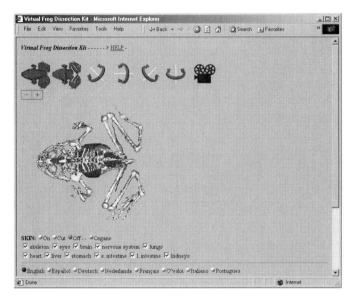

◀ Surprisingly, one of the few frog dissection kits on the Web. In fact this isn't intended to be gruesome – every organ and system can be examined, with full information provided, and not a single frog has to croak!

Paintings at Le Louvre
http://www.paris.org/Musees/Louvre/Treasures/Paintings

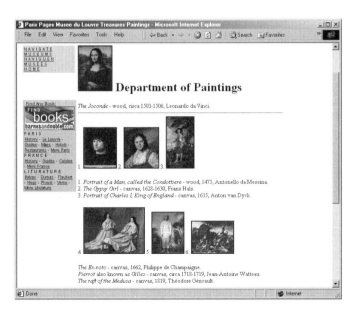

◀ Check out that enigmatic smile while browsing through one of the world's finest galleries. Click on any image to view a larger version and save it to your own hard disk.

The Millennium Experience
http://www.mx2000.co.uk

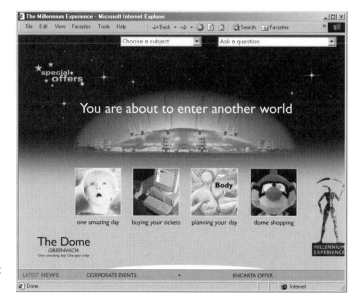

▶ Take a virtual reality tour of the Millennium Dome: it's a lot like 'real' reality, but quicker and cheaper with a lot less queuing.

Crepes Demystified
http://desires.com/2.0b3/Food/Crepes/Docs/crepes3.html

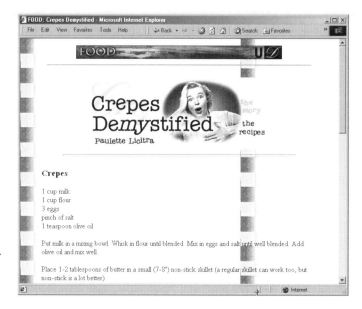

▶ Are you mystified by crêpes? Panicked by pancakes? Let super chef Paulette Licitra better your batter and unscramble your eggs.

Understanding The Web

The World Wide Web is the jewel in the Internet's crown, and the whole reason for the 'Internet explosion'. A large part of the Web's popularity lies in its simplicity: you don't have to be a networking genius or a computer whiz to use it, you just point and click. The 'pages' you find on the Web contain a scattering of words that are underlined and highlighted in a different colour from the text around them. Just move your mouse pointer on to one of these words or phrases (you'll see it change into a hand with a pointing finger as you do so) and click. Hey presto, another page opens. The entire 'web' of pages is being 'spun' by millions of people at the rate of several million new pages per day, and every page includes these point-and-click links to many other pages.

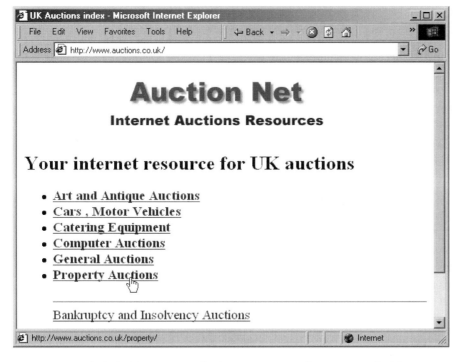

◀ To jump between pages, move the pointer over the coloured hypertext and click to open the related document.

This system of clickable text is called **hypertext**, and you've probably seen it used in Windows help files and multimedia encyclopaedias as a neat way to make cross-references. The Web takes the system a few stages further:

▶ These links aren't restricted to opening a document stored on the same computer: you might see a page from the other side of the world.

Web page

A 'page' is a single document that can be any length, like a document in a word processor. Pages can contain text, graphics, sound and video clips, together with clever effects and controls made possible by programming languages such as Java and ActiveX (I'll tell you a bit about those languages in Chapter 22.)

▶ A hypertext link doesn't have to be a word or phrase: it might be a picture that you click on, or it might be a part of a larger picture, with different parts linking to different pages.

▶ The link doesn't necessarily open a new web page: it might play a video or a sound, download an application, display a picture, run a program… the list goes on.

The Web is made up of millions and millions of files placed on computers called web servers, so no one person or company actually owns the Web itself. The web servers are owned by many different companies, and they rent space (or give it away for free!) to anyone who wants to put their own pages on the Web. The pages are created using an easy-to-use, text-based language called **HTML** (HyperText Markup Language) which you'll learn about in Chapters 23 and 24.

Once the newly created pages are placed on the web server, anyone who knows their address can look at them. This explains partly why the Web became such an overnight success: a simple page can be written in minutes, so a website can be as up-to-date as its creator wants it to be. Many websites with news or sports pages are updated daily, and some may even change every few minutes.

Website

'Website' is a loose term that refers to the pages belonging to an individual or company. A site could be just a single simple page that your Auntie Ethel wrote to share a tasty fruitcake recipe, or it might be hundreds of complex pages belonging to a supermarket chain.

What Do I Need?

To view pages from the World Wide Web you'll need a program called a **browser**. In fact, this single program will be the most powerful weapon in your Internet arsenal, and not just because you'll be spending so much time on the Web – you can use this program to handle many of your other Internet-related tasks as well. Although there are many different browsers available, the most capable is Microsoft's **Internet Explorer**.

If you're connected through one of the online services you'll usually be able to use Internet Explorer. Both MSN and CompuServe provide Explorer by default (although you can switch to something different if you want to); America Online will let you use any browser that takes your fancy.

 The current version of Internet Explorer (v5.5) is included on the free CD-ROM accompanying this book. If you're using Windows Millennium Edition or Windows 98 Second Edition (which should be installed on any PC bought since Autumn 1999) a recent version of Internet Explorer is already installed on your system, and you should see its icon on the desktop (a blue 'e'). A copy of Internet Explorer is included with the original Windows 98 and with some editions of Windows 95 – it may be installed on your computer already, or you may have to install it yourself from the **Windows Setup** tab of Control Panel's Add/Remove Programs applet. It's a rather out-of-date copy, though, so I recommend you install the later version included in the back of this book.

I'm using Netscape Navigator. Will I understand this chapter?

Netscape Navigator is another popular browser. Netscape's buttons and menus differ from those in Explorer, but both tools were designed to do the same job so the methods are very similar. For simplicity, I'm going to assume that you're using Explorer throughout this book, but you'll find the equivalent Netscape options listed in Appendix C.

Start Browsing

When you open Internet Explorer, the first thing you'll see is your **home page**. Unlike a word processor or a paint program, the browser must always display a document, and until you tell it which document you want to look at it will display the document set as its home page. By default, Explorer is set to display the first page of Microsoft's Internet site.

For now this is just a matter of idle curiosity – you've just arrived online, and you're eager to explore, so we'll forget about it for a while. But it could start to get irritating later on: every time you start Explorer you'll have to wait for this page to download before you can go anywhere else! In the 'Customising Your Browser' section of Chapter 6, I'll explain how to swap this page for a different one or replace it with a document on your own disk.

Time to go Home

On Internet Explorer's toolbar you'll see a button with the word 'Home' beneath it. Wherever your Web wanderings lead you, you can just click the **Home** button to return to your home page anytime you want to.

Anatomy Of A Web Page

Now it's time to get acquainted with the basic workings of the browser and with the Web itself. If you look at the home page you should see several hypertext links (underlined, coloured text). Move your mouse pointer on to any link that looks interesting and click. When you do that, your browser sends a message to the server storing the page you want. If everything goes according to plan, the server will respond by sending back the requested page so that your browser can display it.

Spend a little time following links to see where they lead. Don't limit yourself to clicking textual links alone, though – many of the pictures and graphics you see on a page will lead somewhere too. Take a look at the page shown in the following screenshot from *Time Out* Magazine's site (**http:// www.timeout.com**) for a few clues to the type of thing you'll find on a web page.

▲ Some of the main elements that make up a web page.

▶ **Plain Text**. Ordinary readable text. Click it all you like – nothing will happen!

▶ **Hypertext link**. A text link to another page. Hypertext links will almost always be underlined, but their text colour will vary from site to site.

▶ **Image**. A picture or graphic that enhances a website. Like most pictures, it paints a thousand words, but it won't lead anywhere if you click it.

▶ **Hyperlinked image**. Clicking this image will open a new page. In most cases a hyperlinked image will look no different to an ordinary image, but it may have a box around it that's the same colour as any hypertext links on the page.

▶ **Image map**. An image split up into small chunks, with each chunk leading to a different page. In this case, every city name is linked to its own page listing forthcoming events in that city.

▶ **email link**. Click on this link and your email program will open so that you can send a message to the web page's author. The author's address will be automatically inserted into the message for you.

How can I tell an ordinary image from a linking image?

Watch your mouse pointer! When you move the pointer on to any link (image or text), it will turn into a hand shape with a pointing finger. In a well-constructed image map, the different areas of the picture itself should make it clear where each link will lead. Finally, keep an eye on the status bar at the bottom of the browser – as you move over a link of any sort you'll see the name of the linked document or file appear.

Links & Colours

On the home page you were viewing, the text you clicked was probably blue. If you go back and have another look you'll see it's changed colour (probably to purple). This is a neat indicator that helps you keep track of pages you've seen before as you flit from one page to another. These links will return to their original colour after a few days, but it's worth noting that writers of web pages can make their own colour choices, so the colours of visited and unvisited links will vary from one site to another.

Charting Your Course On The Web

By now you should be cheerfully clicking links of all descriptions and skipping from page to page with casual abandon. The problem is, you can only move forwards. If you find yourself heading down a blind alley, how can you retrace your steps and head off in a different direction? This is where the browser itself comes to your rescue, so let's spend some time getting acquainted with its toolbars and menus.

▶ Internet Explorer's button bar and address bar.

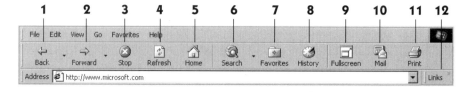

50

1 **Back.** Clicking this button will take you back to the last page you looked at. If you keep clicking you can step all the way back to the first page you viewed this session.

2 **Forward.** After using the Back button to take a second look at a previously viewed page, the Forward button lets you return to pages you viewed later. This button will be greyed-out if you haven't used the Back button yet.

3 **Stop.** Stops the download of a page from the server. This can be useful if a page is taking a long time to appear and you're tired of waiting, or if you clicked a link accidentally and want to stay where you are.

4 **Refresh.** Clicking this tells your browser to start downloading the same page again. See *Sometimes Things Go Wrong…* on page 58 for reasons why you might need to Refresh.

5 **Home.** Opens your Home Page, explained on page 48.

6 **Search.** Opens a small frame in the browser window from which you can choose a web search site and search for pages by subject or keyword. You'll learn about searching for information on the Web in Chapter 7.

7 **Favorites.** Displays the contents of your Favorites list (see below).

8 **History.** Opens a list of the sites you've visited recently, letting you revisit one with a single click (see 'Retracing Your Steps with History' on page 53).

9 **Fullscreen.** Expands the browser window to fill the screen, covering the Windows Taskbar and everything else, and leaving just a tiny toolbar visible.

10 **Mail.** Opens a menu from which you can run your email or newsreader software, or open a blank form to send an email message.

11 **Print.** Prints the current page. You can choose your printer and page setup from the File menu.

12 **Links.** If you double-click on this word a new button bar will slide across revealing links to Microsoft's own site and some useful jumping-off points for your Web travels. To hide the Links bar again, double-click the word 'Address' to its left.

Increase your viewing space

In the best traditions of toolbars, you can find all these options on Explorer's menus as well, and most have keyboard shortcuts. If you'd like to see more of the pages themselves in Explorer's window, head off to the **View I Toolbars** menu and click any entry with a check mark beside it to hide it. Or switch back and forth between Fullscreen and Normal view by pressing F11.

One useful extra tool is a facility to search the page you're viewing for a particular word or phrase. Open the **Edit** menu, choose **Find (on this page)...** (or press **Ctrl+F**), and type the word you're looking for.

Many Happy Returns – Using Favorites

One of the most powerful Explorer tools is the **Favorites** system (known as Bookmarks or Hotlists in other browsers). Any time you arrive at a page you think might be useful in the future, you can add its address to your list of Favorites and return to it by opening the menu and clicking the relevant shortcut. To add the current page to the list, click the **Favorites** toolbar button and click **Add to Favorites**. A small dialog will appear giving a suggested title (you can replace this with any title you like to help you recognise it in future). To place the shortcut directly on the menu, click **OK**.

You can also organise your shortcuts into submenus to make them easier to find. Click the **Create in...** button and **New Folder**, then type a name for the folder. Click the folder into which you want to save the new shortcut and click the **OK** button to confirm. (If it ends up in the wrong place, don't worry! Select **Organize Favorites** from the Favorites menu and you'll be able to move, rename and delete folders and shortcuts, and create new folders.)

When you want to reopen a page that you added to your Favorites list, either select **Favorites** from the menu bar and click the name of the site on the menu, or click the Favorites toolbar button to open a clickable list in a small frame in the left of the browser's window (shown in the screenshot on the page 54).

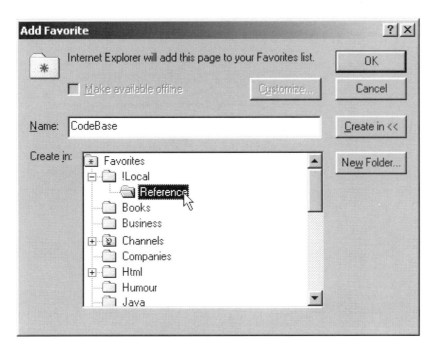

◀ Add a new shortcut to a **Favorites** submenu by clicking the submenu's folder followed by the **OK** button.

Retracing Your Steps With History

The **History** list provides a handy way of finding an elusive site that you visited recently but didn't add to your Favorites list. Internet Explorer maintains this list automatically, and you can open it by clicking the **History** button on the toolbar. The sites are sorted by week and day, with links to the various pages you visited on each site placed into folders. You can revisit a site by finding the week and day you last viewed it, clicking the folder for that site and clicking the page you want to see again. You can choose how long Explorer should store details of visited pages by clicking your way to **Tools | Internet Options | General**.

Are you a furtive surfer?

Explorer's History list can be many things – useful, interesting, nostalgic, to name but a few. It can also be a dead giveaway. Although there's no foolproof way to cover your tracks, clearing the History list is a sensible move if you'd prefer to keep your Web-surfing habits private. You can clear the list by clicking the **Clear History** button on the **Tools | Internet Options | General** page.

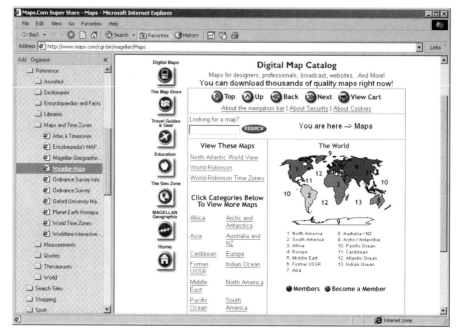

▶ Click the
Favorites button
on the toolbar
and your Favorites
list stays within
easy reach while
you surf.

The Address Bar & URLs

Every page on the World Wide Web has its own unique **URL**. URL stands
for Uniform Resource Locator, but it's just a convoluted way of saying
'address'. You've seen a few of those already – if you skip back to the
beginning of the chapter you'll see the URLs of each website screenshot.

You'll also notice URLs at work as you move from page to page in Explorer,
provided you can see the address bar (if you can't, go to **View | Toolbars |
Address Bar** to switch it on). Every time you open a new page, its URL
appears in this text-bar. You can also type a URL into the address bar
yourself – just click once on the address bar to highlight the address
currently shown, type the URL of the page you want to open, and press
Enter. For example, if you want to look at today's peak time TV listings,
type: **http://www.sceneone.co.uk** into the address bar. In a similar way, if
you find the URL of a site you'd like to visit in an email message or word
processor document, copy it to the clipboard using **Ctrl+C**, click in the
address bar, and paste in the URL by pressing **Ctrl+V**.

Accuracy is everything!

URLs are case-sensitive, so make sure you observe any capital letters. Also, in contrast with the directory paths used in Windows computers, URLs use forward slashes rather than backslashes. Actually these don't matter too much – if you forget and use the wrong type, Explorer will know what you mean.

Understanding URLs

You'll come into contact with a lot of URLs on your travels around the Internet, so it's worth knowing what they mean. As a specimen to examine, let's take the URL for the Radio 1 website at the BBC and break it up into its component pieces. The URL is:

http://www.bbc.co.uk/radio1/index.html

http://   This is one of the Internet's many protocols, and it stands for HyperText Transfer Protocol. It's the system used to send web pages around the Internet, so all web page URLs have the http://prefix.

www.bbc.co.uk/   This is the name of the computer on which the required file is stored (often referred to as the 'host' computer). Computers that store web pages are called web servers and their names usually begin www.

radio1/   This is the directory path to the page you want to open. Just as on your own computer, the path may consist of several directories separated by slashes.

index.html   This is the name of the file you want. The .html (or .htm) extension indicates that it's a web page, but your browser can handle any number of different file types, as you'll see in Chapters 6 and 13.

Why do some URLs contain no filename?

Some URLs finish with a directory name (such as
http://www.bbc.co.uk/radio1) rather than a filename. When your browser
sends this type of URL to a web server, the server will look in the directory for a default file,
often called **index.htm**. If a file exists with this name it will be sent back to your browser; if
not, you'll receive a rather plain looking hypertext list of all the files in that directory (or, more
often nowadays, just a page containing an error message). The index file is usually a
'Welcome' page introducing a website and containing links to other areas of the site.

A little while ago I said your browser was the most powerful tool in your
Internet software armoury, and I wasn't kidding. In later chapters we'll be
looking at other Internet services you can use, and I'll point you towards
some of the best software to help you use them. But your browser is a
multi-talented chap: some of these services can be accessed directly within
the browser itself without the need for any other software, and for those
that can't your browser still makes a great jumping-off point.

A little less typing

When you type the URL of a web page into your address bar you can leave out
the **http://** as most browsers will take that for granted and add it themselves. In
Internet Explorer, when you start typing a URL (or any part of one) that you've visited before, a
list of similar URLs will appear and you can simply click the one you want. So to revisit the
Radio 1 website mentioned earlier, you may be able to type as little as **radio1**.

We've just seen that the World Wide Web service uses a protocol called
HTTP, so all your web page URLs will start **http://** Here are some of the
other prefixes your browser will handle and the results of using them:

Prefix	Result
ftp://	The URL of a library of files on an FTP server. Your browser will display directory and filenames, and allow you to download files. Try typing **ftp://sunsite.doc.ic.ac.uk/computing/systems/ibmpc** into your address bar to visit one of the best software libraries in the UK. For more on FTP, turn to Chapter 11.
gopher://	Gopher was the forerunner of the Web and is now largely ignored, but your browser will still happily access Gopher sites. You'll learn more about this creature in Chapter 12, but you can get a taste by visiting **gopher://wiretap.area.com**
telnet://	Your browser will start your Telnet program rather than accessing the site itself. We'll have a closer look at Telnet in Chapter 12, but in the meantime, type **telnet://qwksilver.com** into your address bar to take part in a brain-twisting, text-based adventure game called MajorMUD.
mailto:	Mailto: links crop up a lot in web pages and I mentioned how they work on page 49. You can also type them into your address bar to open a blank email form with the email address already inserted. For example, to send me a message, type **mailto:rob@codebase.co.uk** (Notice that this prefix and the **news:** prefix below have no // after the colon.) To find out more about sending and receiving email, turn to Chapter 8.
news:	This will be a link to a particular newsgroup for which your browser will start your newsreader software (unless it has its own built-in newsreader) to display the messages in the group. You'll learn about newsgroups in Chapter 9, but for now try entering **news:news.groups** to see a newsgroup for newcomers to the Internet
file:///	Using this prefix you can open a **local** web document, that is a file on your own hard disk that has the .htm or .html extension. Browsers can also open many other types of file (such as images with the .gif or .jpg extension) as we'll see in Chapter 13. In Explorer, unlike most other browsers, you can actually leave out this prefix and just type an ordinary file path like **c:\mydirectory\myfile.htm** In older browsers, you'll have to use this prefix (note the third backslash!), and replace the colon in the drive-name with a pipe symbol, such as **file:///c1\mydirectory\myfile.com**

Sometimes Things Go Wrong...

Things don't always go smoothly when you're trying to open a web page. To begin with, the server might not be running and you'll eventually see a message telling you that the operation 'timed out' – in other words, your browser waited a minute or so for a response from the server and doesn't think anything is going to happen. If the server is running it might be busy. In this case you might get a similar result, or you might get a part of the page and then everything seems to stop dead. You may be able to get things moving by clicking the **Refresh** button on the browser's toolbar, forcing your browser to request the document again, but be prepared to give up, visit a different website, and try this one again later.

And then there's the Mysterious Vanishing Page syndrome. Although all web pages contain links, sometimes the pages those links refer to no longer exist and you'll see an error message instead. The reason is simple: on the perpetually changing landscape of the World Wide Web, pages (and even entire sites) move elsewhere, are renamed, or just disappear. In fact, the average lifespan of a site is a mere 90 days! People putting links to these sites in their own pages have no way of knowing when this happens other than by regularly clicking all the links themselves to check them. By the same token, some of the URLs I've included in this book may be defunct by the time you get to try them. The endless arrivals and departures are a fact of web life, but also a part of its magic.

▶ *So how does anyone find what they're looking for on the Web? Turn to Chapter 7 to find out.*

What Next?

There's much more to the World Wide Web than we've covered in this chapter, but you've seen enough to know what it is and how to move around it. In the next chapter you'll go a stage further, learning how to use other features of Internet Explorer to make your Web-surfing faster, easier and more efficient.

6

MASTERING YOUR WEB BROWSER

In Chapter 5 you learnt the basic moves that let you view web pages, store the location of a useful page so that you can revisit it later, and use your browser to access a few of the other Internet services. But there's a lot more to the Web than I could reasonably fit into a single chapter. In fact, there's more to it than I can fit into *two* chapters! To give you a good head start on the Web, I'm going to linger here a little longer and show you some of the ways in which your browser can power-up your surfing. Later on I'll introduce you to some of the 'sideshows' of the Web such as search engines, multimedia, and online shopping, and I'll show you how to create your own web pages.

Customising Your Browser

Let's start with some browser tips to help you fine-tune your surfing:

▶ **Customise your home page**. If you're content to let your browser download a page every time you run it, you can choose what that page should contain, perhaps to have the latest news stories displayed automatically. Visit **http://home.microsoft.com** and follow the instructions on the page. (If you're using Netscape, go to **http://www.netscape.com/custom/index.html**)

▶ **Use a blank home page**. The problem with the traditional home page is that Explorer will try to download it every time you start up, even if you aren't planning to go online. The other option is to use a blank page from your own disk instead. Go to **Tools | Internet Options | General**, click the **Use Blank** button, then click **OK**.

▶ **Use a different home page**. You can use any page on the Web as your home page. Click your way to **Tools | Internet Options** and either type a URL into the **Address** box at the top of the page, or click the **Use Current** button to set the page you're currently viewing as your home page. (You can even create your own home page if you want to – I'll explain how to do that in Chapter 24.)

▶ **Browse faster without images**. The actual text on a web page downloads very fast; it's the images that you're often left waiting for, and most pages have at least one image. To skip around the Web faster, you can turn off the display of images, and have them replaced by empty boxes or small 'placeholder' icons on the page. To do this in Explorer, go to **Tools | Internet Options | Advanced**, scroll down to the **Multimedia** section and remove the checkmark from **Show pictures**. (You can also prevent sounds, animations and videos playing by using other checkboxes in this section.) If you want to view an image on a particular page, click it with the right mouse button and choose **Show Picture**.

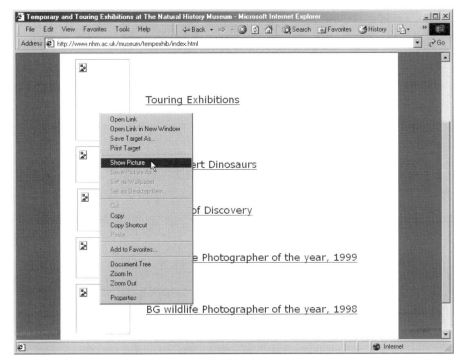

◀ With the automatic display of images turned off, you can right-click the placeholder and choose **Show Picture** to reveal the missing image.

▶ **Rearrange your toolbars**. The toolbar, menu bar and the Address and Links bars have a 'raised' vertical strip to their left. By grabbing the strip with the mouse pointer you can drag the toolbars around. You can even hide them completely, or remove the text labels from their icons using the options on the **View | Toolbars** submenu. To keep everything visible but make it a bit smaller, right-click the toolbar and choose **Customize...**, then choose **Small Icons** from the **Icon Options** box. (You can also choose to remove the text labels from the buttons to shrink the toolbar even more.)

Double Glazing – Opening A New Window

Like most recent applications, web browsers let you open a second window (and a third, and a fourth, as long as your computer has the resources to cope) so that you can run several Web sessions at the same time. There are several reasons why you might find this useful. If you're searching for a particularly elusive piece of information, you can follow two different paths in the two windows and (perhaps) track it down a little sooner. Or you can view a page in one window while waiting for another page to finish downloading. And here's one that I use all the time: if you find a page full of links to sites you want to visit one by one, open each link in a new window, and then close that window when you've finished – the original window is still waiting patiently for you to try the next link on the list. (It really is a lot quicker than using the Back button or the Favorites menu.) You can close one of these windows without it affecting any of the others – as long as Internet Explorer has at least one window open, it'll keep running.

GOOD QUESTION!

Will several windows really turbo-charge my Web-surfing?

Yes and no. If you're downloading a web page in each window, you're ultimately downloading exactly the same amount of data as you would if you used one window and opened the pages one at a time – only a faster modem will make this happen any quicker. However, if you can organise things so that one window is always downloading a page while you're reading the page in the other window, you can stop some of that waiting around.

To open a new window in Internet Explorer, you can use any of these methods:

▶ Click on **File | New | Window** or press Ctrl+N. The new window will start by showing the same page as your original window.

▶ Click any link with the right mouse button and choose **Open in New Window** from the context menu or hold the Shift key while clicking a link.

▶ Type a URL into the address box, and press Shift+Enter.

▶ For non-mouse-fans, press the Tab key repeatedly until the link you want to follow is highlighted, and press Shift+Enter.

Why did it do that?

You may sometimes be innocently clicking links when suddenly a new window opens for a particular page. Web page authors occasionally add an extra piece of code to make a link open in a new window so that you can still find their original page easily. They can also add code forcing your browser not to show toolbars or the status-bar in the new window to give a large viewing area.

Right-click For Easy Surfing

I've already acknowledged the existence of the right mouse button a couple of times in this chapter – you can open a link in a new window or display an image represented by a placeholder by right-clicking and then selecting the appropriate option from the popup context menu. The contents of the menu vary according to the type of item you clicked, but always contains a feast of goodies you won't find elsewhere, so don't forget to use it.

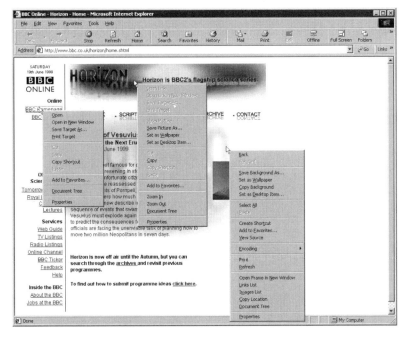

◀ Okay, I admit it: I've cheated here. This composite screenshot shows the context menus that appear after right-clicking a link (left), an image (centre) or the page background (right) in Explorer.

Let's have a look at what some of these options do:

Clicking this	Does this
Copy Shortcut	Places the link's URL on the clipboard ready for you to paste into another application.
Add to Favorites...	Places a shortcut to this page on your Favorites menu. If you clicked the page background, the URL of the current page will be saved; if you clicked a link, the URL referred to by the link will be saved.
Set as Wallpaper	Replaces the wallpaper on your desktop with the web page's background. This will remain on your wallpaper list as **Internet Explorer Wallpaper** for you to choose infuture, but each wallpaper you save in this way will **replace the last.**
Create Shortcut	Places a shortcut to the current page on the desktop. See Using Internet Shortcuts on page 69 to find out more about these.
Save Target As...	Downloads the file to which the link points and saves it onto your disk, but doesn't display it in the browser window. You'll be prompted to choose a location in which to save the file.
Save Picture As...	Stores the image you clicked to a folder on your hard disk. You can also drag the image off the page and on to your desktop to save it.

The last two items lead us neatly into a major area of Internet life, and a likely reason for you wanting to become a part of it: there's lots of 'stuff' on the Web, and most of that stuff you can grab for your own use. So how do you do it?

Saving Files From The Web

There are two groups of files you can grab from the World Wide Web – those that are a part of the web page itself (such as an image), and those that aren't. The second group is huge, covering applications, sound files, videos, spreadsheets, ZIP files, and a whole lot more. Although the methods of saving *any* file are straightforward enough, that second group is going to lead us into a few complications, so let's begin with the first.

Saving Page Elements

▶ **Saving the web page's text**. To save the text from the entire page, open the File menu and choose **Save As…**. Select **Text File** from the **Save as Type** list and choose a name and location for the file. Alternatively, if you need only a portion of the text on the page, you can highlight it using the mouse, copy it to the clipboard by pressing Ctrl+C, and then paste it into another application.

▶ **Saving the entire web page**. If you want to save a copy of the whole page (including images), follow the procedure above but choose either **Web Archive for Email** or **Web Page, Complete** from the **Save as Type** list. The Web Archive is the neater format, but the Complete option may save some elements from the page that the Archive doesn't.

▶ **Saving the web page's source**. The source of a web page is the text you see in your browser plus all the weird codes added by the page's author that make the page display properly. These codes belong to a language called HTML (HyperText Markup Language) which you'll learn about in Chapters 23 and 24. To save the HTML source document, follow the same routine as above, but choose **Web Page, HTML only** from the **Save as Type** list. (If you just want to have a peep at the source, right-click the web page's background and choose **View Source** from the context menu.)

Why would I want to save the HTML source?

As languages go, HTML is a very easy one. It might look a bit daunting on first sight, but the millions of people who've added their own pages to the Web can attest to its simplicity. Most of these people learnt the language by saving the source files of other web pages and then having a look at them in a text-editor such as Windows' Notepad. (Of course, you can also pull bits out to use in your own pages!)

▶ **Saving images from the page**. As you learnt above, it just takes a right-click on any image to save it to disk (or a drag, if you prefer). You can also save the background, a small image file that the browser tiles to fill the entire viewing area. In addition to the **Set as Wallpaper** option mentioned above, you can right-click the background and choose **Save**

Background As... to save the image file to the folder of your choice. You can also copy images or the background to the clipboard with a right-click, ready to paste into another application.

Is that *your* image, Sir?

Although you can easily copy text and images from someone else's page and use them yourself, remember that copyright laws apply to information on the Internet just as they do to information you find anywhere else. Not that people don't 'recycle' stuff they find on the Web of course, but always consider whose it is and how you're planning to use it.

Saving Other Types Of Files

Although most of the links you find on web pages will open another page, some will be links to files that you can download (don't worry – it should be obvious, and if it isn't, just hit the Cancel button as soon as you get the chance!) As I mentioned earlier, this is where things get a bit more complicated. Come what may, the file must be downloaded to your own computer before you can do anything with it all, but how you choose to handle the download will depend upon what you want to do with the file itself. The browser may be multi-talented, but it can't display every type of file that exists!

What it can do, however, is to launch an **external viewer** to display the file. An external viewer is just a slightly technical way of saying 'another program on your computer'. (You'll find some of the best available viewers on the free CD-ROM in the back of this book, and I'll show you where you can find others on the Web in later chapters.) Two vital elements are required for your browser to be able to do this:

▶ You must have a program on your disk that can open the type of file you're about to download.

▶ The browser needs to know which program to use for a particular type of file, and where to find it on your disk.

After you click the link, Internet Explorer will start to download the file it refers to and then show the dialog pictured in the next screenshot. It wants to know what to do with the file when it's finished downloading: do you want to save the file and carry on surfing, or open it immediately using an external viewer?

▶ **Save this file to disk**. If you choose this option, Explorer will present a **Save As** dialog so that you can choose a folder to save the file into, followed by a smaller dialog that will keep you posted on the progress of the download and how much longer it should take. While the file is downloading you can wait, or continue surfing the Web, and there's a handy **Cancel** button you can use if you change your mind halfway through, or if the download seems to be taking too long. The **Save this file to disk** option is the best (and safest) option to use.

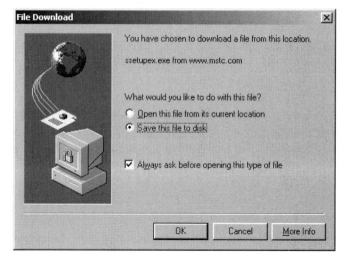

◀ Explorer wants to know whether it should open this file after downloading, or save it to your hard disk.

▶ **Open this file from its current location**. For a file that you want to view or play straight away, you can select the **Open** option. If Explorer hasn't previously been told how to handle files of this type it will then prompt you to choose the program you want to use to view or display the file once it's been downloaded, so click the **Browse** button in the next dialog to locate and double-click a suitable program on your hard disk, and then click **OK**. Explorer will download the file and then launch that program to display the file.

There's also a checkbox labelled **Always ask before opening this type of file**. If you remove the checkmark from this box, Explorer will use the option you select this time whenever you download the same type of file in future. So if you choose to **Open this file from its current location**, and select a program to use, that same program will automatically be used on all future occasions.

You can view and edit the settings for different types of file by opening **My Computer** and selecting **View | Folder Options | File Types**. Click a file type in the list, and click the **Edit** button. If the box beside **Confirm open after download** isn't checked, this type of file will always be opened – you can check this box if you'd like the chance to save this type of file in future or use a different program to open it. To find out which program will open this type of file, click on either **Play** or **Open** in the **Actions** box, then click the **Edit...** button.

Virus alert!

Always run a virus checker before running any program you've downloaded. Although people get a bit too hysterical about it, there's a small risk that a program might contain a virus. It takes only a few seconds to do and might just save a lot of hassle later. I'll show you where to find a virus checker in Chapter 13.

Configuring Your Browser – Automatic Or Manual?

In the routine above, I've assumed that you do actually have a program on your own system that can play or display the type of file you're downloading. Of course, that won't always be the case. Remember that you can opt to save any file so that you know you've got it safe and sound on your disk, and then go hunting for a suitable player or viewer program afterwards. You can then install the new program in the usual way and use it to open this file.

If you do that, you have three possible options for the future:

▶ Every time you come across a file of this type on the Web you can opt to save it, and open it yourself later on in the same way.

▶ You can wait until you find another file of this type on the Web, click on **Open this file from its current location**, remove the tick from the checkbox below and then direct Explorer to the external viewer that you now possess. If you choose this method, your browser will configure itself automatically to use this viewer for this type of file in future.

▶ You can configure Internet Explorer yourself as soon as you've installed the new program so that it knows exactly what to do next time you choose to open this type of file.

I strongly suggest you go for one of the first two options. If you save the file and view it later, you won't be wasting expensive online time looking at something that'll still be there when you disconnect. And if you wait until the next time you find this kind of file, you'll just have to spend a few seconds pointing Explorer to the correct viewer.

If you really do want to configure Explorer yourself, you'll need to know something about file types, extensions, and the way in which particular file types are associated with a certain program. That's the sort of technical stuff I'm not going to venture into here (you'll find it in my book *The UK PC Starter Kit*, also published by Prentice Hall), and it's rarely necessary to configure these settings yourself when your browser makes such a good job of it.

▶ *For more on file types and viewers, skip ahead to Chapter 13. Or turn to Chapter 21 to find some of the best add-ons for viewing the Web's multimedia files.*

Using Internet Shortcuts

We've looked at a few ways that you can go to a particular page on the Web – you can click a link on a page, type a URL into the address bar and press Enter, or select the site from your History list or Favorites. Another method is the **Internet shortcut**.

An Internet shortcut is a tiny file that just contains a web page's URL. You can keep these little files on your desktop (or indeed anywhere on your computer's hard disk) and double-click them to go to the page they point at. In effect, they work in exactly the same way as the links you find on a web page.

Internet shortcuts are my Favorites

If you're using Internet Explorer, you'll find a folder called Favorites inside your Windows folder (or, in Windows 2000, in your personal folder inside the Documents and Settings folder). When you open it, you'll see all the items on your **Favorites** menu. These are all Internet shortcuts - you can create new shortcuts here, and add subfolders, all of which will appear on your **Favorites** menu.

The easiest way to create an Internet shortcut is to click on any link in a web page and (before releasing the mouse button) drag it to your desktop. You can also create your own shortcuts by hand. Open a text editor such as Windows' Notepad and type the following:

> **[InternetShortcut]**
> **URL=***type the URL here*

After the equals sign, type the URL you want this shortcut to point at, such as **http://www.disney.co.uk** Save the file wherever you like with an appropriate name and the extension **.url**. For instance, you might call this example **Disney Site.url** You can create Internet shortcuts that use the other protocols mentioned on page 57, such as a link to a newsgroup, an FTP site, or the email address of someone you contact frequently.

To use an Internet Shortcut, just double-click it. Your browser will start and open the page. If your browser is already running, you can drag and drop a shortcut into its window. You can also copy these shortcuts onto a floppy disk or attach them to an email message so that someone else can use them.

Browse Faster Using The Cache

If you've spent some time surfing the Web and skipping backwards and forwards between pages, here's a phenomenon you might have noticed: when you return to a page you've seen before (perhaps by clicking the Back button) you don't usually have to wait – the page appears almost instantly.

This is the **disk cache** at work. Every page you view, along with its constituent images, is saved to a folder on your own computer's disk. Most browsers simply call this folder **Cache**, but Internet Explorer uses its own, reasonably intuitive, name: **Temporary Internet Files**. For brevity I'm just going to refer to it as the cache folder.

Every web page that Explorer downloads and displays it also saves into the cache folder, along with images and other items on the page (yes, there can be more to a page than just text and images, as you'll learn in Chapter 22). The cache folder will gradually enlarge until it reaches its maximum allowed size, and then the oldest files will gradually be removed to make way for more recent ones.

Whenever you click a link or type a URL into the address bar, the browser looks in the cache first to see if it can grab the files it needs from there instead of downloading them from the Web. Not only does this speed things up for you, it also takes some of the strain off the poor old Internet.

Tweaking The Cache Settings

This isn't a 'must do', but it certainly is a 'might want to do'. Explorer will be set up to use the cache by default, so you're reaping the rewards already. But it might be set up to use a much larger chunk of hard disk space than you really want to sacrifice.

Click your way to **Tools** | **Internet Options** | **General**. On the part of the page labelled **Temporary Internet Files** you'll see two buttons labelled **Delete Files** and **Settings…**. The first of these empties the cache folder letting you regain the disk space it was using, but the real action all takes place on a dialog that appears when you click the **Settings…** button (shown in the screenshot on the next page). From this dialog you can choose how and when Internet Explorer should use the disk cache, and view its contents (letting you selectively delete or copy items from pages you've visited). Here's a quick description of the controls and what they're for.

▶ **Check for newer versions of stored pages**. Choose when Explorer should look in the cache for a page and when it should download it. If you choose **Every visit to the page**, Explorer will never search the cache, even if you looked at this page only two minutes ago. **Every time you start Internet**

Explorer means that if you haven't visited this URL in this web session Explorer should download the page; if you have, it will retrieve it from the cache. **Never** means that Explorer will never try to download the page if there's a page in the cache with the same URL, regardless of its age. **Automatically** leaves Explorer to decide when to check for a newer page, based on its analysis of how often a page has changed over a period of time.

▶ **Amount of disk space to use**. When it's first installed, Explorer will pick what it reckons to be a sensible amount of your hard disk space to hold cached files. Drag this slider to the left or right to reduce or increase this figure.

▶ **Move Folder** lets you move the **Temporary Internet Files** folder elsewhere. This might be useful if you have another drive with more free space.

▶ **View Files** lets you look at all the cached files. This can be every bit as informative as the History list, giving the names of the files, their original URL, the date you last viewed them, and more. **View Objects** gives a similar view of a folder named **Downloaded Program Files**, which contains ActiveX controls that were installed on your PC by web pages you've visited (more about ActiveX controls in Chapter 14).

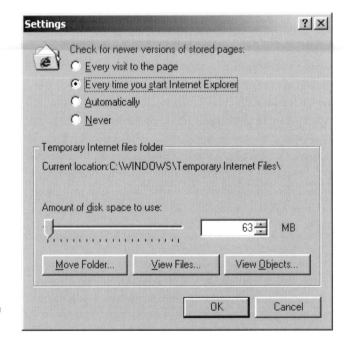

▶ Alter Explorer's use of the disk cache and take a look at the files in the cache folder.

Your files are downloading anyway!

Because Explorer uses the files' original names and locations in the cache folder, you can open it any time you want to and copy files from it for your own use. So instead of saving text, source and images from a page as you surf, you could just come back to the Settings dialog after disconnecting and click View Files to locate them.

Which Option Should I Use?

So which of the four **Check for newer versions** options is the best? It really depends upon the types of website you visit most often, and whether you visit the same ones regularly. Sites specialising in news, weather and stock quotes might change by the hour, or even by the minute, so you'd want to choose **Every visit to the page** to always see the latest version. However, if you tend to visit and revisit sites that rarely change, you can speed things up a lot by selecting **Never** and loading the page from the cache every time.

I chose 'Never'. How can I see if the page has changed?

You don't need to go back and change the cache settings. Just click the **Refresh** button on the toolbar (or press F5). This forces Explorer to download and display the current version of the page from the server, and store it in the cache to replace your old copy.

Internet Explorer sets itself to the **Automatically** option by default. This is irritating if you'd like to know when you're seeing a new page and when you're not, but it does speed up your surfing by maximising the use of the cache.

If in doubt, the safe 'middle option' is **Every time you start Internet Explorer**. This way you'll always see the latest version of the page when you first visit that site in a web session, but if you return to it later in that session it will be opened from the cache.

Do Your Browsing Offline

Try this: open Internet Explorer and choose **File | Work Offline** (or click the **Offline** toolbar button) and click the **History** button. If you look at the pages listed, you'll see that some are greyed-out to indicate they're not available offline, with others appearing in black. Clicking on any of the black entries will open the corresponding page from the cache folder.

This is **offline browsing** – the ability to surf the Web (some of it, anyway) without going online. We've already seen how the cache works, and the majority of items in the History list should still be in the cache and available for viewing offline.

GOOD QUESTION!

Why are some of the pages in History unavailable?

When web authors write a web page, they can set a date when the page should expire. When that date comes around, browsers remove the page from the cache folder regardless of the settings you chose. If a particular page is expected to change frequently, its author may specify a date in the past to ensure the page is never cached - that way you'll see the latest version on each visit. The result is that the page is properly included in the history list but never makes it into the cache for offline viewing.

But offline browsing is a little more powerful than that. You can create a list of pages that you'd like to browse offline, send Internet Explorer online to retrieve them in a quick burst of activity, and then log off and browse them in your own time. Although the same amount of information has to be downloaded, you're not pausing at each page to read it so your online time is cut dramatically.

There are two ways to make pages available offline. The first is used when you add the page to your Favorites list (see page 52). Click the checkbox labelled **Make available offline** and then click the **Customize** button to choose from related options. The second method is for items already on your Favorites list. Choose **Organize Favorites** from the Favorites menu, click once on the chosen page and you'll see the same checkbox (shown in the screenshot below). When you click this checkbox, a **Properties** button will appear to let you decide how and when the page should be retrieved.

The options you can choose from after clicking the Customize or Properties buttons are many and varied, but the defaults are well suited to UK users with their eye on the phone bill. The **Schedule** tab allows you to set a schedule for automatic downloading of pages at precise times, but the better choice is to download (or *synchronize*) all pages manually by choosing **Tools** | **Synchronize**.

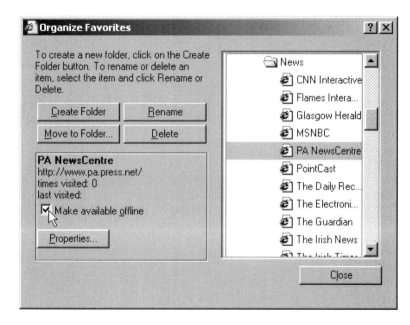

◄ Use the Organize Favorites dialog to make pages available for offline browsing.

On the **Download** tab you can choose how deeply into the site the downloading should travel. When set to 0 (the default) only the selected page will be retrieved. Setting this value to 1 will download this page and every page linked to it. You can set this option to trawl through up to three levels of links, but this could add up to hundreds of pages so regard 1 as the maximum until you're sure you know what you're doing! By clicking the **Advanced** button, you can choose whether elements such as images and videos should be ignored which will help to speed the synchronization process and save some disk space.

FINDING YOUR WAY ON THE WEB

Armed with the information we've covered in the last two chapters you're ready to venture out onto the Web and start surfing. And almost immediately you'll hit a predicament: how on earth can you find what you're looking for? As you probably guessed, the Internet is one jump ahead of you on that score. Whatever you're looking for, there's no shortage of tools to help you find it. Choosing the best tool to use will depend largely on the type of information you want to find, but don't panic: these search tools are easy to use, and you'll probably use several of them regularly. And, yet again, all you need is your trusty browser.

Finding A Search Site

Anything you can find on the World Wide Web you can find a link to at one of the Web's search sites. Although finding a search site on the Web is easy (especially as I'm about to tell you where the most popular ones are!), picking the one that's going to give the best results is never an exact science. Essentially there are two types of site available: **search engines** and **directories**.

▶ **Search engines** are indexes of World Wide Web sites, usually built automatically by a program called a spider, a robot, a worm, or something equally appetising (the AltaVista search engine uses a program it endearingly calls Scooter). These programs scour the Web constantly, and return with information about a page's location, title and contents, which is then added to an index. To search for a certain type of information, just type in keywords and the search engine will display a list of sites containing those words.

▶ **Directories** are hand-built lists of pages sorted into categories. Although you can search directories using a keyword search, it's often as easy to click on a category, and then click your way through the ever-more-specific sub-categories until you find the subject you're interested in.

Search engines have the benefit of being about as up-to-date in their indexes as it's possible to be, as a result of their automation. The downside is that if you search for **pancake recipe** in a search engine, the resulting list of pages won't all necessarily contain recipes for pancakes – some might just be pages in which the words 'pancake' and 'recipe' coincidentally both happen to appear. However, the robot programs used by the search engines all vary in the ways they gather their information, so you'll quite likely get results using one engine that you didn't get using another.

Directories don't have this problem because they list the subject of a page rather than the words it contains, but you won't always find the newest sites this way – sites tend to be listed in directories when their authors submit them for inclusion.

Below is a short list of popular search engines and directories to get you started. When you arrive at one of these, it's worth adding it to Internet Explorer's **Favorites** menu so that you can get back again whenever you need to without a lot of typing.

Search site	URL
AltaVista	http://www.altavista.digital.com
Dogpile	http://www.dogpile.com
Excite	http://www.excite.co.uk
Google	http://www.google.com
HotBot	http://www.hotbot.com
Infoseek	http://www.infoseek.com
Lycos UK	http://www.lycos.co.uk
searchUK	http://www.searchuk.com
UK Plus	http://www.ukplus.co.uk
Yahoo! UK & Ireland	http://www.yahoo.co.uk

Using A Search Engine

For this example I'll pick Excite, but most search engines work in exactly the same way, and look much the same too. Indeed, directories such as **Yahoo** and **Infoseek** can be used like this if you like the simplicity of keyword searches.

When you arrive at Excite you'll see a page like the one shown in the next screenshot. For the simplest sort of search, type a single word into the text box, and click on **Search**. If you want to search for something that can't be encapsulated in a single word it's worth reading the instructions – you'll probably see a link on the page marked Help or Search Tips or something similar – but there are a few tricks you can use that most search engines will understand (and those that don't will generally just ignore them).

One for the kids

The Internet is fairly teeming with websites for children, and Yahoo has a sister site called Yahooligans at **http://www.yahooligans.com** dedicated to these sites alone. The format is the same as Yahoo's main site, but all the links lead to pages for, or by, kids, along with some useful advice and information for their parents.

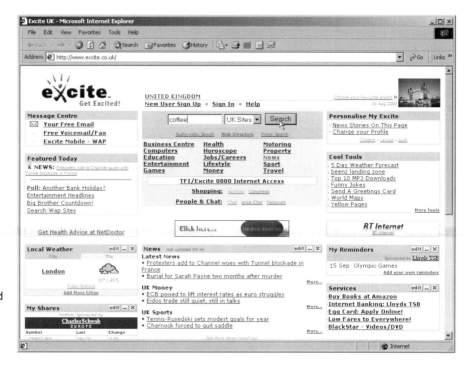

▶ Type a keyword into the search engine's text box and click Search.

▶ If you enter several keywords, type them in descending order of importance. For example, if you want to find pictures of dolphins, type **dolphin pictures**. The list will then present good links to dolphin sites before the rather more general links to sites just containing pictures.

▶ Use capital letters only if you expect to find capital letters. Searching for **PARIS** may find very little, but searching for **Paris** should find a lot. If you don't mind whether the word is found capitalized or not, use lower case only (**paris**).

▶ To find a particular phrase, enclose it in "quote marks". For example, a search for **"hot dog"** would find only pages containing this phrase and ignore pages that contained just one word or the other.

▶ Prefix a word with a + sign if it must be included, and with a – sign if it must be excluded. For example, to find out more about tourism in Paris, you might search for **paris+tourism**. Constructing very specific searches can make a huge amount of difference. A general search for **racing** produced 200 000 matching pages that probably covered everything from horse racing to barge racing. Refining the search to **racing+ "formula 1" +car** reduced this to under 10 000 pages – in other words, removing 190 000 pages I probably wouldn't have found useful.

After entering the text you want to search for and clicking the **Search** button, your browser will send the information off to the engine, and within a few seconds you should see a new page like the one pictured below listing the sites that matched your search criteria. I used the keyword **coffee**, and Excite has found 297 031 different pages. It's worth remembering that when some search engines say they've found pages *about coffee*, they've found pages that contain the word 'coffee' somewhere within the text. Many of these pages may be *about* something entirely different.

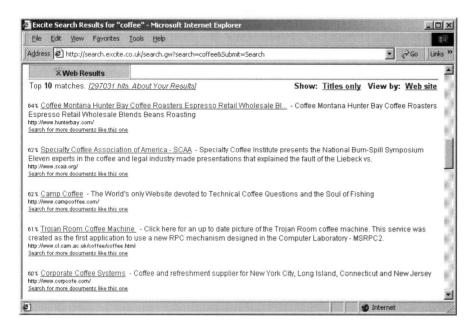

◀ A search for 'coffee' finds more than enough results to keep me up all night.

Of course, you won't find all 297 031 pages listed here. Instead you'll see links to the ten most relevant pages, with a few words quoted from the beginning of each. At the bottom of the page you'll find a button that will lead you to the next ten on the list, and so on. In true Web style, these are all hypertext links – click the link to open any page that sounds promising. If the page fails to live up to that promise, use your browser's **Back** button to return to the search results and try a different one.

Save your search for later

When the search results appear, you can add this page to Internet Explorer's **Favorites** menu. Not only is the URL of the search site stored, but also the keywords you entered for the search. It's a handy option to remember if you don't have time to visit all the pages found in the search straight away.

Most search engines give the pages a score for relevancy, and these are worth keeping an eye on. In many cases, a page scoring below about 70 per cent is unlikely to give much information. If you can't find what you want using one search engine, always try another – because their methods are different, their results can vary dramatically.

▶ *A search engine may be able to find a program for you by name (such as* **WSFinger***), but it may not be as successful if you enter a filename (such as* **WSFNGR.ZIP***). To find a file by name, try using one of the FTP search engines mentioned on page 171, or use an Archie search, as explained on page 181.*

Searching The Web Directories

Top of the league of web directories is Yahoo, which now has a 'UK & Ireland' site at **http://www.yahoo.co.uk** When you first arrive at the Yahoo site, you'll see a search engine-style text box into which you can type keywords if you prefer to search that way. However, you'll also see a collection of hypertext links below that, and these are the key to the directory system. Starting from a choice of broad categories on this page, you can dig more deeply into the system to find links to more specific information.

To take an example, click on the **Computers and Internet** link. On the next page, you'll see the list of sub-categories, which includes **Graphics**, **Hardware**, **Multimedia**, **Training**, and many more Computer- and Internet-related subjects. Click on the **Multimedia** link, and you'll see another list of multimedia-related categories, shown in the following screenshot. Below this list of categories, you'll see another list: these are links to multimedia-related sites rather than more Yahoo categories. To find out more about multimedia generally, you might click one of these to visit that site; to find out more about a specific area of multimedia such as sound, video or virtual reality, you'd click that category in the upper list.

It's a 404!

Sometimes you'll click a link on a search results page, only to see a dull grey screen and a **Not Found** message. This is due to the constant rise and fall of websites that I mentioned on page 58. Some search engines are more reliable than others in this department, and some seem to offer almost nothing but out-of-date links. (The '404', incidentally, comes from a similar message, now rarely seen, for a page that couldn't be found: **HTTP Error 404**.) In popular Net jargon, almost anything that can't be found is said to be 404'd rather than lost.

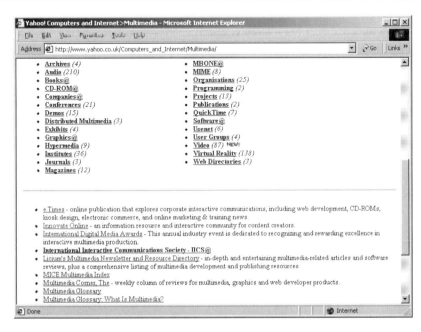

◀ Choose a more specific Yahoo category from the upper list, or a direct link to a website from the lower.

The layout is pretty easy to follow when you've browsed around for a few minutes, but Yahoo has simplified it further by using bold and plain text to help you identify where you're going. Bold text means that this is a link to another Yahoo category; plain text indicates that it's a link to a page elsewhere on the Web that contains the sort of information you've been searching for. Beside most of the bold category links, you'll also see a number in brackets, such as **Pictures (448)**. This number tells you how many links you'll find in that category.

Why do some of the categories finish with an '@' symbol?

The '@' symbol indicates a cross-reference to a different main category. For example, click on **Companies@** and you'll be moving from the **Computers and Internet** heading to the **Business and Economy** heading. You'll find links to multimedia companies here, but other categories will be more related to business matters than to computing.

Which Search Site Is Best?

So should you use a search engine or a directory? And which one should you choose? There really isn't a 'best site', of course, though you'll probably come across a few candidates for the 'worst search site' title on your travels. Most users try a few search sites in their early days on the Web, settle on one or two they like best and stick with them. Here are quick introductions to four popular but very different sites, all well worth a look.

Lycos UK

Lycos has long been one of the 'heavyweight' US-based search engines, and now has a UK site at **http://www.lycos.co.uk** A simple dropdown list lets you search for sites in the UK and Ireland only or worldwide, and you can also search for sounds, pictures and books. In many ways, Lycos barely differs from other search engines such as Excite and AltaVista – search results are presented in a similar way, there are links to news stories and recommended sites, and you'll find a few categories that give the impression of being a Yahoo-like web directory until you see how limited they are. Lycos expects to be used for keyword searches, and it has one very useful option that its opposition doesn't: after entering your keywords, you can choose whether the engine should find matches containing all the words you entered, any word, or the exact phrase.

Mirago

The main Mirago page at **http://www.mirago.co.uk** looks a lot like any other search engine, but its big difference is a Kids Only button at the top of the page. Clicking this button takes you to **http://www.mirago.co.uk/zone**, a family-friendly version of the search engine that filters out links and site descriptions you wouldn't want your kids to see (you may not want to see them yourself, for that matter). Whichever version of Mirago you use, you can carry out powerful UK-specific searches for web pages, images, video, multimedia or someone's name, and set a variety of other searching and sorting options.

◀ Mirago, a much-needed 'family friendly' search engine.

Yahoo! UK & Ireland

Yahoo was the site that invented the whole Web-searching concept, and it's still a well-loved and widely used workhorse. Its UK and Ireland site at **http://www.yahoo.co.uk** has all the variety, speed and reliability of its US-based counterpart, but it also lets you choose between searching the entire Web or just the UK and Ireland sections of it. Even if you choose to search the whole Web, any UK or Irish sites found will be placed at the top of the list and indicated by flags to grab your attention. You'll also see a sunglasses icon beside sites that the folk at Yahoo thought were especially 'cool'. The layout is plain and functional, to the point of being dull, and site descriptions range from short to non-existent, but its power is hard to beat. Be warned though: both Yahoo and its kids' counterpart at **http://www.yahooligans.com** can be addictive! If you start exploring those categories, rather than running a quick keyword search and going away again, it's easy to lose track of the time you've spent online!

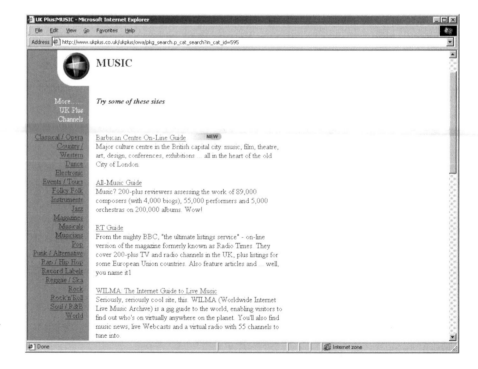

▶ UK Plus: a smart and straightforward starting point for finding UK sites.

UK Plus

Like Yahoo, UK Plus at **http://www.ukplus.co.uk** uses a directory format in which you pick a category from its front page and dig deeper into the sub-categories until you reach the subject you're looking for. Apart from being a much more attractive site than Yahoo, there are a couple of more important differences. First, you'll find nothing but UK sites here, and second, every site is accompanied by a useful description. Although the UK Plus directory is tiny by Yahoo standards, it's probably the best and simplest place to start looking when nothing but a UK site will do.

▶ *If you're looking for truly specialised information and the traditional search engines and directories can't help, turn to page 280 for a site that may. For more details about finding people or locating newsgroups, turn to Finding People On The Net on page 118 and Searching The Newsgroups on page 138.*

Searching Made Faster & Friendlier

If you're searching for a particularly elusive website or nugget of information, one option is to work through every search engine you can think of until you track it down. A better option is to use a **meta search** site. These look a lot like any other search site, but they submit your keywords to a bundle of different search engines at once and then gather all the results together on a single page for you to browse through. Two of the best meta search sites on the Web are MetaCrawler at **http://www.metacrawler.com** and HotBot at **http://www.hotbot.com** Better than either is Copernic from **http://www.copernic.com**, shown in the next screenshot. Copernic is a free meta search program that you install on your PC. It works just like a web-based search engine, but has useful options that let you customise the way it works and look through old search results without going back online.

I mentioned a few pages back that you can improve the relevance of the search results by constructing your search properly (using quote marks, plus and minus symbols, and so on), but wouldn't it be nice if you could just ask something in normal English and be taken to the answer? Well you can! Go to Ask Jeeves at **http://www.ask.co.uk** (or the oddly-named children's version, Ask Jeeves for Kids, at **http://www.ajkids.com**) and type in a question like "When was Beethoven born?" The results will list all the similar questions Jeeves knows the answer to, and you can pick the one that's closest to what you're looking for.

▶ Search the Web using over a dozen search engines at once with Copernic.

Any portal in a storm?

A 'portal' is a search site that's expanded to offer a bit of everything – news, weather, finance, shopping, kitchen sink, etc. Portals would like to be your 'start' page, the page you look at first when you go online. The result is that old favourites like Lycos, Excite and AltaVista now all carry identical clutter on their pages, leading many users to abandon them in favour of the simpler approach offered by search sites like Google and raging.com.

Yellow Pages – Searching For Businesses

So far we've been looking at fairly general searches – you want a particular type of information and you don't mind where it is or who put it there, and consequently the results can be hit-and-miss. Searching for a specific business or service is different; either you find it or you don't. But businesses want to be found, to the extent that they'll pay to be listed in specialised 'yellow pages' directories, so these searches will almost always yield results. Two of the most useful for finding UK businesses are Yell.com (the Yellow Pages we all know and love, in its online incarnation), and Scoot.

Yell.com at **http://www.yell.com** (perhaps you guessed?) is an ideal place to begin a search for a UK company or business. Type in a 'what' or a 'who' (such as *boutique* or *Jailhouse Frock*) and a 'where' (such as *Chelmsford*) and click the Search button to get started. The results show all the expected contact details, plus links to the company's website, if it has one, and local area maps to help you find your way on the ground.

The Scoot site, at **http://www.scoot.co.uk**, works in a slightly different way from Yell.com. Although you can click the Company Name link to find a specific company, Scoot specialises in locating a particular *type* of business in your chosen area. This is a great way to search if, for example, you need a plumber and you're currently too damp to care which plumber it is.

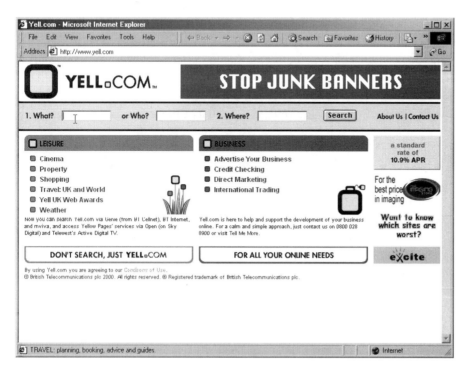

◀ Yell.com, the ideal place to find the websites and contact details of UK businesses.

Guesswork is good

BY THE WAY

If you can't trace the URL of a company's website, try typing a few guesses into your browser's address bar. Most companies use their own name as their domain name, so if you're looking for a company called Dodgy Goods plc, try **www.dodgygoods.com** or **www.dodgygoods.co.uk**. If you look at the company URLs given throughout this book, you'll see how likely this is to get a result.

If you haven't found the company yet, it's either American or it doesn't want to be found! To search for US companies, head off to Excite at **http://www.excite.com** and click the **Yellow Pages** button. Enter a company name and category description, together with location details if known, and click the search button. If the category you have chosen doesn't match an Excite category, you'll be given a list of similar categories to choose from. You can also try **http://www.companiesonline.com**, a new addition to the Lycos search engine family. If you're looking for financial or performance-related information about a company, visit Infoseek and select **Company Profiles** from the dropdown list to search through almost 50 000 US companies. Finally, of course, there's the good old workhorse, Yahoo. Visit **http://www.yahoo.co.uk/ Business_and_Economy/Companies** and you'll be presented with a list of over 100 categories. The sites you'll find in Yahoo's categories cover the UK and Ireland as well as America and elsewhere.

Easy Web Searching With Internet Explorer

To reach a search site quickly in Internet Explorer, click the Search button on the toolbar (a globe icon with a magnifying glass). A frame will appear at the left of Explorer's window, similar to the Favorites and History list panels, displaying a mini version of a search engine. Explorer chooses the search engine for you, but you can choose a different one by clicking the **New** or **Customize** buttons. Type in your query, click the obvious button and the results will appear in the same frame with the usual **Next 10** button at the bottom.

Instant searching

Instead of clicking the **Search** button and waiting for the search page to load, Internet Explorer offers a quicker method. In the address bar, type the word(s) you want to search for then press Enter. If a matching website can be found, Explorer will open it; if not, your words will be passed to the search engine and the search frame will appear to display the results.

The great benefit of this method of searching is that you can click any entry in the list to open it in the main part of the window without losing track of the search results. For a brief description of each site found, hold your mouse pointer over the link for a moment as shown in the screenshot below.

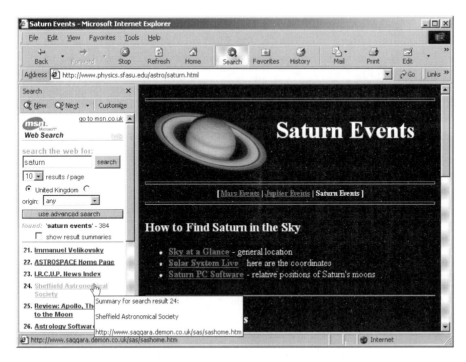

◀ Internet Explorer's search panel keeps your results visible as you work your way through the most promising links.

Surf's Up! Now Where Shall I Go?

All dressed up and nowhere to surf? The sheer unpredictability of the World Wide Web will almost certainly tempt you at times, even if there's nothing in particular you need to do or find. For those moments when you've just got to surf, here's a brief list of sites that give you somewhere worth surfing to. The official term for these, sad to relate, is 'cool sites'. On the Web, you have to aspire to being 'cool'.)

▶ **Cool Site Of The Day**. A single cool site every day. And every day the entire universe goes to visit the lucky recipient of the title. You'll also find The Still Cool Archive, The Cool-O-Meter, and Cool Site Of The Year. Bucketloads of cool, and you'll find it all at **http://cool.infi.net**

▶ **Top 50 UK Web Sites**. A simple list of sites numbered 1 to 50 according to how many visitors (or 'hits') each site has had in the last week. You'll find a huge variety of stuff here, but they must all be good, mustn't they? Skip off to **http://www.top50.co.uk**

▶ **PC Magazine's Top 100 Websites.** Top sites chosen by the magazine's editors and sorted into 20 categories, but now buried at the less-than-catchy URL **http://www.zdnet.com/pcmag/stories/reviews/0,6755, 2394453,00.html**

▶ **The Weekly Hot 100**. Links sorted into 60 categories from the obvious (Sport, Music, Travel) to the not-so-obvious (Auctions, Wine, Jobs). The sites are sorted by how many visits they get. Head for **http://www. 100hot.com**

▶ **Jacob Richman's Hot Sites**. 32 categories of useful links sniffed out and sorted by Jacob himself, including Humour, Education, Law and Music. Although he has no greater claim to fame than any other web surfer, Jacob has a keen eye for good sites and a well-organised collection of links. Find this at **http://www.jr.co.il/hotsites/hotsites.htm**

Finding more cool sites

The Web abounds with sites that are cool (or sites whose authors think they're cool!) – run a search for **cool sites** at any search engine to find more coolness than you can shake a stick at.

The World Wide Web is an art form, and like any form of art, some people can do it and some people can't. Depending on your viewpoint, bad art can be far more entertaining than good art: there are countless websites out there which, far from being 'cool', have been caught with their trousers round their ankles. If you've overdosed on cool, try these as an antidote:

▶ **The Worst Of The Web**. Click on the large image to take a trip through the current 'worst sites', accompanied with comments from your three cartoon hosts. Alternatively, follow the links below the image to see previous award winners in this category. Visit **http://www.worstoftheweb.com** for this 'bland bombshell'.

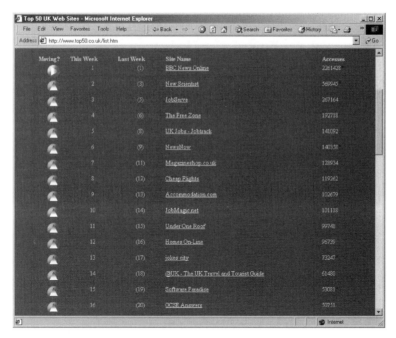

◀ The Top 50 UK Web Sites, as chosen weekly by several million people!

▶ **Totally Useless.** Links to dozens of useless sites, including *50 Years of Band-Aid*, *Beard Research* and *The Electric Pole Shrine*, all at **http://www.ambitweb.com/useless/useless.html**

▶ **Worst Web Sites**. Links to some of the best 'dead flies' that litter the Web, at **http://webworst.miningco.com**

8

EXCHANGING MESSAGES BY EMAIL

▶ **IN THIS CHAPTER**

What's so great about email anyway?

Choose and set up your email software

Send and receive your first email message

Take the mystery out of sending files by email

Learn the secret language of the Internet – emoticons and acronyms email is the old man of the Internet, and one of the reasons the network was constructed in the first place. It's one of the easiest areas of Net life to use, and one of the most used – for many people, sending and receiving email is their only reason for going online. By the end of this chapter you'll be able to send email messages and computer files to millions of people all over the world (well, perhaps not all of them!) in less time than it takes to stick a stamp on an envelope.

Why Should I Use email?

First, it's incredibly cheap. A single first class stamp costs 27p and will get a letter to a single, local (in global terms) address. But for a local phone call costing 5p you can deliver dozens of email messages to all corners of the world. Second, it's amazingly fast. In some cases, your email might be received within just seconds of your sending it. (It isn't always quite as fast as that, however: on occasions, when the network conspires against you, it might take several hours.) Third, it's easy to keep copies of the email you send and receive, and to sort and locate individual messages quickly.

Snail mail

A popular term for ordinary mail sent through the land-based postal service, whose speed is closer to that of a certain mollusc than email.

There's a possible fourth reason, but it should be regarded with some caution. If you agonise for hours over ordinary letter writing, email should make life easier for you. An inherent feature of email is its informality: spelling, grammar and punctuation are tossed to the wind in favour of speed and brevity.

Everybody's First Question

Whenever the subject of email comes up with Internet beginners, the same question is guaranteed to arise within the first minute. So that you can concentrate on the rest of the chapter, I'll put your mind at ease by answering it straight away. The question is: *What happens if email arrives for me and I'm not online to receive it?*

The answer: email arrives at your service provider's computer (their **mail server**) and waits for you to collect it. In fact it will wait there a long time if it has to: most mail servers will delete messages that remain uncollected for several months, but if you take a week's holiday you can collect the week's email when you return.

Newbie

You're a newbie! It's okay, I'm not being abusive. It just means that you're new to the Internet. You wouldn't be proud to describe yourself as a newbie, but you might want to do so when appealing for help in a newsgroup, for example, to keep responses as simple as possible.

Understanding email Addresses

There are two easy ways to spot an Internet 'newbie'. The first is that their messages begin 'Dear...' and end 'Yours sincerely'. The second is that they tell you their 'email number'. Don't fall into either trap! I'll tell you how to avoid the first pitfall later in the chapter; in the second case, you definitely have an email *address*!

Email addresses consist of three elements: a username, an '@' symbol, and a domain name. Your username will usually be the name in which your account was set up, and the name that you log on with when you connect. The domain name is the address of your ISP or online service. For example, if your user name were **joe.bloggs** and you set up an account with Virgin Net, your email address would be **joe.bloggs@virgin.net** Other companies do things slightly differently: your account name comes after the '@' sign, and you can have unlimited email addresses by putting whatever you like *before* the '@' sign. Joe Bloggs could have the email address **joe@joebloggs.**

freeserve.co.uk, and his wife could be **jane@joebloggs.freeserve.co.uk** (though she might be less than thrilled at the prospect!).

Quoting your email address

If you have to say your email address out loud, replace the dots with the word 'dot' and the @ sign with the word 'at'. The email address of Joe Bloggs, mentioned above, would be pronounced 'joe dot bloggs at virgin dot net'.

email Addresses & Online Services

The email address of someone using an online service is structured in a similar way, although CompuServe calls the username a 'User ID' and AOL calls it a 'Screen Name'. If you have an account with an ISP and you want to send email to an AOL member, use the address *ScreenName*@**aol.com**. To send to a member of MSN, use *username*@**msn.com**, and for CompuServe members use *UserID*@**compuserve.com**.

Members of online services can also send email out on to the Internet to someone with an ISP account. In fact, for members of AOL and MSN they can use the email address without making any changes to it. If you're a CompuServe member, though, you'll have to insert the word 'Internet:' (including the colon) before the address. To send the fictitious Joe Bloggs a message, for example, a CompuServe member would use the address **internet:joe.bloggs@virgin.net** The word 'internet' isn't case-sensitive, and it doesn't matter if you leave a space after the colon.

If you're a member of an online service, and you want to email another member of the same service, all you need to enter is the username (or User ID, or Screen Name) of the person you want to email.

What Do I Need?

If you have an account with an online service such as CompuServe or AOL, you don't need anything more – the software you use to connect to and navigate the service has built-in email capability. If you have an ISP account, you'll need an email client (geek speak for 'a program that works with email'). There are many of these to choose between, and your ISP might have provided one when you signed up. There are three major factors to consider when choosing an email program:

▶ it's compatible with the protocols used by your email account (I'll explain that in a moment);

▶ it will let you work offline;

▶ it will let you organise incoming and outgoing messages into separate 'folders'.

Offline

JARGON BUSTER

Software that lets you work offline allows you to read and write your messages without being connected to your ISP or online service and clocking up charges. You only need to go online to send your messages and receive any new email. The earliest email had to be written online, which is why speed mattered more than spelling.

Oh dear, more of those protocols again. This isn't too tough though. There are two protocols used to move email around: **SMTP** (Simple Mail Transport Protocol) and **POP3** (Post Office Protocol, which is currently in its third version). SMTP is the protocol used to send email messages to the server. Although SMTP can also handle the delivery of messages too if it has to, POP3 is the protocol of choice for the job. What you need to know is whether you have a POP3 email account, and your ISP should have made that quite clear. There are several dull, technical reasons why a POP3 account is better than an SMTP-only account, but the reason you care about right now is that you'll have a far wider range of email software available to choose from.

If you do have a POP3 account, the most popular email clients on the Internet are:

▶ **Outlook Express**. This Microsoft package gives you an email and newsgroup program in one, and integrates neatly with

IT'S ON THE CD

Internet Explorer. In fact, when Internet Explorer (or Windows) was installed, Outlook Express should have been installed with it and you can probably see its icon on the desktop – an envelope with a blue arrow wrapped around it. The current version (5.5) is included on the CD-ROM in the back of this book, and you can check for newer versions at **http://www.microsoft.com/windows/ie/download**

▶ **Eudora**. This popular program offers a choice of modes: light, sponsored or full. Light mode is free, but has fewer features. Full mode has all the features but it's only available after purchasing a license from **http://www.eudora.com** Sponsored mode has all the features of full, and it displays adverts instead of charging you money.

▶ **Pegasus Mail**. A neat, free, email program that you can download from **http://www.pmail.com**

What about Microsoft Exchange?

Exchange (also known as Windows Messaging) is included in recent versions of Windows, but I don't recommend using it: it's bloated, slow, and unfriendly. However, if you have Microsoft Outlook (also included in the Microsoft Office suite) I suggest you try that and see how you get on. It's the big brother to Outlook Express and offers a range of extra features well suited to busy offices such as a contacts manager and appointments scheduler.

If you don't have a POP3 account…

▶ **Tetrix Reader Plug**. This is simple and neat, and doubles as a newsreader program. Type the following URL into your browser's address bar and press Enter to start the download: **ftp://ftp.euro.net/d3/Windows/winsock-l/mail/trp110.zip**

If you use the Netscape Navigator browser, you may have an email program already. Navigator is part of an integrated suite of programs named Netscape Communicator, and this suite includes Netscape's own email program. You can find Communicator on Netscape's site at **http://www.netscape.com** but, just as with Internet Explorer, if you prefer to use an unrelated email program the choice is entirely yours.

Setting Up Your email Program

Before you can start to send and receive email, your software needs to know a bit about you and your email account. This simply involves filling in the blanks on a setup page using some of the information given to you by your service provider (see pages 30–31). The first time you start the program it should prompt you to enter this information (unless it was entered automatically when you signed up with your ISP), but it's worth knowing where to find it in case you ever need to change it in the future.

▶ In **Eudora**, go to **Tools | Options**. Click the icons in the left pane to open the various option pages. The settings you're concerned with at this point are scattered over the first five pages. On the **Sending Mail** page, remove the checkmark from the **Immediate Send** box.

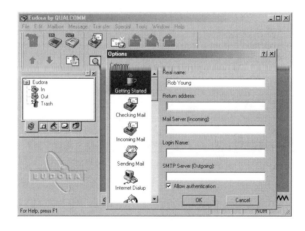

◀ Entering personal email account details into Eudora.

▶ In **Pegasus**, click **Tools | Internet Options** and work through the four tabbed pages filling in the details.

▶ In **Outlook Express**, choose **Tools | Accounts** and click the **Mail** tab.

In the first two programs especially, you'll find a bewildering array of checkboxes and options. Ignore them! Just fill in personal details about your email address, POP3 account name and password, SMTP and POP3 mail server addresses, and so on. In Outlook Express there are one or two options worth changing. Go to the **Tools** menu and choose **Options**. On the **General** tab, remove the checkmark beside **Send and receive messages at startup**. This prevents your PC dialling up every time you open Outlook Express, which can be annoying when you just wanted to read or reply to a message. You might also want to check **When starting go directly to my 'Inbox' folder**, bypassing the friendly 'overview' screen that appears when you start the program. On the **Send** tab, remove the checkmark beside **Send messages immediately**. Finally, click **OK**.

JARGON BUSTER

SMTP server, POP3 server

There are two protocols computers use to move email around, SMTP (used to *send* email messages) and POP3 (used to *deliver* messages to you). Your email program needs to know the name of the computers handling these things (the *servers*). They may both be the same, something like **mail.myprovider.net**, or they may be the equally intuitive **smtp.myprovider.net** and **pop.myprovider.net** If you need to know, your ISP can tell you, but you may prefer to try these first and perhaps save the cost of a premium call to the support line.

▶ *Turn to Appendix G to find out more about working with email accounts in Outlook Express.*

Sending An email Message

You probably feel an overwhelming temptation to email everyone you know and tell them you've 'joined the club', but hold that thought for a moment. Start by sending a message to yourself instead – that way you can check that everything's working, and learn what to do when you receive a message as well.

Fire up your email program or your online service's software and click the button that opens a message window. You'll usually find this button at the left of the toolbar with a label or tooltip that reads **New Message**.

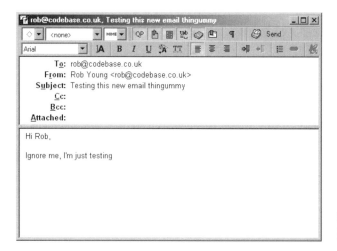

◄ Writing a test message in Eudora.

Although all of these email programs look a little different, the important features are the same:

To: Type the email address of the person to whom you want to send the message. In Outlook Express, as you type the first few letters, the program will try to match the name with an entry in your Address Book (see page 111).

CC: Carbon copy. If you want to send the message to several people, type one address in the **To** field and the rest in the **CC** field. Using this method, all recipients will know who else received a copy of the message.

BCC: Blind Carbon Copy. If you want to send the same message to several people and you don't want any of them to know who else is getting a copy, place their addresses in this field instead of the CC field.

From: You'll rarely see this in the message window, and the email software will enter your email address automatically from the information you entered when you set up the program. This tells the recipient who to reply to.

Subject: Enter a short description of your message. In some email programs you can send a message with a blank subject line, but avoid doing this. Although most people will open any email they receive (even if the subject is blank), this entry really comes into its own when the recipient is looking for this message again in six months time.

Attached: Lists the names of any computer files you want to send to the recipient along with the message. You'll learn about attaching files later in this chapter.

Below these fields is the area in which you type the message itself. Because you're going to send this message to yourself, type your own email address into the **To** field, and anything you like in the **Subject** field (just to get into the habit!), and then write yourself a welcoming message.

GOOD QUESTION!

Where's the BCC box in my program?

In Pegasus click the **Special** tab and you'll find the field is labelled **Blind CC**. In Outlook Express the BCC field is hidden by default: choose **All Headers** from the View menu and the BCC field will be shown for all future messages you write.

Now you need to send the message. Once again the programs differ here, but look for a button marked **Send** on the toolbar. Some programs will send the mail immediately, and try to log on to your service to do so; most add mail to a 'queue' (or Outbox) of messages to be sent all together when you're ready. You may even have two Send buttons with a choice of Send Now or Send Later. Clicking the Send button in the message window will store the message you've written in the Outbox. If you have more messages to write, you can follow the same steps again, still without going online.

When you've finished writing (or replying to) messages, you're ready to send everything waiting in the Outbox in one short online session. Your email program will have a **Send** or **Send & Receive** button on its toolbar. When you click this, your email program should go online and you'll see some indication that the messages are being sent. Finally, in Outlook Express and other programs with a combined Send & Receive button, the program will check for incoming mail and deliver anything it finds to your Inbox.

Don't hold your breath!

If your program sends and receives mail in a single operation, the email you're posting to yourself may came back to you instantly. On the other hand, it may not. Although email messages usually take just seconds to get to where they're going, glitches in the Internet network may delay a message by minutes or even hours.

I've Got New Mail!

You really feel you've arrived on the Internet when you receive your first message, but how do you know there are messages waiting for you? You don't, unfortunately – your email program has to go and look. With an online service account, you'll see an on-screen indication that new mail is waiting after you log on, and you can retrieve it by clicking the obvious button. With an ISP account, if you're using one of the email programs mentioned earlier, you'll have a button labelled something like **Check for new mail**, or you might have the more useful combined **Send & Receive** button.

◀ When you log on to CompuServe a message at the bottom of the screen informs you of new messages. Click the envelope button beside it to retrieve them.

Most email programs use an Inbox/Outbox system: email waiting to be sent is placed in the Outbox, and new mail will arrive in the Inbox. When new mail arrives, all you'll see is a single entry giving the subject line of the message and the name of the sender (although some programs give a wealth of information including dates and times of sending and receiving the message, its size, and the number of attached files). To read the message, double-click this entry.

The dubious automation feature

Each of the programs mentioned here can be set to check for mail automatically at regular intervals (usually entered in minutes) and give an audible or visual prompt when new mail arrives. Useful as it sounds, this is a feature best suited to busy offices with a leased line connection (unless you have ADSL or some other form of unmetered access).

At this point you can decide what to do with the message. You can delete it if you want to, and until you do it will remain visible in the program's Inbox or main folder. You should also be able to print it on to paper. Good email programs allow you to create named folders to store and organise your messages more efficiently (you might, for example, want to create a Business and a Personal folder), and you can move or copy messages from the Inbox to any of these folders. In addition you might be able to save a message as a separate file on to your hard disk or a floppy disk.

Replying & Forwarding

One of the things you're most likely to do with an incoming message is send a reply, and this is even easier than sending a brand new message. With the message open (or highlighted in your Inbox) click on the program's **Reply** or **Reply to Author** button. A new message window will open with the sender's email address already inserted and the entire message copied. Copying the original message this way is known as **quoting**, and it's standard practice in email. The program should insert a greater than sign (>) or something similar at the beginning of each line, and you can delete all or any of the original message that you don't need to include in the reply.

What's the point of quoting in replies?

The main reason is that it helps the recipient to remember what it is you're replying to. For example, if someone sends you a list of questions you can type the answer after each quoted question, saving the recipient the need to refer back to his previous message. Remember that the aim of quoting is not to build up a message containing your entire conversation, though – remove anything being quoted a second time (>>), and cut the rest down to the bare memory-jogging essentials.

The Reply button also inserts the word **Re**: at the beginning of the subject line, indicating to the recipient that it's a response to an earlier message. Although you can change the subject line of a reply, it's often best not to – many email programs have search and sort facilities that can group messages according to subject (among other things) making it easy to track an earlier email 'conversation' you've long since forgotten about.

You can also send a copy of a received message to someone else, and you'll probably have a **Forward** button on the toolbar that does the job. Enter the recipient's email address and any extra message you want to add, then click the Send button. Just as in new messages, you can include **CC** or **BCC** addresses when replying or forwarding. Forwarded messages usually have **Fwd**: inserted at the start of the subject line.

Getting Attached – Sending Files Via email

Ordinary email messages are plain text (7-bit ASCII) files, and have a size limit of 64Kb. While 64Kb is an awful lot of text, it's a pretty small measure in terms of other types of computer file you might want to send with a message. And most other types of file are **binary** (8-bit) files, so you'd expect your email program just to shrug its shoulders and walk away. Until recently it would do just that, and many people still delight in telling you that attaching binary files to email messages is a job for the brave or the foolish.

It may be text to you...

Remember that a text file is just that – plain ASCII text. A formatted document created in a modern word processor may look like ordinary text but it needs to be encoded to be sent as an attachment. The acid test is: will the file look exactly the same if you open it in a text editor such as Windows Notepad? If not, it's a binary file and must be encoded.

However, most modern email programs are much more capable: you choose the file or files you want to attach, your emailer converts them to ASCII ready to be sent, and the recipient's emailer converts them back again at the other end. In most cases it really should be as simple as that. The only blot on the landscape is that there are several methods used to do it, and both sender and recipient must be using the same method.

▶ **UUencode**. The original (rather messy) conversion system for PCs. The file is converted into ASCII and, if necessary, broken up into chunks to get around the email size restriction. It looks like pure gobbledegook until converted back by a **UUdecoder**.

▶ **MIME**. A modern successor to UUencoding, now also used on the Web for transferring files. It can identify the type of file you're sending and act appropriately, and the whole system works completely unaided at both ends.

▶ **BinHex**. A conversion system used mostly on Macintosh computers, similar to UUencoding.

Which method should I use?

If at all possible, use MIME. If your email program can't handle MIME, replace it with one that can. If you have a choice of methods on your Options page, set MIME as the default. Use a different system only if your recipient doesn't have a MIME-compatible email program (and refuses to do the sensible thing!). Online services now handle MIME attachments, making it easy to send files to members of the same service, a different service, or an Internet email account.

If you know that your software and that of your recipient both use the same system, attaching files is simple: look for a toolbar button with a paperclip symbol and click it (in Outlook Express and Pegasus you'll find the button in the New Message window itself). You can then browse your computer's directories to find and double-click any files you want to attach; the software will handle the rest itself.

Receiving attachments in incoming email should be just as simple and transparent, especially if your email program recognises both MIMEd and UUencoded attachments, as many do. Eudora, for example, will decode attachments and put them in a directory called Attach; Outlook Express will show an attached file as an icon just below the Subject field at the top of the message window.

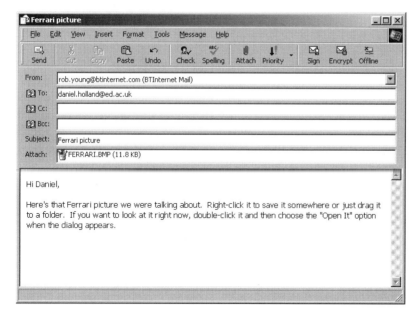

◄ Attachments in Outlook Express appear as file icons. Right-click the icon to open or save the attached file, or drag it to your desktop or a directory on your hard disk.

Fatal attachment

Despite the occasional scare stories about so-called 'email viruses', email messages are just plain text and therefore can't harbour computer viruses. But files included as attachments may be executable programs or documents that can contain executable macros such as Microsoft Word files, and these certainly can carry viruses. You should always check these attachments with a virus checker utility before running them, and be especially wary of attachments in messages from someone you don't know – there are some weird people out there!

Attachments That Use a Different Conversion Method

Although you've got the whole attachment business sorted out, and you're happily MIME-ing files to all and sundry, you may still receive a UUencoded file from someone else, or need to UUencode a file for someone who doesn't have MIME. Even if your email software can't handle the conversion for you, there are utilities available that you can use to do the job yourself. Two of the best (both of which handle MIME and UUencode as well as several other methods) are WinZip and ESS-Code. You'll find WinZip on the CD-ROM accompanying this book, and you can look for a later version at **http:// www.winzip.com** ESS-Code can be downloaded directly by typing the following into your browser's address bar: **http://www.salftrans.co.uk/ECD77W95.ZIP**

An emotional attachment

If there's someone special in your life, why not send them a kiss, a card, or even a proposal as an email attachment? Turn to page 268, 'It Must Be Love', to find out how.

What Else Should I Know About email?

Like most simple tools, email software has grown to offer a lot more than the basic requirements of writing, sending, receiving and reading. Once you feel comfortable using the program you've chosen, spend a little time reading the manual or Help files to see what else it offers. (Remember that you can keep sending yourself test messages to find out if or how an option works.) Here's a selection of options and issues worth knowing about.

Address Books

An address book is simply a list of names and email addresses. Instead of typing the recipient's address into a new message (risking mistakes and non-delivery), you can click the Address Book button and double-click the name of the intended recipient to have the address inserted for you. (In Outlook Express, click the little address book icon beside each field to pick a name from the Address Book.) You may be able to add new addresses to the book by right-clicking on a message you've received, or the name of the sender, and selecting an **Add to address book** option. Many programs will allow you to create multiple address books, or to group addresses into different categories, for speedy access to the one you want.

GOOD QUESTION!

How can I find someone's email address?

Believe it or not, the only truly reliable way is to ask! But there are search facilities on the World Wide Web that can find people rather than places, and you'll learn where to find them and how to use them later in this chapter.

A similar option is the **address group** (known by different names in different programs). You can send the same message to all the addresses listed in a group by simply double-clicking the group's name. This is an option worth investigating if you need to send an identical memo or newsletter to all the members of a team or club. When you do this, always put the name of the address group in the BCC field, and in the To field put an imaginary name (such as "Snail Farming List") followed by your own email address between < and > signs. Along with ensuring the privacy of the people on your list by not sending their name and email address to everyone on the list, it also keeps the size of the message to a minimum: the message-header won't now contain an immense list of names and email addresses! The name you enter in the To field is the name that recipients will see, so make sure you pick something relevant.

Signatures

An email 'signature' is a personal touch to round off an email message. You'll find a **Signature** option on one of your program's menus that provides a blank space for you to enter whatever text you choose, and this will be added automatically to the end of all the messages you write.

A signature commonly gives your name, and might also include the URL of your website if you have one, your job description and company if you're sending business mail, and (very often) a quotation or witticism. Try to resist getting carried away with this, though – eight lines is an absolute maximum for a signature.

Emoticons & Acronyms

Emoticons, otherwise known as 'smilies', are little expressive faces made from standard keyboard characters used to convey feelings or to prevent a comment being misunderstood in email messages, newsgroup postings and text chat. Here's a little bundle of the more useful or amusing emoticons. (If you haven't come across emoticons before, look at them sideways.)

Symbol	Meaning	Symbol	Meaning
:-)	Happy	:#)	Has a moustache
:-(	Sad	:-)>	Has a beard
:-))	Very happy	(-)	Needs a haircut
:-((	Very sad	(:-)	Bald
;-)	Wink	:-)X	Wears a bow tie
>:-)	Evil grin	8-)	Wears glasses
:-D	Laughing	:^)	Has a broken nose/ Nose put out of joint
:'-)	Crying	:-w	Speaks with forked tongue
:-O	Surprised	:-?	Smokes a pipe
:-&	Tongue-tied	:-Q	Smokes cigarettes
:-I	Unamused	*-)	Drunk or stoned
:-II	Angry	<:-)	Idiot
X-)	Cross-eyed	=:-)	Punk rocker

Another commonly used abbreviation (although not a smiley) is **<g>**, meaning 'grin', often used to say to the reader 'Don't take that too seriously, I'm just kidding'. The angle-brackets are a way of adding asides and sound-effects to plain text: you might come across **<giggle>**, **<bang>**, **<wipes away tear>** and so on.

Communicate or confuse?

BY THE WAY

You can really go to town on these emoticons, and you could turn just about any phrase you like into an 'acronym'. Just because you know that IJBMS stands for 'I just burnt my sausages' doesn't mean that anyone else does! Similarly, an emoticon meant to indicate that you're an angry, cross-eyed punk rocker with a beard might just look like you've sat on the keyboard.

Acronyms came about as a result of Internet users having to compose their email while online and clocking up charges. Although messages are now mostly composed offline, these acronyms have become a part of accepted email style, and have been given new life by the emergence of online text chat which you'll learn about in Chapter 10.

In fact most of these aren't acronyms at all, but they fall under the banner of TLAs (Three Letter Acronyms). Er, no, they don't all consist of three letters either.

Acronym	Meaning	Acronym	Meaning
AFAIK	As far as I know	KISS	Keep it simple, stupid
BCNU	Be seeing you	L8R	Later (or See you later)
BST	But seriously though	LOL	Laughs out loud
BTW	By the way	OAO	Over and out
FAQ	Frequently asked question(s)	OIC	Oh I see
FWIW	For what it's worth	OTOH	On the other hand
FYI	For your information	OTT	Over the top
GAL	Get a life	PITA	Pain in the a~!#
IMO	In my opinion	ROFL	Rolls on the floor laughing
IMHO	In my humble opinion	RTFM	Read the f*%£?!# manual
IMNSHO	In my not so humble opinion	TIA	Thanks in advance
IOW	In other words	TNX	Thanks

Another common need in email and newsgroup messages is to emphasise particular words or phrases, since the usual methods (bold or italic text, or underlining) aren't available. This is done by surrounding the text with asterisks (*never*) or underscores (_never_).

Undelivered email

If an email message can't be delivered it will be 'bounced' straight back to you, along with an automatically generated message telling you what went wrong. If the address you typed doesn't exist, or you made a mistake, the message should come back within seconds or minutes. In some cases a message might be returned to you after several days, which usually indicates that the problem lies in delivering the message at the other end. If this happens, just send the message again. If the problem persists, try altering the address so that it looks like this:

[**SMTP:***username@domain*]

(including those square brackets) or send a message addressed to **postmaster@***domain* (using the domain of the person you were trying to contact) asking if there's a problem with email delivery and quoting the email address you were trying to send to.

Other email Bits & Pieces

▶ **Filtering**. Modern email programs offer filtering options (sometimes known as 'Rules') that let you decide how to handle certain types of incoming email. You might choose to have all messages from a particular person moved to a special folder as soon as they arrive, for example.

▶ **Formatting**. Many email programs allow you to add formatting to your email as if it were a word processed document, choosing fonts, colours, layout styles, and even themed background pictures, creating a result that looks a lot like a web page and is sent in the same format. The problem is that your recipient must be using an email program that can understand all this formatting or he'll just receive a plain message with all the formatting codes placed in a meaningless attached file. More and more email programs do understand these formats now, however, so the problem crops up a lot less often. It's best not to add background images though – some people receive dozens of messages every day and don't want to wait ten times as long for one of yours to download!

▶ **Delete on receipt**. As soon as you collect your email it should be deleted from your access provider's mail server. The reason for this is that your provider won't give you unlimited space for email on the server: when your mailbox is full, mail will just be bounced back to the sender. Your email software may give you an option to delete retrieved messages, but it will usually be switched on by default. (Of course, this means that you can only retrieve a message once, so think carefully before deleting a message from your own system!)

Yes, it's electronic mail, but...

It's not supposed to look like a letter. You don't need to put the date or the recipient's postal address at the top, or use any letter writing formalities. On some occasions you might want to include your own postal address and phone number, but do this only when the recipient really needs to know them.

▶ **Writing style**. Don't start with 'Dear…' or end with 'Yours sincerely'. You might send a message that starts 'Hi Rob', or 'Hello Rob' if you really want some sort of salutation, or you could just start 'Rob,'. But it's perfectly acceptable just to get straight into the message, and not be regarded as rude. Similarly you might sign off with 'Regards' or 'Best wishes', but there's no need to put anything at all but your name. (You might find it a hard habit to break – I know I do – but don't think people rude when they do it!)

▶ **Identities**. This is a useful new option added to Outlook Express. By choosing **File | Manage Identities**, you can create a new 'identity' for each member of your family and choose which should be used each time Outlook starts (or pick **Ask Me** to be prompted to choose an identity). Outlook will display only that user's messages and folders, switch to that email account and add the appropriate signature to outgoing email. For security, you can password-protect an identity to keep your messages private.

▶ **Digital signatures**. Not to be confused with ordinary email signatures mentioned a few pages ago, a digital signature (or digital ID) is a type of electronic 'certificate' that guarantees you're the person you're claiming to be. By digitally signing messages, you confirm to the recipient that the message really was sent by you. A number of companies can provide you with a digital ID, including Verisign (**http://www.verisign.com**) and BT Trustwise (**http://www.trustwise.com**) but a popular choice is Thawte (**http://www.thawte.com**) who provide personal certificates free.

▶ A Thawte digital ID certificate. By digitally signing an email message you can verify its origin and optionally encrypt the message too.

email Netiquette

The term 'netiquette' is an abbreviation of 'Internet etiquette', a set of unwritten rules about behaviour on the Internet. In simple terms, they boil down to 'Don't waste Internet resources' and 'Don't be rude', but here are a few specific pointers to keep in mind when dealing with email:

▶ Reply promptly. Because email is quick and easy, it's generally expected that a reply will arrive within a day or two, even if it's just to confirm receipt. Try to keep unanswered messages in your Inbox and move answered messages elsewhere so that you can see at a glance what's waiting to be dealt with.

▶ DON'T SHOUT! LEAVING THE CAPS LOCK KEY SWITCHED ON IS REGARDED AS 'SHOUTING', AND CAN PROMPT SOME ANGRY RESPONSES. IT DOESN'T LOOK AT ALL FRIENDLY, DOES IT?

▶ Don't forward someone's private email without their permission.

▶ Don't put anything in an email message that you wouldn't mind seeing on the news! Anyone can forward your email to a national newspaper, your boss, your parents, and so on, so there may be times when a phone call is preferable.

Web-based email

At the beginning of this chapter I mentioned that you don't have to worry about missing an important email message by being on holiday for a couple of weeks – you just grab any waiting messages when you return. But what if that message is so important that you can't wait until then to read it?

In these days of mobile computing, one answer is to take a laptop or handheld computer with you and look for a handy phone socket on your travels. You can buy a credit card-sized modem to plug into the computer for under £150, and a few handheld PCs have a modem built in. But this may still leave you making a long-distance – or, worse still, an international – phone call to your ISP when you go online.

A much cheaper solution is Web-based email. Instead of using a dedicated email program, just create a free account with an email service such as Hotmail (**http://www.hotmail.com**) or Yahoo Mail (**http://mail.yahoo.com**) and you'll be given a new email address similar to *yourname*@hotmail.com. Being Web-based, you can read and write email messages simply by visiting the service's website and logging in using your personal username and password. You can do this from anywhere in the world, of course, and your only problem is in finding a cyber café, hotel or library with an Internet-connected computer.

You need to give your friends and colleagues your Web-based email address, of course, and tell them to use it if they need to contact you while you're away. If you spend a lot of time on the move, you may find it simpler to ignore the email address given to you by your ISP and stick to your Hotmail or Yahoo Mail account even when you're home.

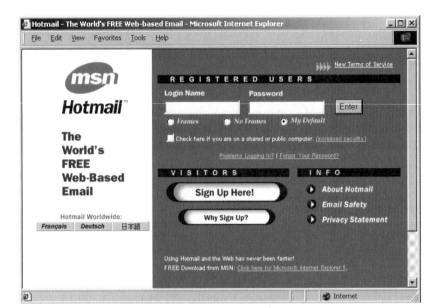

▶ Create a free
Hotmail account
and handle all
your email on the
Web.

Web-based is better!

The problem with the typical email account is that if you switch to a different ISP, your email address will change (see page 219) and your old ISP is unlikely to forward email to your new email address. One advantage of Web-based email services is that you have a permanent unchanging email address, removing the risk of email going astray when you change to a new service provider.

Finding People On The Net

Finding people on the Internet is a bit of a black art – after all, there are in excess of 100 million users, and few would bother to 'register' their details even if there were an established directory. In addition, of course, if you move your access account to a different online service or ISP, your email address will change too (more on that in Chapter 15). So it's all a bit hit and miss, but let's look at a few possibilities.

Flick Through The White Pages

In the UK, the term Yellow Pages is synonymous with finding businesses. White pages is a type of directory listing people (what we usually just call a phone book), and the Internet has a few 'white pages' directories that may turn up trumps. Some of these rely on people actually submitting their details voluntarily; others take the more crafty approach of searching the newsgroups and adding the email addresses of anyone posting an article. Searching white pages is just like using any other search engine, usually requiring you to enter the user's first and last names and click on a Search button.

▶ **Bigfoot** at **http://uk.bigfoot.com** Don't be fooled by the URL – the search engine itself is in America – but this is the directory most likely to find the email address of a UK Internet user. It's a very useful site that will be mentioned again in later chapters.

▶ **Yahoo! People Search** at **http://people.yahoo.com** (or **http://ukie.people.yahoo.com** to find folk in the UK and Ireland.) The biggest and most popular 'people locator' in the States, which searches the Internet for email addresses and accepts individual submissions. Details found here may include a user's hobbies, postal address and phone number, but most entries are from the USA.

▶ **Infospace**. Go to **http://www.infospace.com** and click the **Find People** link. Choose the appropriate country (but ignore the State/Province box unless you're searching for someone in the US or Canada) and enter any other details you can, such as name and city. Infospace also has a handy Phone Numbers lookup, reached by scrolling to the bottom of the page, which can often provide a postal address and other details.

GOOD QUESTION!

Are there any other white pages I can search?

On the Internet there's always more of anything! Head for **http://dir.yahoo. com/Reference/Phone_Numbers_and_Addresses** for links to white pages sites covering email addresses, phone books, Yellow Pages and more.

If you're prepared to wait a little while for a result, you might find them at MIT (Massachusetts Institute of Technology), which regularly scans Usenet archives to extract names and email addresses. Send an email message to **mail-server@rtfm.mit.edu**, with the text **send usenet-addresses/***name* as the body of the message (remembering not to add your email signature on the end). Provided that the person you're trying to trace has posted a message to a newsgroup in the past, you should receive a reply containing the email address. As an example, it should be possible to retrieve my email address by sending the message: **send usenet-addresses/Rob Young**. (It's worth remembering that this will work only if the person has posted an article to Usenet using their own name; some users frequent the type of newsgroup in which it's common to post under an alias.)

GOOD QUESTION!

Can I find the email addresses of famous people?

If they've ever posted an article to a newsgroup you may be lucky, although you may get a list of dozens of Hugh Grants or Jennifer Anistons. One site to try that keeps a handy list is called simply Celebrity Email Addresses. Although there are no guarantees of accuracy, if you want to email Shania Twain, Brad Pitt or Madonna (among others) head for **http://celebrityemail. hollywood.com** or **http://www.addresses.site2go.com**

Back To The Search Engines

Most of the popular search engines and portals have their own 'people finder' options too. Both Excite and AltaVista have an easy-to-find People Finder link near the top of their homepages, Infoseek has a People Search link, and Dogpile has a White Pages button you select when searching.

Although the thrust of the last few pages has really been to find email addresses, here's one final site that may be able to help you track down all kinds of information about a person, such as their phone and fax number, their address, or even their hobbies. Go to **http://www.phonenumbers.net**, select the country you want to search in, and you'll find links to all the most relevant sources of information.

▶ *Although the only truly reliable way of finding someone's email address is to ask, you could try using Whois as a last resort, covered on page 183.*

NEWSGROUPS – THE HUMAN ENCYCLOPAEDIA

▶ **IN THIS CHAPTER**

What are newsgroups all about?

Choose a newsreader and download a list of available newsgroups

Start reading (and writing) the news

Send and receive binary files with news articles

Mailing lists – have your news delivered by email

News, as we generally think of it, is a collection of topical events, political embarrassments, latest gossip, and so on. All of that, and more, can be found on the Internet, but it's not what the Net calls 'news'. The newsgroups we're talking about here are more formally known as **Usenet discussion groups**; there are over 50 000 of them (and counting!) covering everything from accommodation to zebrafish.

Newsgroup discussions take place using email messages (known as **articles** or **postings**), but instead of addressing articles to an individual's email address they're addressed to a particular group. Anyone choosing to access this group can read the messages, post replies, start new topics of conversation, or ask questions relating to the subject covered by the group.

How Does It Work?

Your service provider has a computer called a **news server** that holds articles from thousands of newsgroups that form part of the Usenet system. This collection of articles will be updated regularly (perhaps daily, or perhaps as often as every few minutes) to include the latest postings to the groups. Using a program called a **newsreader**, you can read articles in as many of these groups as you want to, and post your own articles in much the same way that you compose and send email messages. Messages you post will be added to the server's listings almost immediately, and will gradually trickle out to news servers around the world (the speed with which this happens depends upon how often all the other servers update themselves).

Although there are currently more than 50 000 groups, you won't find every group available from your access provider. Storage space on any computer is a limited commodity so providers have to compromise. In addition, many providers are now taking a moral stance against groups involving pornography and software piracy (among others) and these are unlikely to be available. But if you really needed access to a group concerned with grape-growing in Argentina (and one existed), most reasonable providers would subscribe to it if you asked nicely. If a suitable group doesn't exist, and you think the world is itching to discuss the Argentine grape with you, you could even talk to your ISP about setting up the newsgroup yourself in the 'alt' hierarchy (more about that below).

If my ISP doesn't subscribe to it, how can I find out if it exists?

If you're looking for a group dedicated to tortoise farming and your ISP doesn't seem to have one, use your browser to search the lists of newsgroup names at the following websites, using the keyword 'tortoise'. If you find a promising group, ask your ISP to subscribe to it.

http://alabanza.com/kabacoff/Inter-Links
http://www.magma.ca/~leisen/mlnh

Newsgroup Names

Newsgroup names look a lot like the domain names we met in earlier chapters – words separated by dots. Reading the names from left to right, they begin with a **top-level** category name and become gradually more specific. Let's start with a few of these top-level names:

comp   Computer-related groups such as **comp.windows.news**.

rec   Recreational/sports groups like **rec.arts.books.tolkien**.

sci   Science-related groups such as **sci.bio.paleontology**.

misc   Just about anything – items for sale, education, investments, you name it…

soc   Social issues groups such as **soc.genealogy.nordic**.

talk   Discussions about controversial topics such as **talk.atheism or talk.politics.guns**.

uk   UK-only groups covering a wide range of subjects including politics, small ads and sport.

A little moderation

Some newsgroups are moderated, meaning that the creator of the group (or someone else appointed to run it) reads all the messages and decides which to post. The aim is to keep the topics of discussion on course, but they often tend to weed out deliberately argumentative or abusive messages too.

One of the largest collections of groups comes under a completely different top-level heading, **alt**. The alt groups are not an official part of the Usenet service, but are still available from almost all service providers. Because almost anyone can set up a group in the alt hierarchy they're sometimes regarded as anarchic or somehow 'naughty', but in truth their sole difference is that their creators chose to bypass all the red tape involved in the Usenet process. Here's a taste of the breadth of coverage you'll find in the alt hierarchy:

alt.culture.kuwait	alt.education.disabled
alt.fan.david-bowie	alt.games.dominoes
alt.ketchup	alt.paranormal.crop-circles
alt.windows95	alt.support.spina-bifida

What Do I Need?

You need two things: a program called a **newsreader** and a little bit of patience. We'll come to the second of those in a moment; first let's sort out the newsreader. These come in two flavours. First, there's the **online newsreader** – you don't want one of those! Reading and posting articles all takes place while connected and clocking up charges. Second is the **offline newsreader**, and that's definitely the type you want, but offline readers also vary. Some offline readers download automatically all the unread articles in your chosen group so that you can read them and compose replies offline; the problem is that in a popular group you may have to wait for several hundred articles to download, many of which you won't be interested in. The second (and by far the best) type of offline reader just downloads the

headers of the articles (the subject line, date, author and size). You can select the articles you want to read, based on this information, and then reconnect to have them downloaded.

If you don't already have a good offline newsreader, here are my recommendations:

▶ **Outlook Express**. As mentioned in the previous chapter, this integrates nicely with Microsoft's Internet Explorer browser, and gives you an email client too. If you have Windows 98, you should have Outlook Express already installed. Windows 95 users can install Internet Explorer from the CD-ROM in the back of this book which will set up Outlook Express at the same time.

▶ **Agent or Free Agent**. A popular newsreader available in two versions – one is free, the other you'll have to pay for (guess which is which!) Free Agent is included on the CD-ROM. Point your browser at **http://www.forteinc.com** for the extra features built into Agent.

▶ **TIFNY**. A stylish, colourful and oddly named newsreader that packs a lot of handy information into a small space. You can download a free copy from **http://www.tifny2.com**

Having got your hands on one of these, the setting up is fairly simple. The program should prompt you for the information it needs the first time you run it, which will include your name, email address, and the domain name of your news server (usually **news.***serviceprovider.co.uk***). You'll probably see other options and settings, but don't change anything just yet.

Now switch on your patience circuits! Before you can go much further, your newsreader has to connect to the server and download a list of the newsgroups you can access. How long this takes will depend upon the number of groups available, the speed of your modem, and how fast a connection you have. It might take only two or three minutes, but it might take 15 or more.

▶ While your
newsreader
downloads a list
of groups, you'll
have to sit tight
and count to ten.
Lots of times.

That was the bad news. The good news is that you'll need to download the group list only once, as long as you don't decide later that you want to use a different newsreader. In future, when your newsreader connects to the server to download new articles, it will automatically fetch the names of any new groups that have been created and add them to the list.

Newsgroups and online services

To access newsgroups in AOL, use the keyword **newsgroups**; in CompuServe, use the Go word **usenet**. When you look at the list of groups your online service provides, many may be missing (such as the entire 'alt' hierarchy). In many cases you can access these, but you need to 'switch on' access to them yourself. For example, AOL has an Expert Add function for this. Check the Help files for details, or contact the service's support line.

Subscribing To Newsgroups

Before you can start reading and posting articles, you need to subscribe to the groups that interest you. ('Subscribing' is the term for letting your newsreader know which groups to download headers from – there are no subscription fees!) Although you can scroll your way through the thousands of groups in the list, it's easier to search for a word you'd expect to find in the group's name. In Outlook Express, click the Newsgroups button on the toolbar (or press Ctrl+W), and type a keyword into the box above the list; in Agent, click the toolbar button with the torch symbol and type a word into the dialog box.

To subscribe to a newsgroup in Outlook Express, click its name, and click the **Subscribe** button. When you've subscribed to all the groups you want, click **OK**. In Agent right-click a newsgroup's name and click **Subscribe**.

▶ *If you need to find out whether a newsgroup exists on a particular topic, or you want to search the newsgroups for information, turn to Searching The Newsgroups on page 138 to find out how to do it.*

Can't get the group you want?

If you want to subscribe to a group that your service provider doesn't (and won't) subscribe to, you may be able to access it through one of the public access news servers instead. Visit **http://www.newzbot.com** for a list of public servers. There are no lists of the groups covered by each server; you'll have to configure your newsreader to connect to it, download a list of groups, and see if the group you want is there.

Reading The News

When you've chosen the groups to which you want to subscribe, you're ready to download the headers from one of the groups. In Outlook Express, click the name you chose to describe your news server in the Outlook Bar on the left, and then double-click the name of one of your subscribed newsgroups in the upper window. The program will connect to your news server and download the headers from articles in the selected group (shown in the next screenshot). By default, Outlook Express will download 300 headers at a time (as long as there are that many articles in the group), but you can change this figure by going to the **Tools** menu, selecting **Options** and changing the figure shown on the **Read** tab.

In Agent, click on **Group | Show | Subscribed Groups** (or click the large button marked **All Groups** until it says **Subscribed Groups**). You'll see the list of newsgroups you subscribed to, and you can double-click one to download its headers. Agent will present a dialog asking if you want to collect all the headers, or just a sample of 50. Some popular newsgroups have several thousand articles, so it's best to start with a sample just to get a flavour of the group first. Change the figure if you want to, and then click the button marked **Sample Message Headers**.

To download and read an article immediately in the preview window, click the header once in Outlook Express, or double-click it in Agent.

Usually you'll want to download articles to read offline, and Outlook Express makes this easy: just tell it which articles you want. If you want to grab every article in the group, click **Tools | Mark for Offline | Download All Messages Later**. If you just want selected articles, either right-click each article separately and choose **Download Message Later**, or hold the Ctrl key while clicking all the required articles and then right-click on any of them and choose **Download Message Later**. Beside the headers for messages you've marked you'll see a blue arrow indicator so that you can tell what you've chosen at a glance. You can now select another group to download headers for, and mark those in the same way. When you've finished marking the articles you want in all groups, open the **Tools** menu and click the appropriate **Synchronize** button. Agent (and most other newsreaders) use similar methods. To mark a message for download in Agent, highlight it and press M, or right-click it and choose **Mark for Retrieval**. Once you've marked all the articles you want to download, click the toolbar button with the blue arrow and thunderbolt symbol and Agent will fetch them for you and mark them with a little 'page' icon.

Why can't I download some of the articles listed?

Although the headers are displayed, you might find that some of the articles are no longer available. To make room for new articles, older ones have to be deleted. In the most popular groups, receiving several hundred messages per day, articles might vanish within a matter of days.

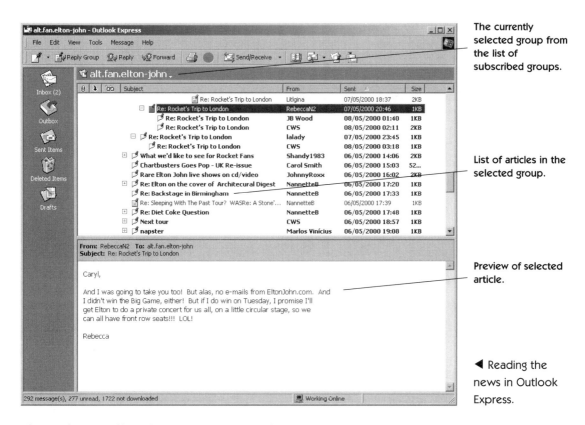

The currently selected group from the list of subscribed groups.

List of articles in the selected group.

Preview of selected article.

◀ Reading the news in Outlook Express.

Threads – Following A Conversation

Although a newsgroup is dedicated to one *subject*, there may be dozens (or hundreds) of different conversations going on. Fortunately all newsgroup articles have a subject line just like email messages, so all messages with the same subject line will be part of the same conversation, or in newsgroup parlance, the same **thread**. Most newsreaders let you choose how you want to sort the list of articles (by date or by sender, for example), but the best way to view them is by thread so that articles from one conversation are listed together.

So how do threads work? When you post a brand new message to a newsgroup, you're starting a new thread. If someone posts a reply, their newsreader will insert the word **Re**: in the subject line (just as in email replies). Your newsreader gathers together the original message and all replies (including replies to replies) and sorts them by date. The original message will have a little '+' icon beside it indicating that it's the beginning of a thread and you can click this to reveal the other articles in the thread.

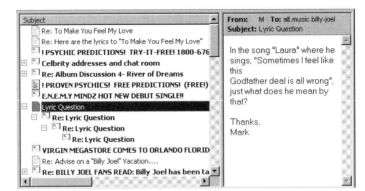

▶ Click the '+' icon to reveal the rest of the thread, or the '−' icon to hide it.

Why does this message have nothing to do with the subject line?

Some threads go on and on for months and may eventually have nothing to do with the article that started it all, despite the subject line. All it takes is for someone to raise a slightly different point in a reply, and someone else to pick up on it in their reply, for the entire thread to veer on to a whole new course.

Marking Messages

In most newsreaders, as soon as you open an article to read it the article will be marked as **Read**. (In Outlook Express the read articles turn from bold type to normal; in Agent they turn from red to black.) You can also mark a message as Read even if you haven't read it, or mark an entire thread as Read (perhaps you read the first couple of articles and decided everyone was talking rubbish). In modern newsreaders this just acts as a useful way to remember what you've read and what you haven't – you might just as easily delete messages you've read if you won't want to read them again.

If you want it, save it!

Modern newsreaders automatically store the list of downloaded headers, and all downloaded articles, but they'll eventually delete them before they swallow up too much of your hard disk. If there are particular articles you want to keep for future reference, you can usually save them to a special folder, or to any directory on your hard disk. You should also be able to print an article, or copy it to the clipboard to be pasted into another application.

Older newsreaders don't store the headers: they download them, display them, and then forget them again when you move to a different newsgroup or log off. All they know is which messages are marked as Read. Next time you open this newsgroup, the unread headers will be downloaded, so it makes sense to mark as Read any headers that you're definitely not interested in so that they're not continually being downloaded. (You can even mark every message in the group as Read so that you'll see only any newer messages that appear.)

Pure Gobbledegook – ROT13

Once in a while, you might come across a message that looks a bit like the one shown in the next screenshot – they could be words, but they don't seem to mean anything. Yes, it might be a transcript of a party political broadcast, but it's more likely that it's been encrypted with **ROT13**.

ROT13 stands for Rotated 13, and it's a pretty simple encryption system: every letter is replaced with the one thirteen steps along in the alphabet, so E becomes R, H becomes U, and so on. Simple. (Or rather, Fvzcyr.) But working it out that way could start to lose its novelty value after a while. Most newsreaders have a menu option called **Unscramble ROT13** which will do it for you (and you might be able to use the same option to scramble your own messages.)

If it's so easy to decode, why encrypt a message with ROT13 at all?

ROT13 is used to prevent anyone from accidentally reading a message that may offend or disgust them. In other words, if you see a message like this, you can decide for yourself whether you really want to read it. But don't say I didn't warn you – it could be pretty nasty.

▶ A ROT13-encrypted message in Outlook Express (No, this one isn't offensive, just a bit dull. I've encrypted it as an example.)

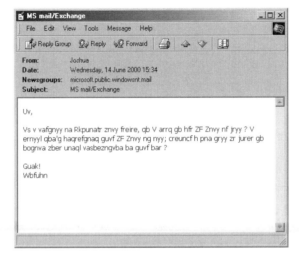

Posting Articles To Newsgroups

It's a funny old language really. Newsgroup messages work just like email: the only difference is that the address you use is the name of a newsgroup, not an email address. But even though you *send* an email *message*, you *post* a newsgroup *article*. Don't ask why, just accept it!

Although just reading articles can be very addictive, sooner or later you'll want to get involved. There are various ways to post articles, and they're common to just about every newsreader you'll come across. In the following list I'll take Microsoft's Outlook Express as an example, but if you're using something different you'll still have all the same options (although their precise names may vary).

Test the water first

Before posting an article to a 'proper' newsgroup where everyone can see it, you probably want to send a test message first as you did with your email program in the previous chapter. You can send a message to alt.test, but it's worth checking to see if your access provider has its own 'test' group. You might even get a reply from another newcomer. Allow at least a few minutes before checking the group to see if your message is listed.

▶ To reply to a message you're reading, click the **Reply Group** button, or right-click the header and choose **Reply Group**. (In many newsreaders, a reply is called a **Follow-up**). A new message window will open with the name of the group already entered, and the same subject line as the message you were reading. Type your message and click the **Send** button (or press Alt+S).

▶ To reply to the author of the article privately by email, click the **Reply** button and follow the routine above. In this case the article won't be posted to the newsgroup.

▶ To reply to the newsgroup and send a copy of your reply to the author by email at the same time, go to **Message | Reply to All**. Once again the routine is the same as above.

▶ To create a new message (and start a new thread), click the **New Post** button (or press Ctrl+N). A new message window will open with the currently selected newsgroup shown. To send to a different newsgroup, or to more than one group, click the newspaper icon beside the name to add and remove groups from the list. Enter a title for the article on the **Subject** line, and then write your message.

Don't change the subject!

When replying to an existing thread, don't change the subject line at all! If just one character is different, newsreaders will regard it as the start of a new thread and won't group it with the other articles in the thread.

In keeping with email, any replies to newsgroup articles automatically **quote** the original article (see page 106). Make sure you delete any of the original article that doesn't need to be included. Remember that newsreaders list earlier messages in the thread in a well-organised fashion, so most people will have already read the message you're replying to.

Attachments & Newsgroup Articles

At the risk of being boring, let me just say again: newsgroup articles and email messages are so similar even their mother couldn't tell them apart. A case in point is that you can send and receive computer files as part of a newsgroup article just as you can with email. So I'm going to assume that you've read the section on attachments in the previous chapter, (pages 107–10).

In most newsreaders, attaching a binary file to an article is a simple case of clicking a button marked **Attach File** (often marked with a paperclip icon), browsing your directories for the file you want to send, and double-clicking it – your newsreader should do the rest. Most modern newsreaders, including those mentioned earlier in this chapter, will also decode any attachments in an article you open, with no need for intervention on your part: these may be saved automatically to a directory on your computer, or you may have to click a button on the toolbar (as in Agent) to view them. Outlook Express displays news attachments as an icon at the top of the window in the same way as it handles email attachments (see page 109).

GOOD QUESTION!

How can I tell if an article has an attachment by looking at the header?

Newsreaders show the number of lines in an article as part of the header information in the list. Even a long text-only article shouldn't run to more than about 60. An attached picture or sound file will usually range from about 200 up into the thousands. Only newsgroups that have the word 'binaries' somewhere in their name should have articles that include attachments, so you'll probably be expecting to find a few if you're in one of these groups. Outlook Express helpfully lists the size in kilobytes rather than the number of lines.

On occasion, an attached file might be split into several messages due to its size (known as a **multi-part attachment**) and the subject lines for each message will include additions like [1/3], [2/3] and [3/3] to number the parts of a three-part file. In many newsreaders, if you try to open any one of these it will realise that the file isn't complete and automatically download the other two as well and piece them together. In the remaining few programs, you'll have to select all three parts in advance.

If you have a problem with attachments at all, it'll be that you open an article with an attached file that uses a format your newsreader can't handle (not all newsreaders can decode both UUencode and MIME files). In this case you'll see line upon line of textual gibberish in the article. Unlike ROT13-encrypted articles, mentioned earlier, these characters will be in an endless stream, and will often use more symbols than letters and numbers. In this case you'll need to decode the attachment yourself by saving the message onto your own disk, and using one of the programs mentioned on page 110.

Newsgroup Netiquette & Jargon

Newsgroups are pretty hot on netiquette, the 'rules' you should follow when using them, and Usenet has invented its own brand of weird language to go with some of these.

▶ It's good practice to lurk a while when you visit a new group (especially as a newcomer to the whole idea of newsgroups). So what's 'lurking'? Reading newsgroups articles without posting any yourself. Get an idea of the tone of the group, the reactions of its participants to beginners' questions, and the types of topic they cover.

▶ Before diving in and asking a question in the group, read the FAQ. This stands for Frequently Asked Question(s), and it's an article that tells you more about the group, its topics, and other related groups. Many groups post a FAQ every few weeks, but if you don't see an article with 'FAQ' in its header, send a short message asking if someone could post it.

▶ Don't post 'test' articles to any newsgroup that doesn't have the word 'test' in its name.

▶ Don't post articles containing attachments to any newsgroup that doesn't have the word 'binaries' in its name. This is out of respect for people whose newsreaders give them no choice but to download every article and who don't expect to spend five minutes downloading an attachment they don't want.

▶ Don't spam! Spamming is a lovely term for sending the same article to dozens of different newsgroups, regardless of whether it's relevant. These messages are usually advertising mailshots, get-rich-quick schemes, and similar stuff that no one finds remotely interesting. The risk is greater than just being ignored though: you might get mail-bombed – many people will take great delight in sending you thousands of email messages to teach you a lesson! So, why 'spamming'? Monty Python fans might remember a sketch about a certain brand of tinned meat... try asking for a copy of the script in **alt.fan.monty-python**!

▶ When replying to an article requesting information, or an answer to a question, it's good practice to also send the author a copy by email, in case your newsgroup reply doesn't get noticed. By the same token, if someone asks for answers by email, post your answer to the group as well – it may be of interest to others.

▶ Don't rise to flame bait! Some people delight in starting arguments, and deliberately post provocative articles. Personal attacks in newsgroups are known as 'flames', and on occasions these can get so out of hand that the whole groups descends into a 'flame war', with little else going on but personal abuse.

Searching The Newsgroups

There's more value to searching Usenet newsgroups than there appears at first. For example, with so many thousands of groups to choose from, a quick search for the keywords that sum up your favourite topic might help you determine the most suitable newsgroup to subscribe to. Or perhaps you need an answer to a technical question quickly – it's almost certainly been answered in a newsgroup article.

One of the best places to search for newsgroups and articles is Deja News on the Web at **http://www.deja.com**. Deja News looks just like any other search engine you've come across on your travels except that there's a choice of two textboxes for keywords. If you're looking for a *newsgroup*, enter a keyword into the lower of the two to find groups that discuss the subject you want. If you're looking for individual *articles*, use the upper text box. The search results list 20 articles at a time (with the usual button at the end of the page to fetch the next 20), and include authors' details and the names of the newsgroups in which the articles were found. Click on one of the articles to read it and you'll find a handy button-bar added to the page that lets you view the topic's thread, read the next or the previous article, and post replies to the newsgroup or to the article's author by email.

Stick to what you know

If you search Deja News for newsgroups, you can click any newsgroup you find on the results list to read its articles. But although it's possible, it's not the easiest way to navigate a newsgroup – you'll find it simpler to run your newsreader program and read the articles from the chosen group with that instead.

The great value of Deja News is that articles are available here long after they were first posted to Usenet. The only possible fly in the ointment is that the group you want may not be covered. If it isn't, head for Infoseek's search engine and choose **Usenet** from the drop-down list.

Mailing Lists – More Discussions

You may feel that a choice of over 50 000 discussion groups is about enough, and I wouldn't disagree. But let's round off this chapter with a look at a different system that can add another few thousand to that total: **mailing lists**.

A mailing list is like a newsgroup that arrives by email: once you've subscribed, all the messages from the group are delivered automatically to your mailbox for you to download when you like. In most cases, you can opt to receive a *digest* version which gives a single, large daily or weekly message rather than a constant stream of separate ones. To subscribe to a mailing list takes a single email message, as does unsubscribing.

Mailbox mayhem

Be very wary of mailing lists – if you like the general idea, start by subscribing to one list and see how things go. Popular lists generate a huge amount of email, and it's not a good idea to be subscribed to half a dozen of those while you're still finding your feet!

Mailing lists come in many shapes and forms, but the two primary systems are **Listserv** and **MajorDomo**. Like most mailing list systems, these are automatic, run by a program on a computer that reads the email you send to subscribe and adds your email address to its list. For automatic lists, your email message must be constructed in a certain way.

Listserv Mailing Lists

Listserv is one of the major automated systems, and requests for information and subscriptions are made by sending an email message to one of the computers on the Listserv system. All Listserv computers are linked together, so it doesn't matter which one you use for requests; if you don't know of any other, send your messages to **listserv@listserv.net** The request message you send needs nothing in the **Subject** line, although if your email program insists you enter something, just type a dot. The message itself must contain nothing but the request (so make sure you turn off your email program's Signature option).

To do this	Type this request in your email message
Subscribe to a list	SUB *listname your name*
Unsubscribe to a list	SIGNOFF *listname*
Get information about a list	INFO *listname*
Receive the digest version of a list	SET *listname* DIGEST
Get a list of request commands	HELP
Find all lists on this system	LIST
Find all Listserv lists in existence	LISTS GLOBAL

Be a bit wary of that last option – the message you'll receive containing a list of all the mailing lists available will be about half a megabyte in size!

Most Listserv lists can also be read using your newsreader – you'll find them in the **bit.listserv** hierarchy.

To send messages to a list you've subscribed to, you'll need to know which computer runs that list (the **sitename**, which should be in the details that are returned to you). You can then take part in the discussion by sending messages to *listname@sitename*. Make sure you don't get these two addresses confused. The first address I gave above is only for making requests and queries about lists; the second address is only for messages that you intend every subscriber to read. If you send your requests to the second address, a copy will be sent to everyone on the list, but the request itself won't be processed!

MajorDomo Mailing Lists

The MajorDomo system is similar to Listserv, but each computer on the system is independent so you need to know which computer handles the list you're interested in (the **sitename**). Armed with this information, send an email message to **majordomo@***sitename* containing one of the following requests:

To do this	Type this request in your email message
Subscribe to a list	subscribe listname
Unsubscribe to a list	unsubscribe listname
Find all lists on that computer	list

More mailbox mayhem

If you're going on holiday for a while and won't be able to download your email, consider unsubscribing from your mailing lists while you're away. Otherwise you might be faced with a barrage of email when you next log on!

▶ Pick one of hundreds of subjects to choose from thousands of lists.

There May Be An Easier Way...

I mentioned a moment ago that you can get a flavour of some of the Listserv lists before subscribing by using your newsreader. Many mailing lists also have their own page on the World Wide Web giving information about the list, and a simple form you can fill in online if you want to subscribe. To find lists of mailing lists on the Web, use your browser to go to **http://www.liszt.com** (where you can search for a mailing list by typing in a keyword) or **http://paml.net** (where you can choose a subject from a list of hundreds, as shown in the screenshot above).

CHAT & TALK WITHOUT MOVING YOUR LIPS

▶ **IN THIS CHAPTER**

Chat, talk and VON – what's it all about?

Using chat rooms on the World Wide Web

Take part in IRC chat sessions on the Internet

Spice up your chat sessions with cartoon characters

Cut your phone bill using Talk and Voice over the Net

Talk to your buddies while you surf with Instant Messaging

Chat *and* talk? Am I losing my marbles? No, I'm not (or at least, if I am, you couldn't count this as evidence). In Internet speak, chatting and talking are two different things, but what they have in common is their immediacy: you can hold conversations with people from all over the world at a speed almost comparable with talking on the phone. In most cases, you won't know who these people are, and you may never 'meet' them again.

Reactions to this area of cyberspace vary considerably. Many people find it exciting or addictive, to the point of spending hours every day 'chatting'. Many more find it inane, frustrating or offensive. Quite simply, these services bring Internet users into the closest possible contact with each other, and are used by many to meet members of the opposite sex. However unsatisfying you might imagine cybersex to be, it's very real, and all potential 'chatters' should be aware of its existence before taking part. That being said, chatting and talking can also be sociable and fun, practical and informative – to a large extent, the choice is yours.

What Are Chatting & Talking?

Chatting means holding live conversations with others by typing on your keyboard. You type a line or two of text into a small window and press Enter, and the text is visible to everyone else taking part almost instantly. They can then respond by typing their own messages, and you'll see their responses on your own screen almost instantly. Chatting usually takes place in a chat room, and the room may contain just two or three people, or as many as 50.

GOOD QUESTION!

Doesn't everyone talk at once in a chat room?

Sometimes, yes. Sometimes no one seems to talk at all. Sometimes there are two or three conversations going on between little groups of people, with all the messages appearing in the same window, and things can get a bit confusing. But although there may be 35 people in a room, many are just 'listening' rather than joining in.

Talk is a little different. Although the method of sending messages to and fro is the same, 'talk' usually takes place between just two people, and in a more structured way. Using a talk program, you'd usually enter the email address of the person you want to talk to, and if that person is online (and willing to talk to you!) the conversation begins. To cloud the issue a bit, *chat* programs also allow two people to enter a private room and 'talk', and many *talk* programs will allow more people to join in with your conversation if you permit them to enter.

Finally there's Internet telephony, otherwise known as Voice Over the Net, by which people can *really* talk to each other using microphones. Along with dedicated Internet telephony programs, many talk programs now have options to plug in a microphone and communicate by voice rather than text.

Chat Rooms On The Web

One of the major reasons for the early popularity of online services was their built-in, easy-to-use, chat systems. The major online services put a lot of effort into improving their chat facilities, and also now offer parental controls that can bar access from certain chat areas. As a measure of how seriously they regard these facilities, online services regularly enlist celebrity guest speakers to host chat sessions and answer questions. Both AOL and CompuServe have a variety of chat rooms geared towards different age groups and interests, and some of the chat rooms aimed at young people are **moderated** (a representative of the service is 'listening in', able to keep things friendly and remove troublemakers).

BY THE WAY

Socially challenged?

If you're of a shy disposition, you'll probably have a great time with chat. When no one can see you (and you can easily escape if you feel foolish!) you can pretend to be anyone you like. In fact, the adoption of a whole new persona is part of the fun for many users. But if you really don't want to get involved, it can still be very entertaining just to 'lurk' and watch.

The rest of the online world has learned everything it knows about chatting from the online services, and hoards of websites now include 'chat rooms' for their visitors. These 'rooms' are actually chat programs running on the website, and they can differ from one site to another: some sites use one of the many off-the-shelf chat systems available to Web designers while others pay for a custom-built service. The general workings of chat rooms never vary much, though, so you shouldn't have any trouble understanding how to use any of them.

One of the simplest and friendliest of online chat sites is the Warner Brothers Chat Complex at **http://chat.warnerbros.com**. Pick a chat room from the dropdown list and click the **Log in as a Guest** button. If there's no one in the room you chose, click **Who's Online?**, see which room is most popular and visit that instead.

Here are a few other Web-based chat rooms to try:

▶ **http://www.talkcity.com/chat** A popular site with a huge number of chat rooms covering all age groups and topics.

▶ **http://www.chatshack.net** 10 chat rooms with names such as Sports Talk, The Lobby, The Games Room and The Hot Tub.

▶ **http://www.ichatzone.com/teen-chat-rooms** A friendly site with 6 chat rooms intended for 13 to 19-year olds.

▶ **http://www.lifebegins.net** An online magazine site for 'discerning 50-somethings' with its own chat room.

▶ A typically friendly chat at Freeserve (www.freeserve. com/chat)

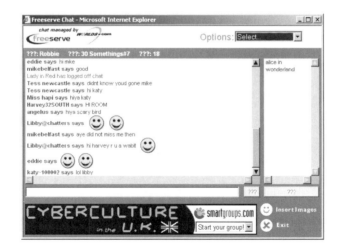

When you visit one of these sites, you'll sign in by entering your name (or choosing an alias or nickname) and perhaps choosing one or two other options. Once inside a chat room you can watch the conversations unfold in the upper portion of the window, or participate by typing text into the space at the bottom and pressing Enter. (Don't type your nickname before each line – the chat program handles that automatically.) Some chat programs display a list of all the people in the room, and you may be able to click on a name and get more information about a person, or open a small window and invite someone to 'talk' privately with you.

Where do those chat room names come from?

At any chat site, the rooms are often given names like 'Hot Tub', 'Singles Bar', and 'Sports Shack'. These names are chosen to attract particular types or age groups of people, and they give a clue to the folk you'll find inside and the kind of chat that's likely to be going on. Obviously anyone could enter a room called 'Sports Shack', but non-sports fans would probably find the conversation a bit dull.

Chatting On The Internet

Away from the chat rooms that have sprung up on websites in recent years, the Internet has its own long-established chat system called Internet Relay Chat, or **IRC**. Like all the other Internet services, you'll need to grab another piece of software to use it. One of the best, and the easiest to use, is **mIRC** from **http://www.mirc.co.uk** and included on the free CD-ROM in the back of this book. The first time you run mIRC, you'll see the dialog shown in the following screenshot into which you can enter the few details needed by the program.

Enter your name and email address in the appropriate spaces, and choose a nickname (or *handle*) by which you'll be known in chat sessions. A nickname can be anything you choose: it may give an indication of your hobby or job, or a clue to your (adopted?) personality, or it may just be meaningless gibberish, but it can't be more than nine characters in length. Finally choose a UK server from the list and click **OK**.

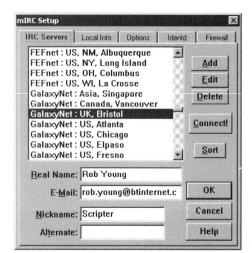

▶ Fill in three boxes, choose a server, and you're ready to start chatting.

Channels

In the weird world of IRC, which bases its jargon heavily on CB radio, a channel is the term for a chat room.

Now you're ready to connect and start chatting. Make sure you're connected to your service provider first (mIRC won't start the connection for you), and then click the thunderbolt button at the extreme left of the toolbar. As soon as you're connected, you'll see a small dialog box listing a collection of channels that mIRC's author thought you might like to try. You could double-click one of those to enter that channel, but now is a good time to use one of the many IRC commands. Close the little list of channels, type /**list** in the box at the bottom of the main window, and then press Enter. A second window will open to display all the channels available on the server you chose (shown in the next screenshot). There could be several hundred channels, so this might take a few seconds. Beside each channel's name you'll see a figure indicating how many people are on that channel at the moment, and a brief description of the channel's current subject of discussion. Choose a channel, and double-click its list entry to enter.

Some long-time IRC users can be a bit scathing towards newcomers, so it's best to choose a beginners' channel while you take your first faltering steps.

Good channels to start with are **#beginners**, **#mirc** (for mIRC users), **#irchelp** or **#ircnewbies**. You may see some more channel names that refer to help, beginners or newbies – try to pick a channel that has at least half a dozen people in it already so that you won't feel too conspicuous!

When a channel window opens, you'll see your nickname listed among the channel's other occupants on the right, with the conversation taking place on the left. As soon as you enter the channel, your arrival will be broadcast to everyone else (you'll see this happen when others arrive and leave) and you may receive an automated Welcome message, or someone might even say Hello. To join in with the chat, just start typing into the text box at the bottom and press Enter to send. If you want to leave a channel, type the command/**leave** and press Enter.

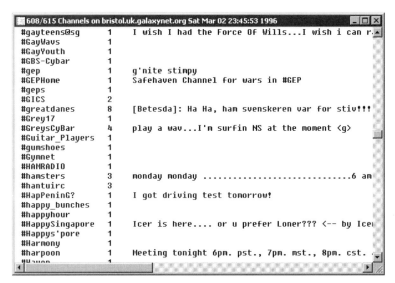

```
608/615 Channels on bristol.uk.galaxynet.org Sat Mar 02 23:45:53 1996
#gayteens@sg      1    I wish I had the Force Of Wills...I wish i can r.
#GayWavs          1
#GayYouth         1
#GBS-Cybar        1
#gep              1    g'nite stimpy
#GEPHome          1    Safehaven Channel for wars in #GEP
#geps             1
#GICS             2
#greatdanes       8    [Betesda]: Ha Ha, ham svenskeren var for stiv!!!
#Grey17           1
#GreysCyBar       4    play a wav...I'm surfin NS at the moment <g>
#Guitar_Players   1
#gumshoes         1
#Gymnet           1
#HAMRADIO         1
#hamsters         3    monday monday .............................6 am
#hantuirc         3
#HapPeninG?       1    I got driving test tomorrow!
#happy_bunches    1
#happyhour        1
#HappySingapore   1    Icer is here.... or u prefer Loner??? <-- by Ice
#Happys'pore      1
#Harmony          1
#harpoon          1    Meeting tonight 6pm. pst., 7pm. mst., 8pm. cst.
#Havan            1
```

◀ The complete channel listing from GalaxyNet's Bristol server. Choose any channel from 615 possibles!

GOOD QUESTION!

How can I start chatting without 'butting in'?

Whenever you arrive in a channel there's likely to be a conversation going on. If no one brings you into the chat, it's a good idea to 'lurk' for a few moments to see what it's all about, but it's quite acceptable to type something like Hi everyone, how's it going? and you'll usually get a friendly response from someone. If you don't, follow the conversation and try to interject with something useful.

IRC Commands – Chat Like A Pro

The IRC system has a huge number of commands that you can learn and put to good use if you're really keen, and mIRC includes a general IRC help file explaining how they work. You certainly don't need to know all of them (and mIRC has toolbar buttons that replace a few), but once you feel comfortable with the system you can experiment with new ones. Here's a few of the most useful to get you started.

Type this	To do this
/help	Get general help on IRC.
/list	List all the channels available on the server you're connected to.
/list –min *n*	List all the channels with at least *n* people in them (replace n with a figure).
/join #*channel*	Enter a channel (replace channel with the name of your chosen channel).
/leave #*channel*	Leave the specified channel (or the channel in the current window if no channel is specified).
/quit *message*	Finish your IRC session and display a message to the channel if you enter one (see below).
/away *message*	Tell other occupants you're temporarily away from your computer, giving a message.
/away	With no message, means that you're no longer away.
/whois *nickname*	Get information about the specified nickname in the main window.

So what are those 'messages'? When you quit, you might want to explain why you're leaving, by entering a command like /**quit Got to go shopping. See you later!** Similarly, if you suddenly have to leave your keyboard, you might type /**away Call of nature**. Type **BRB** to indicate that you'll be back in a minute if anyone tries to speak to you. (BRB is a common shorthand for 'Be right back' – turn to page 113 for a few more of these). When you return, just type /**away** to turn off this message again.

An easy way to make a fool of yourself

All commands start with a forward slash. If you type the command without the slash it will be displayed to all the participants in your channel, and give everyone a good giggle at your expense.

You can also 'talk' privately to any of the participants in a channel. If you want to start a private talk with someone called Zebedee, type the command /**query Zebedee Can I talk to you in private?** (of course, the message you tag on the end is up to you). Zebedee will have the opportunity to accept or decline the talk: if he or she accepts, a separate private window will open in which the two of you can exchange messages.

Easy window management

You can keep windows open in mIRC as long as you want to. The program places each new window on a task-bar so that you can switch between open channels and lists to your heart's content. Many people even keep several 'chats' going at once in this way!

Starting Your Own IRC Channel

If you always connect to the same server, and always use the /**list** command to get a list of channels you might notice that the number of channels varies. Channels are dynamic – anyone can create a new one, and when the last person leaves that channel it ceases to exist. Here's how to create your own channel.

1   Pick a channel name that doesn't already exist and enter it. To create a channel called Skylight, type /**join #Skylight**.

2   To put yourself in charge of this channel you have to promote yourself to 'channel operator' status. Do this by typing /*op nickname* (entering your

own nickname). As operator, your nickname will be displayed with an '@' prefix to indicate your status to anyone who enters your channel.

3 Now set a topic that will displayed in the channel list and (with luck!) attract some passers-by. Type **/topic** followed by a description of what your channel would be discussing if there was someone else to discuss it with. As people join your channel and the discussion moves to different areas, use the **/topic** command to update the description.

As channel operator you are all-powerful: you can invite people into your channel using **/invite** followed by their nickname and the name of your channel (for example, **/invite Zebedee #Skylight**), and you can kick someone out if their conduct is offensive or disruptive using **/kick #Skylight Zebedee**. You can also use the **/op** command to promote other visitors to channel operator status if you wish to.

Chatting Can Be Comical

Simple though it is, chatting can be very addictive. But it's still plain text, and in Internet-land that just won't do. The latest thing is graphical chat software in which you choose a cartoon character called an **avatar** to represent yourself. These programs offer you a list of avatars to choose from, and some even let you create your own if you're handy with a graphics program. The following screenshot shows one of the most popular graphical chat programs, **Microsoft Chat** (which also supports ordinary textual chat if those avatars get on your nerves!). Chat is included on the

 Windows 98 and Me CD-ROMs, and the latest version is included with Internet Explorer 5.5, which you can install from the CD in the back of this book.

Turn off your avatar

Microsoft have set up their own chat rooms for Microsoft Chat, but you can also connect to the usual mIRC channels, and Chat will assign other occupants an avatar so that you can still take part using avatars rather than plain text. If you do connect to an IRC channel, though, go to Chat's **View | Options | Settings** page and check the box beside **Don't send Microsoft Chat specific information**, or the rest of the channel will see some very strange stuff alongside your typed text!

◀ Microsoft's visual Chat program lets you choose an avatar, and select different emotions to match your text.

If you get a taste for this type of chat, this program is just the tip of a whole new iceberg. On the CD-ROM that accompanies this book, you'll find details of programs that you can use to access sites on the World Wide Web that use avatars and virtual reality to combine chat with the exploration of 3D worlds. In fact, some of these worlds are so amazing, you won't even want to stop and chat!

Finally on the subject of chat, a word about personal security: never give out personal details other than your name, age, sex and email address. After chatting with someone for a while, it's easy to forget that you really know nothing about them but what they've told you (and that may not be true!).

Internet Telephony – Talk Really *Is* Cheap!

The sort of chat we've looked at so far is 'unplanned' – you arrive in a channel or chat room and chat to whoever happens to be there. If you get on well enough, you might invite someone else to have a private chat (a 'talk') in a separate window. But what if there's someone in particular you want to talk to? Until recently, your options were limited: you could agree to meet in a chat room at a certain time and take it from there, or you could pick up the phone.

Now there are a couple of other options: instant messaging, which we'll meet a little later, and Internet telephony (otherwise known as Voice Over the Net or **VON**). As you'd expect, VON is the Internet equivalent of a telephone: you start the program, choose an email address to 'dial', and start talking. But in this case, talking is really *talking*. You can hold live conversations with anyone in the world by speaking into a microphone and hear their responses through your speakers or a headset.

Will they be online?

BY THE WAY

You can only talk to someone else if they're online and have their VON software running. Many American users have access to free local phone calls and can stay online all day, but if you want to contact another UK user you might still have to arrange to be online at a pre-specified time.

So how does Internet telephony differ from an ordinary telephone conversation? First and foremost, the price – because you're only dialling in to your local service provider, you're only paying for a local phone call although you may be speaking to someone in Australia. But it's the extra goodies that VON programs offer that make them valuable. Depending on the program you use, you can send computer files back and forth, hold conferences, use a whiteboard to draw sketches and diagrams, and you can even take control of programs on the other party's computer (if they're happy to let you do that). Recent programs have even made the fabled 'video phone' a reality at last – admittedly the pictures are small, rather jerky (especially with a slow modem) and a bit blurred, but you can finally see and be seen while you talk! Of course, you'll need a digital video camera (a so-called 'webcam') and software, but these can be bought for less than £100.

Sounds Good, What's The Catch?

The downside is that the other party must also be online to receive the 'call', so you'll both pay phone charges, but even added together these could amount to less than ten per cent of an international call charge. In fact, there are already programs such as Net2Phone (from **http://www.net2phone.com**)

that allow you to dial someone's phone number rather than email address, making it possible to make these cheap international calls to someone who doesn't even have an Internet account!

A second catch (at the moment) is that you must be using the same program as the person you want to talk to. If you talk to a lot of people, you might need several different programs that do the same job just because they all use different programs. Fortunately some of these programs are free, so it's probably easiest to pick a free one and then convince your friends to grab a copy themselves! Before long, the various software companies involved will probably get their act together on this as they have with the other Internet services.

What Do I Need?

Unlike the other services you use on the Net, VON programs have some definite hardware requirements. To begin with, you'll need a soundcard. It doesn't need to be a flashy, expensive card since the quality of these voice calls isn't high, but look out for a **full duplex** card. You need a reasonably fast computer too (preferably at least a Pentium II) with a bare minimum of 32Mb RAM. And you'll need a microphone and speakers plugged into your soundcard; the quality of these doesn't matter too much and any computer peripherals store can supply them very cheaply.

JARGON BUSTER

Full duplex

There are two choices: full duplex and half duplex. A full duplex card can record your voice while playing the incoming voice so that you can both talk at the same time if you want to (ideal for arguments, for example!). With a half duplex card you can either talk or listen, but not both – you'd normally switch off your microphone after speaking as an indication you'd finished (rather like saying 'Over' on a walkie-talkie).

Next there's your Internet connection and modem to consider. You might just get by with a 28.8Kbps connection, but you'll get much better results from a 56Kbps modem and if you have a faster connection option available, it'll pay dividends. Finally, of course, you need the software. There are many different programs to choose from, some of which are aimed more at business rather than personal use, but here's a brief selection, all of which you'll find on the CD-ROM that accompanies the book.

▶ **PowWow**. A very friendly, free program from Tribal Voice which we'll look at in a moment. You can download this from **http://www.tribal.com**

▶ **NetMeeting**. Microsoft's free VON program aimed largely at business users, but (seemingly) used more by personal talkaholics. NetMeeting supports video, voice, and multi-user conferences, and you can use programs on the other person's computer by remote control. If you don't already have NetMeeting (it's included with Windows 98, Me and 2000) it can be installed along with Internet Explorer from the CD-ROM, or you can download it as a separate item from **http://www. microsoft.com/netmeeting**

▶ **Web Phone**. A multi-talented, and very stylish, VON program based on a mobile phone design with features such as video, text chat and answerphone, as well as four separate voice lines. You'll need to 'activate' the evaluation copy (an unusual way of saying 'pay for') to unlock some of its smartest features by visiting **http://www.itelco.com** Although inexpensive, Web Phone is targeted more at the business user than are NetMeeting or (particularly) PowWow.

▶ **Internet Phone**. A true VON program, in that it has no 'text talk' or whiteboard facilities so it'll be no good to you without soundcard, microphone and speakers. Until you pay for your copy, your talk time will be limited. You can register the evaluation copy by pointing your browser at **http://www.vocaltec.com**

Don't be out when the call comes in!

To get the most from any chat, talk or VON program, make sure you run it every time you go online; if you don't, it's like leaving your phone permanently off the hook – no one will be able to contact you! Even if you just plan to do a bit of web-surfing, run the program and then minimize it. If someone wants to talk, a dialog will appear to ask if you'd like to accept.

Start Talking

As usual, most VON programs have similar features, although their names and toolbar buttons vary. It's probably an inescapable fact of life that the most popular VON programs are the free ones, so let's take a look at Tribal Voice's **PowWow** as a representative example.

When you first run PowWow you'll be prompted to enter your name, email address and a choice of password. The program will then dial up and register these in the main PowWow database and you're ready to start. Click the **Connect** button at the left of the toolbar and type in the email address of the PowWow user you want to contact. To save their details to the Address Book for future use, fill in their name or nickname and click **Add**. Make sure you're connected to your ISP and click the **Connect** button. If the other person is online and running PowWow (and willing to speak to you, of course) the main window will split into two and you'll see their reply. Just as in any Chat program, you simply type your side of the conversation and press Enter.

GOOD QUESTION!

How can I tell who's online and available for chat?

It depends on the program. In some programs you can't – you have to send a request and see if you get a response. In other programs, such as NetMeeting and Internet Phone, as soon as you connect you'll see a list of users currently online, so take your courage in both hands and double-click one!

To speak to someone using your microphone, click the **Voice** button. Although PowWow lets you text chat with up to seven people, you'll only be able to have a voice conversation with one at a time. Here's a brief run-down of features you'll find in PowWow (and most other VON programs):

▶ Transfer files by clicking the **Send File** button and choosing a file to send. You can continue to talk while the file is being transferred.

▶ Set up an answering machine message that will be sent to anyone trying to contact you when you're unavailable. Some programs (such as Web Phone) can also record messages left by anyone trying to contact you.

▶ Send a picture of yourself to the other user by entering its location in PowWow's setup page. Most programs can send images to be displayed on the other user's screen without interrupting the conversation.

▶ If you have a webcam attached to your computer (a small, cheap digital camera, available from around £50), many programs can transmit live pictures, allowing the other party to see you while you speak. These neat devices can also take still snapshots to be saved as computer files, or short movies you can attach to an email message as 'video email'.

▶ Click the **Whiteboard** button to collaborate in drawing pictures using a similar set of tools to those found in Windows' Paint.

▶ Host a conference with up to 50 people taking part in text chat.

▶ If you have your own website, you can add a PowWow link to your page to tell visitors that you're online and available to chat. This is a slightly unusual feature, but Internet Phone users have a similar option. Visitors to the page can click the link to start their own software and invite you to talk.

▶ Stuck for someone to call? Click the **White Pages** button in PowWow and your web browser will open the main Tribal Voice page. Click a button to see a list of users currently online, then click one of the names to request a chat

Punctuate your chat with WAV audio files by clicking the **Sound** button. PowWow comes with its own set of sound files such as 'Applause', 'Hi', 'Cool' and 'Bye', and lets you choose between a male or female voice. Provided the same sound file is on the other person's system too, you'll both hear it.

A matter of fax

So you can use the Internet as a telephone – that's been possible for a while, so it's not wildly exciting any more. Here's a new one: go to **http://www.faxme.co.uk**, create a free account, and give the number you receive to your friends and colleagues. They can send faxes to that number which will be forwarded to you as email attachments. All you need is an ordinary email program and an image viewer that can handle these TIFF-format fax images.

Tiny Talk – Instant Messaging

From the topsy-turvy mix of chat, talk and voice software out there, one type of program has emerged as a firm favourite: the **instant messenger** service. It all started with a program called ICQ (I Seek You, geddit?) and other well-known companies have since jumped on board offering their own instant messengers.

The idea is simple: download the software, create a list of friends, and every time you connect to the Net the software will tell you which of your friends are online. In the same way, your friends will know that you're online. To send an instant message (or an 'IM' in the jargon), double-click a name and start typing.

Here are the five best-known IM programs, all of which are free. The first four are all fairly simple to set up and use, making them a good choice for beginners or for personal use. ICQ tries to do far more than the others and may be a bit off-putting, despite giving a choice between Simple and Advanced modes, but it's still the most widely accepted: you'll even see ICQ numbers on people's business cards!

▶ **AOL Instant Messenger** (or AIM) from **http://www.aol.co.uk/aim**

▶ **AltaVista Messenger** from **http://www.altavista.com**

▶ **MSN Messenger** from **http://www.msn.co.uk**

▶ **Yahoo! Messenger** from **http://messenger.yahoo.com**

▶ **ICQ** from **http://www.icq.com**

One thing that may colour your choice of IM software is whether or not it's compatible with what your friends and colleagues use. AltaVista and some of the other companies involved are promoting an 'open standard' in instant messaging – they feel that users should be able to choose the software they like best and still be able to contact users who prefer a different IM program (in keeping with the Web, email, newsgroups, IRC, and so on). You can find out more about the ongoing bun-fight, and who the good guys and bad guys are, by visiting freeIM at **http://www.freeim.org**

GRABBING THE GOODIES WITH FTP

FTP – a bunch of initials. Why did they have to do that? The Web is the Web, email is email. Why couldn't this be called 'Dave' or something? Perhaps then you wouldn't feel like skipping this chapter. FTP really deserves a much simpler name – it's one of the easiest Internet services to use, and if you've been surfing the Web you know something about using it already. So don't be fooled by the name, come on in and meet 'Dave'!

What Is FTP?

Imagine you've been left alone in a room full of computers with huge hard disks. You can root around as much as you like, grab any files you want, and take them home with you. If that sounds like a little slice of happiness, you'll like FTP – that's what it's for. FTP stands for File Transfer Protocol, and it works a lot like Windows Explorer or File Manager. You can open directories by clicking them, browse around, and click on any file to copy it to somewhere else. There's just one difference: on your own computer you might copy a file from one directory to another, or to a floppy disk, but FTP copies the file to a different computer – your own.

We've already looked at links to files on the World Wide Web in Chapter 6. What you didn't realise is that you were already using FTP just by clicking these links and letting the file download. Some of the files are stored on a web server, others are stored on an FTP server, but you don't need to know what the main job of the computer is: you click the link, the file is sent, end of story. (If you're interested, move your mouse pointer on to the link and look at your browser's status-bar to see where the link points. If the address starts with **ftp://** you'll know it's an FTP site. It might be worth knowing, as you'll learn in a moment.)

GOOD QUESTION!

I couldn't connect to the site. What went wrong?

It might be closed, or it might be very busy. Some FTP sites put a limit on the number of people that can visit at once, and others don't allow anonymous logins during business hours, so try again later. It's good netiquette to avoid accessing FTP sites during their local business hours (some knowledge of time zones is helpful here!), and you'll usually get a much faster service too. Of course, you might just have typed the address wrongly – always a good place to start!

Using Your Browser for FTP

FTP addresses look a lot like web addresses: they begin with the name of the computer, and continue with the directory path to the file you want. To use your browser to visit an FTP site, you'll usually need to prefix the whole thing with **ftp://** (the only exception is when the name of the computer starts with 'ftp', but you can still use the prefix in these cases if you prefer to). To get acquainted with FTP using the browser, let's visit an FTP site. Start up your browser, type the following address into the address bar, and press Enter:

ftp://sunsite.doc.ic.ac.uk

Addresses, names and numbers

Sometimes you'll see an FTP site address given as a bundle of numbers and dots (an IP address) instead of a name. Instead of **sunsite.doc.ic.ac.uk** you might see **193.63.255.1** Don't worry about it – they work the same way. You could type **ftp://193.63.255.1** to get to this site.

Once you're connected to the site, you'll see a plain white background with a plain black welcoming message. (This is how the whole World Wide Web looked until a few years ago!) Scroll downwards in the window and a list of blue hypertext links will come into view. In true Web style, the blue text is clickable and will lead somewhere else. To the left of each hypertext entry you'll see either **Directory** or a set of figures. The word Directory indicates that this is a link to another directory (like clicking a folder icon in Windows); the figures show that the entry links to a file and give its size. Further to the left you'll see the date and time that the file was placed on the computer. On some FTP sites, you might see friendly icons next to the hypertext links – a folder icon for a directory, and a page icon for a file.

To get to the directory shown in the screenshot, click on the directory entry **computing**. Explorer will display the contents of the **computing** directory and you can then click on the **systems** directory, followed by **ibmpc**, and then **windowsnt**. From here, you could click on another directory to open it, or click on one of the files to start downloading it. To go back to the **ibmpc** directory you just left, click the text at the top of the list that reads **Up to higher level directory**.

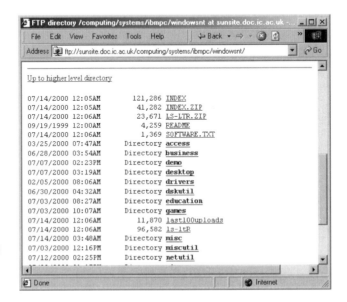

▶ One-click browsing through an FTP site using Internet Explorer.

Avoiding the scenic route

If you know exactly where you need to go, don't waste time clicking your way through all the directories. For example, to get to the 'windowsnt' directory in the example, type **ftp://sunsite.doc.ic.ac.uk/computing/systems/ibmpc/windowsnt** into the address bar. Better still, if you know the name of the file you want to download from this directory, add /***filename*** on the end. Explorer will connect and start downloading the file, but won't waste time showing you the FTP directory.

Keep a look out for files called **Index**. These will tell you something about the site you're visiting, and give a list of all the files on the site or in the current directory (depending on the individual site – some give more detail than others). As you can see in the screenshot, there are two Index files. One is a text file that you could read in any word processor or in your browser's window; the other is a *compressed* version of the same file (indicated by its **.zip** extension and much smaller size) and needs a program like WinZip to decompress it, which you'll learn about in Chapter 13. It's well worth grabbing Index files to read offline: they usually include a brief description of each file to supplement the rather cryptic filenames you see listed on the screen.

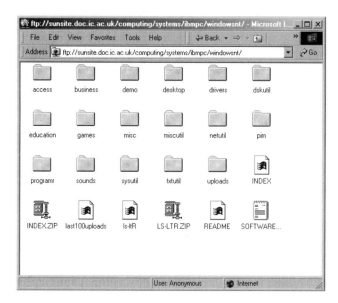

◀ The same FTP directory shown using Internet Explorer's 'folder view'.

If the rather plain text listing of directories and files puts you off, recent versions of Internet Explorer offer a more familiar way of presenting the same information: a 'folder view' that looks just like the view of folders on your own computer, shown in the screenshot above. Go to **Tools** | **Internet Options** | **Advanced** and check the box labelled **Enable folder view for FTP sites** to use this view in future.

Private Sites & Anonymous Sites

To gain access to any FTP site you have to log in, just as you do when you connect to your ISP or online service. Some of these sites are private, and you'll need a username and password to get access. For example, a company might allow you access to their site in order to upload information or files rather than sending them by email. If you create your own website and upload the files by FTP, you'll have a username and password to prevent anyone else having access to your directory and tampering with your web pages.

Heading straight for the pub

Many anonymous sites will give free access only to certain areas; some directories will be 'roped off' and you won't be allowed into them. Keep a look out for a directory called **pub**, which will contain all the files and subdirectories available to anonymous visitors.

Many other sites are accessible to the public, and anyone can log on and delve in. These are known as *anonymous* sites, because the system doesn't need to find out who you are before letting you in. To access these sites, you'll log in with the username **anonymous** and give your email address as the password. Using your browser, this is handled automatically and you won't be prompted to enter anything. Using an FTP program, as you'll learn in a moment, you just click a box labelled **Anonymous** to have the details entered for you.

Using A 'Real' FTP Program

So if the browser can cope with FTP, why would you want to use anything different? Quite simply, a 'real' FTP program is custom built for the job. With a few minutes' practice, it's actually easier and friendlier to use, and it can usually connect to an FTP site faster than your browser can, speeding up the transfer of files that you download. It also gives you more information about the progress of downloads from FTP sites than your browser does. Finally, it will let you upload files as well as download them which, at the moment, browsers can't do.

Why would I want to upload files?

GOOD QUESTION!

If you've logged in anonymously you won't be able to upload any files. The main time you'll want to do this is when you've created your own website, and have to copy the files to your service provider's web server. You'll learn more about doing that in Chapter 25.

First you'll need to grab a copy of an FTP program, and three of the best are listed below. For the rest of this chapter I'm going to assume you're using FTP Explorer, but don't worry if you're not: all three programs have very similar features.

▶ **FTP Explorer**. A neat program for Windows 95 and later, shown in the screenshot on page 170 and found at **http://www.ftpx.com**

▶ **CuteFTP**. No more cuddly than the others, but every bit as good. If you choose to use this program for more than 30 days, head for **http://www.cuteftp.com** to register it

▶ **WS_FTP Professional**. One of the most popular programs, despite the dull name. You can download an evaluation copy from **http://www.ipswitch.com**

Setting up FTP Explorer couldn't be easier: when you first start it up, you'll be asked to enter your email address, and that's it. A dialog will appear to ask if you'd like some 'sample profiles' to be created, and it's worth clicking the **Yes** button: this puts a list of useful FTP sites just a couple of clicks away, and you'll see this list in the next window that opens, the **Connect** dialog.

If there's a particular site you want to visit and you know you'll only want to visit it once, you can cancel this dialog and use the Quick Connect option instead. Click the toolbar button with the lightning flash, type the URL of the site and click **OK**, and FTP Explorer will try to connect you.

Can't I use the FTP program in my Windows directory?

Well you could, yes. But it's like nailing jelly to the ceiling. It's an MS-DOS program with an unfriendly set of commands, and takes a lot of very precise typing. I'd give it a miss.

The more practical way of working is to create a new 'profile' for the site. This can be saved so that you can use it again in the future (rather like Internet Explorer's **Favorites** menu). As an example, let's set up a profile for the SunSite FTP site we visited earlier. In the **Connect** dialog, click the **Add** button and follow these steps.

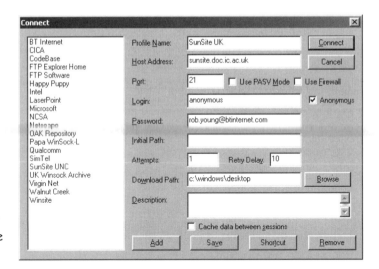

▶ Creating a new connection profile in FTP Explorer.

1 In the **Profile Name** box, type any name that will help you recognise the connection to this FTP site in future, such as **SunSite UK**.

2 Type the address of the computer you want to connect to in the **Host Address** box – in this case **sunsite.doc.ic.ac.uk**

3 If you're visiting a private site, type your logon name in the **Login** box and your password in the **Password** box. SunSite, like most of the sites

you'll visit, is a public site, so click the checkbox marked **Anonymous**. This will fill in those two boxes for you automatically.

4 In the **Initial Path** box, you can type the path to the directory you want to see after connecting, such as **/computing/systems/ibmpc** (not forgetting that first forward slash!). If you leave this blank, you'll arrive at the root directory of the SunSite computer.

5 In the box marked **Download Path**, you can type the path to a directory on your own computer that you want any files to be downloaded into. This directory will be selected for downloads every time you connect to this site.

6 Click **Save** to add this new profile to the list on the left. In future you can click the **Connect** button on the toolbar to see this dialog again, choose 'SunSite UK' from the list and click Connect to visit it. For now, as the dialog is already in front of you, click Connect and FTP Explorer will dial up (if necessary) and try to connect to the site.

FTP and the online services

The major online services will also let you transfer files by FTP. In America Online, use the keyword **ftp**; in CompuServe, use the Go word **ftp**. In either program you can click on the big **Internet** button on the main desktop and choose FTP from the next menu.

If the connection is made successfully, you'll see the window as shown in the next screenshot. Exploring the contents of the FTP computer is as easy as exploring your own hard disk: use the tree structure in the left pane to select directories and open directories, and view their contents in the right pane. Select the file or files you want to download and click the Download button on the toolbar to copy it to the directory you entered into the **Download Path** box. A small dialog will keep you posted on the transfer progress. You can also drag and drop files from FTP Explorer's main window to your desktop or elsewhere to download them. If you find an Index or text file that you'd like to read immediately rather than store, right-click it and choose the **Quick View** option.

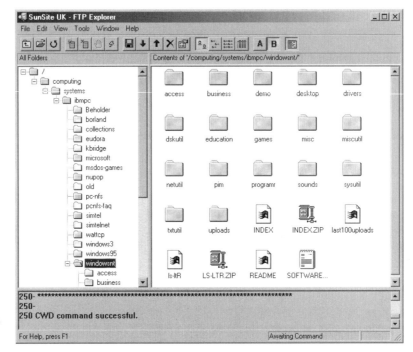

▶ Browsing directories on the remote computer with FTP Explorer's familiar layout.

Which mode should I use?

GOOD QUESTION!

Most FTP programs give you a choice of two modes, **ASCII** and **Binary** (FTP Explorer has buttons marked A and B on its toolbar for this). ASCII mode can only be used to download plain text files and will do so faster than Binary mode. But since text files tend to be small anyway, the time difference is negligible. It's simplest to stick to Binary mode for everything, unless you come across an FTP server that insists on using ASCII mode for its text files.

Uploading files is just as easy as downloading them. You can click the Upload button on the toolbar and choose one or more files from a standard file dialog, or simply drag them from one of your own directories and drop them into FTP Explorer's main window. You can also drag folders into this window and the folder will be uploaded along with its contents. To create a new directory on the server, right-click on a blank area in the main window, choose **New** and **Folder**, and type a name. You can then just double-click this new folder to open it and start copying files into it.

Finding The Stuff You Want

The big trick with FTP is to actually locate what you're looking for. There may be dozens of directories, all containing more directories, and the structure may not always be as intuitive as the way you structure your own hard disk. Let's look at several things you might want to do, and come up with some solutions.

▶ If you know the name and location of the file you want, type it into your browser's address bar, or type the path into FTP Explorer's **Initial Path** box and look for the file when the directory's contents is shown.

▶ If you know the location of the file you want, but not its name, visit that directory and either 'Quick View' or download one of the Index files which should give a short description of each file in that directory.

▶ If you don't know the location of the file (or the location you were given is wrong), but you know its name, there are several options. One is to see if it's listed in an Index file. Another is to use an Archie search (you'll meet Archie in Chapter 12). A third possibility is to use your browser to visit FTP Search at **http://ftpsearch.lycos.com** (pictured in the next screenshot). Type the name of the file into the **Search for** box and click the **Search** button. (If FTP Search doesn't do the trick, a similar search at **http://www.snoopie.com** may yield different results.)

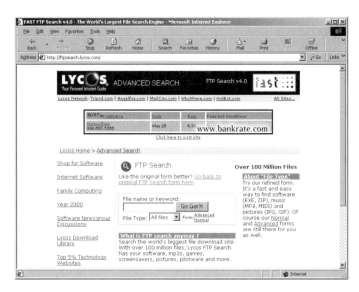

◀ Track down elusive files using the FTP Search page.

GOOD QUESTION!

Why can't I get to ftpsearch.lycos.com?

You're probably not typing the **http://** prefix at the start. Fair enough, I told you that you didn't have to. Unfortunately this URL begins with the letters 'ftp', so Internet Explorer is trying to find it as an FTP site (**ftp://ftpsearch.lycos.com**) and failing. To prevent it doing that, type the URL as **http://ftpsearch.lycos.com**. (This appears to be a bug in recent Internet Explorer versions: previous versions far more sensibly looked for URLs starting with 'ftp' *followed by a dot.*)

▶ Even if you're not looking for anything in particular, it's fun just browsing through directories until you come across something interesting. Directory names tend to become more specific as you dig deeper. For example, if you were looking for email programs, start in the pub directory, and from there you might find a 'computing' directory, which would lead you to 'software', then 'internet', then 'email'. If the pub directory has an Index or Readme file, grab that first – it may contain a listing of all its subdirectories and an explanation of what each contains.

Another, often better, way to find a file is to run an Archie search. What's that all about? Keep reading – all will be revealed in Chapter 12.

12

EXTRA TOOLS & UTILITIES

▶ **IN THIS CHAPTER**

Research and exploration with Gopher

Play adventure games by remote control with Telnet

Let Archie take the strain of finding elusive files on the Internet

Find information about people and companies using Whois and Finger

Iron out connection problems with Ping

Since the Internet's popularity explosion in 1994, the main attractions for newcomers to the Net have been the World Wide Web and email, with newsgroups and chat close behind. Of course, you don't have to use any part of the Internet you're not interested in, but there's plenty more treasure to be found if you like digging around. In this chapter, we'll take a look at some of the backwaters of the Internet, and a few extra utilities that may one day come in handy.

Searching Gopherspace

I'm going to tell you this up front – you probably won't like Gopher. A few years ago, though, you'd have loved it. Until that time, the Internet was an unfriendly place that had to be navigated with complicated text commands, and Gopher came along to solve everyone's problems by grouping everything into a series of menus. Clicking a menu entry might lead to another menu on another computer somewhere in the world, or it might lead to a file or document. It was a great leap forward, and was heralded as the future of the Internet. So what happened? The World Wide Web came along, and few people wanted to use a menu-driven system any more, whether it had a cute name or not.

JARGON BUSTER

Gopherspace

The Gopher system consists of many computers around the world acting as Gopher servers (just as there are web servers, FTP servers, news servers, and so on). When you look at a document from a web server, you're using the World Wide Web. Connect to a Gopher server, and you're said to be 'in Gopherspace'.

Nowadays you won't find many Gopher sites on the Internet; most have become websites instead. And for any that you do come across, your web browser can access them without needing any outside help. But although links to Gopher sites are not plentiful on the Web, there are still many useful documents stored on Gopher servers, and the easiest way to find them is to use a dedicated Gopher program. The best is WSGopher, which seems to come and go from the various software-download sites but was last spotted at **http://www.enet.it/mirror/WWW/ winsock/win95/gopher.htm** – there's a copy included on the CD-ROM too.

Once you've installed WSGopher, it's easy to set up – there's nothing to do at all! I would make two suggestions though. Before you do anything else, select **Edit | Fonts** and choose a smaller font for the first three items on the list. Next, click your way to **Edit | Preferences | Home View** and choose any window layout that shows bookmarks (you'll understand that as soon as you see the Home View page). As soon as WSGopher has connected to your Home site (a Gopher server listed in **Edit | Preferences | Home Gopher**) you'll see a list of directories containing links to menus and files in the Directory List. Click on the '+' sign to expand a directory and see its subdirectories, or click on any directory to see its contents in the Document List window and then double-click a document to download and open it.

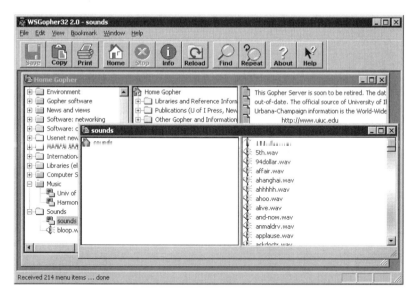

◀ Use WSGopher's supplied bookmarks to find your way to some of the best Gopher sites.

WSGopher has its own bookmarks system that works like Internet Explorer's Favorites menu. Best of all, the program's author has thoughtfully supplied a ready-sorted bundle of bookmarks, but you'll see these only if you chose the window layout I suggested a moment ago. These are a great place to start: expand one of the bookmark directories and double-click on any of the entries. An excellent site to try is **Gopher Jewels** listed in the **Gopher services** directory. If you find any sites that you'd like to add to the bookmarks list, right-click them, choose **Add**, and select a Category in which to store the bookmark (or create a new Category by typing a name for it and clicking **Create** followed by **OK**).

Is Gopherspace as exciting as the World Wide Web?

No; by comparison it's like watching paint dry. Although you can find sound and picture files to download, Gopher is still a text-based system. It can be extremely useful for research purposes though – many of the remaining Gopher sites belong to universities, libraries, government departments, and other organisations who choose to publish their information widely in a simple form.

Taking Control With Telnet

Telnet is yet another rather dull way to get at information on the Internet, and it's another service that's been overshadowed by the World Wide Web. The reasoning is if you want to do it, and it can be done on the Web, why would you choose the difficult way instead? But, like Gopher, there are places you can get to only by 'Telnetting' there, and some of them hold a few surprises.

Telnet is a system that lets you use programs running on another computer, or explore their files and databases. To do this, you'll need a Telnet program – this is one of the few talents your web browser doesn't have. If you use Windows 95, 98, Me or 2000 you already have a good Telnet program: click **Run** on the Start Menu, type **telnet** and press Enter. For this section I'm going to assume you're using the Windows offering, but you'll also find a much smarter and friendlier Telnet program, NetTerm from **http://starbase.neosoft.com/~zkrr01**, on the CD-ROM.

Read the rules!

All Telnet sites are different, and what you see after connecting will vary from a plain text display to a lavish graphical interface – you take pot luck. For the same reason, the commands you use will vary too, so it pays to read any helpful notices you can find when you arrive. If all else fails, try typing **help** followed by Enter.

There are several ways to connect to a Telnet site: if you click a Telnet link on a web page, your browser will start your Telnet program automatically to connect to it (if it can't locate a Telnet program, the browser will ask you to specify its location). Similarly, you could type the URL of the Telnet site you want to visit into your browser's address bar, prefixing it with **telnet://**. Finally, you can start the Telnet program yourself, click on **Connect | Remote System**, and then type the site's address into the **Host Name** box and click the **Connect** button. When you've finished a Telnet session and want to log off, try typing **quit** or **exit** followed by Enter. If you get no response, go to the **Connect** menu and choose **Disconnect**.

If you want to give Telnet a go, use your web browser to visit the HYTELNET site at **http://library.usask.ca/hytelnet**. Click the **Other Resources** link or either of the **Library Catalogs** links to see a list of Telnet sites you can try. At some Telnet sites you'll have to log in using an account name and give a password, but many of these sites still allow public access so HYTELNET will usually tell you the account name and password to use.

Telnet and the online services

Both America Online and CompuServe have built-in Telnet support. In both cases, the Go or keyword is **telnet**. If you're a Virgin Net or MSN user, you'll need to use the Windows Telnet program or install a different program such as NetTerm.

Fantasy & Adventure By Remote Control

One of the few reasons for Telnet's continuing survival is a type of role-playing game called a MUD (short for Multi-User Dungeon). You'll also come across MUCKs, MUSHs, MOOs and a few more, but to the non-purist they all mean much the same. These are usually science fiction or adventure games in which the program might give you information like *You are in a large room with a door to the West. In front of you is a table. On the table is a book.* You control the action yourself by typing commands such as **get book**.

These games are incredibly popular and could keep you online for days at a stretch if you get a taste for them. A good MUD for beginners can be found at **anguish.org:2222** This program takes you through the game's commands step by step, so take time to read the text carefully at the beginning. If you fancy trying some more of these, point your browser at **http://www.chaco.com/lists** for a hypertext list.

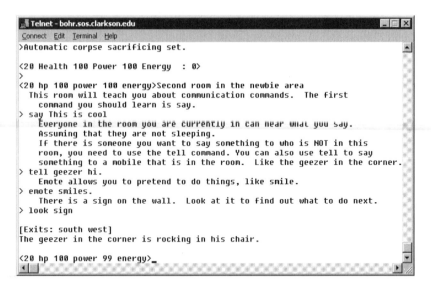

▶ Role-playing MUD games – the most popular use of Telnet.

Finding Files With Archie

Once you've found the file you want, downloading it with FTP is a simple job of clicking one button, as you learnt in the previous chapter. And exploring the directories of FTP servers can lead you to some weird and wonderful files. The big puzzle with FTP is how to find the particular file you need without spending hours searching countless computers, and this is where **Archie** steps in to help.

Why is it called Archie?

The Archie system stores a list (or archive) of the files it finds, and Archie is just 'archive' minus the 'v'. But Archie also happens to be a famous cartoon character, so two later search systems were named 'Veronica' and 'Jughead', characters from the same cartoon show. See? Even Internet geeks have a sense of humour!

The Archie system consists of a bunch of computers around the world that regularly examine the contents of FTP servers and store a list of the files they find. Using an Archie program, you can connect to one of these computers and ask it to search its list for a particular file name. Two of the best programs, both of which are free for personal use, are:

▶ **WSArchie**. This program works hand in hand with your FTP program to make downloading quick and easy. You can grab a copy of WSArchie from **http://dspace.dial.pipex.com/town/square/cc83**

▶ **fpArchie**. Going one step further, fpArchie doesn't need a separate FTP program: if it locates the file you want, it can download it for you too. You can visit its web page at **http://www.fpware.demon.nl**

Setting up these programs is a quick job. If you opted for WSArchie, go to **Option | Ftp Setup**, and tell the program where to find your FTP program (click the **Browse** button to locate and double-click the program). In fpArchie, go to **View | Options** and click the **FTP** tab. Fill in your email address and, if you wish, enter a folder to which all downloaded files should be saved. (Turn to 'Downloading – Choose Your Folder' on page 192 for a suggested way of organising your folders.)

Not all Archie servers are the same

Although all Archie computers in the system do much the same job, some find files that others don't. If you run a search and get no results, click WSArchie's **Archie Server** tab (or fpArchie's **Servers** tab), and choose a different server to search from the dropdown list. You may find that you can't connect to a particular server at all if you were unlucky enough to choose a busy time.

To find a file using one of these Archie programs, go to the **Search For** (or **Name & Location**) tab, and type the name of the file you want to look for. If you know the exact name of the file, you can speed up the search by selecting **Exact** (or **the exact name**). If you only know a part of the filename, type it in and select **Substring** (or **a part of the name**). For example, if you're looking for a program called ABC101.EXE, but you think it might have been replaced by a newer version called ABC102.EXE, just enter ABC10.

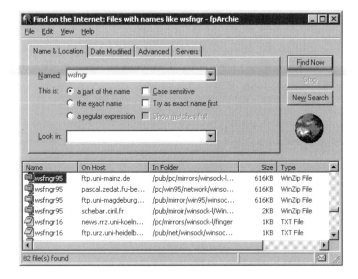

▶ Using fpArchie to search for files containing the characters 'wsfngr'.

If either program finds any files matching the text you entered, you'll see the filenames displayed in the main window, together with their sizes, and details of the FTP server on which each file was found. If one of the files listed is the one you want, just right-click on the filename and choose

Retrieve – as long as the FTP server isn't too busy, the program will handle the download for you automatically. If the file you want is listed as being available on several different FTP servers, you'll usually get the quickest download time by choosing the FTP server geographically closest to you.

Archie on the Web

If you really don't want another program just to handle the occasional search for a file, you can find Archie on the World Wide Web too. Go to **http://cui.unige.ch/archieplexform.html** and type the name of the file you're looking for using similar options to those covered here. If the search is successful you'll see a page of hypertext links to all the files that match the text you entered – just click one to download it.

Quickfire Extras

For this last little batch of utilities I'm going to move into 'quickfire mode'. The odds are that you'll never want to use these programs unless you like to experiment with software and you're not put off by technical gibberish like 'IP address' and 'name server'. If that doesn't sound like you, skip this section by all means!

Using Your Finger

Finger is a program that might be able to give you some information about an Internet user if you know their logon username and domain name. Of course, if you know that, you probably know their email address too, and you could get the information pretty easily by asking them for it. However, some people set up a special file to provide instant access to certain information (a business might provide product details, for example) that you can retrieve by fingering them. To finger someone, just enter *username@domain* and click **OK**. There are many Finger programs available with varying features, but the most popular is WSFinger32, a free program that you can download from **http://www.empire.net/~jobrien/wsfinger.htm** or install from the CD-ROM at the back of this book. Finger is also one of the bundle of features included in WSPing ProPack shareware program covered overleaf.

Shareware

Shareware is a popular method of selling software on the Internet. You can download the program and try it out for a while, but if you choose to continue using it beyond a specified period you should *register* it (in other words, pay for it). Shareware has become a generalised term encompassing nagware, crippleware and others, which you'll learn about in Chapter 13.

Give 'Em A Ping

Ping is a little utility used to test a connection by sending a short message to a chosen computer to see if it responds and, if it does, how quickly. This can be handy for two purposes. First, if you're not sure whether your own connection to your ISP is working, start your Ping program and type in the domain name of any computer (such as **www.btinternet.com** or **ftp.tcp.com**). Second, if you're trying to connect to a particular site and it's not responding, try Pinging it instead. The program will send out several short messages, and the results will show whether the Ping was successful and tell you how long the computer took to respond.

Windows users already have a Ping program – open the Start Menu, choose **Run**, and type **ping** followed by an Internet address (for example, **ping www.microsoft.com**). A more capable Ping program is WSPing ProPack, available from **http://www.ipswitch.com/** and included on the CD-ROM. Select the Ping tab, type the name of the computer whose connection you want to test into the **Host name** box, and click the **Test** button.

WSPing has a couple more tricks up its sleeve. Select the **TraceRoute** tab and type an address into the **Host name** box as above. The program will show you all the computers in the chain linking you to that computer, and the time each takes to respond. Apart from its initial novelty value, if a link in this chain has failed, you'll see straight away why you're unable to connect. (Windows users have this facility too – follow the same routine as you did for Ping, but replace the word **ping** in the command with **tracert**.) Among its many other features, WSPing can also translate between domain names (such as www.microsoft.com) and IP addresses (such as 207.68.137.65). Using the **Lookup** tab, type either into the **Hostname** box, and click the **Start** button.

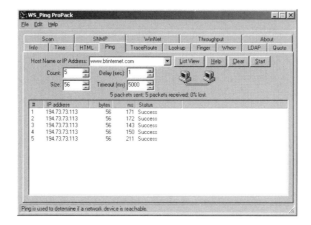

◀ Using Ping to test and time an Internet connection.

Whois...?

In theory at least, a Whois program will tell you someone's email address. In reality, it probably won't, since the Whois service lists less than one per cent of Internet users, but it can give you some useful information about businesses on the Internet. The neatest Whois program around is WinWhois by Steven Doyle, which you can install using the link on the CD-ROM that accompanies this book. As soon as you start WinWhois, a small text box will open into which you can type the name to search for. You can start further searches by clicking the 'paper' icon on the toolbar, or selecting **File** | **New**.

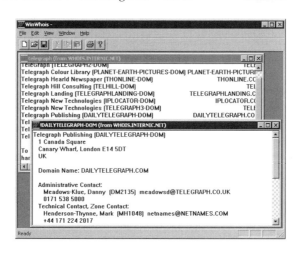

◀ A quick and simple Whois search can give a comprehensive set of contact information on a business or name.

In the screenshot above, a Whois search for **telegraph** yields an entry for the *Daily Telegraph* newspaper, among others. Following the simple instructions that WinWhois helpfully provides on the screen, a further search for **!DAILYTELEGRAPH-DOM** gives postal address, telephone number, and a contact name and email address.

3

USING THE INTERNET

▶ **IN THIS PART**

SHAKING THE SOFTWARE TREE

▶ **IN THIS CHAPTER**

Unravel the mysteries of shareware, nagware and postcard-ware

Explore the top software collections on the Web

Organise your directories and simplify your life

Compressed archives and software installation

Viruses, file types, and the Top 5 file viewers

The Internet is knee-deep in software, and much of it is free. I've already pointed you towards some of the best Internet programs and utilities, but these are just the tip of the software iceberg; you can find just about any type of file you want, from screensavers to word processors, icons to personal organisers. And with just a single click, you can download them and start using them immediately.

The Internet is reckoned to be the software supply-line of the future. Soon we could be purchasing and downloading almost all our software over the Internet and programs will update themselves automatically when newer versions and improvements become available. In fact, Windows 98 and later operating systems have a **Windows Update** utility which already provides this 'self-updating' feature via the Web, and a growing number of software applications are adding similar options. One bonus of this is that software should become much cheaper by removing the middleman and the need for flashy packaging. The downside, as you're sure to discover pretty soon, is that you'll spend all the savings you make on ever-larger hard disks to hold all these goodies!

Shareware, Freeware, Everyware

Every piece of software you find on the Internet is something ware, and the two terms you'll come across the most are **freeware** and **shareware**. Freeware is easily explained – it's free! If you like it, you keep it, no questions asked. However, there are usually a few limitations: the author will usually retain copyright, and you won't be allowed to sell copies to anyone.

GOOD QUESTION!

Why is 'freeware' free? Doesn't it work?

Freeware is often as good as an equivalent product you'd pay for. For many programmers, the reward comes in knowing that their creation is being used and appreciated. On a more fundamental level, perhaps, the administration involved in collecting money from all over the world takes up a lot of time that could be more enjoyably spent programming something else!

Shareware is an economical method of selling software that bypasses packaging, advertising and distribution costs, resulting in a much cheaper product for us and a much easier life for its author. The most important benefit of the shareware concept is that you get the opportunity to try out the software before you buy it, but the understanding is that you should pay for it if you continue to use it beyond the specified trial period (known as **registering** the software). In return for registering, you'll normally receive the latest version, and you might be entitled to free upgrades as they become available. Apart from shareware and freeware, there are a few more terms you'll come across in reference to software.

Term	Meaning
Postcard-ware	Instead of paying for the software, you send the author a picture postcard of your home town.
Nagware	A type of shareware program that nags you to register it by regularly displaying a little 'Buy Me' dialog that has to be clicked to make it go away. Only money can stop it doing that.
Save-disabled/Crippleware	The software is crippled in some way that prevents you making full use of it until you pay, usually by removing the options to save or print anything you create with it. Sometimes less politely referred to as 'crippleware'.
Time-limited	You have full use of the program for a set period (usually 30 days) after which the software won't run until you enter a valid registration number.
Alpha versions	These are very early versions of a program which may (or may not) be unreliable, but are released to anyone willing to try them. The author hopes that you'll report any problems you find so that they can be fixed. Unless you're a very experienced computer-user, avoid any software labelled as an alpha.
Beta versions	Later, and usually more stable, versions of a program than alphas, but still not regarded as a saleable product. You might prefer to wait a little longer for the finished article.

Most of the software you download will include several text files that you can read in a text editor such as Windows Notepad or any word processor. Keep a lookout for a file called **Readme.txt** or **Register.txt** that will tell you about any limitations of use, provide installation details, and explain where and how to register the software.

Where Can I Find Software?

The best places to find software are all on the World Wide Web. If you're feeling adventurous, you could visit an anonymous FTP site (see page 166) and root around its directories and Index files, but that's not the easiest way to go about it. (Okay, adventurers, go to the Imperial College site at src.doc.ic.ac.uk for oodles of software, fast response times, and very informative Index files.) Most of the software sites on the Web use a directory layout from which you select the type of software you're looking for, browse through a list of software titles and descriptions, and click a link to start downloading the file you want. (For more on downloading files with your browser, skip back to page 66). Here's a quickfire list of some of the best software sites on the Web.

JARGON BUSTER

Mirror site

The most popular websites are those that give something away, and software sites are top of that list. If everyone had to visit the same site, that server would slow to a crawl and no one would be able to download anything. So exactly the same collection of files is placed on other servers around the world to spread the load, and these are called mirrors. When you get a choice of sites to download from, you'll usually get the quickest results by choosing the site geographically closest to you.

▶ **Tucows.** The definitive site when you want to find Internet applications for Windows. Tucows has mirror sites all over the world, but visit **http://tucows.mirror.ac.uk** for a good, responsive connection in the UK. And a few pictures of cows.

▶ **Shareware.com.** One of the best sites for software of all types, located at **http://www.shareware.com** This has a keyword search facility to help you track down a particular program by name, or find a type of program.

▶ **WinFiles.com.** An excellent site providing all kinds of software for
Windows 95 and later, found at **http://www.winfiles.com**

Apart from directories of software (and you'll find links to more of those on
the CD-ROM), there are a number of other avenues worth exploring. If you
visit **http://dir.yahoo.com/computers_and_internet/software/shareware**
you'll find a long list of links to shareware pages, most accompanied by
useful descriptions. Or go to one of the search engines mentioned in
Chapter 7 and use the keyword **software** or **shareware**. If there's a
particular type of program you're looking for, such as an appointments
calendar, try searching for **freeware shareware +calendar**.

◀ Navigate the
WinFiles.com site
by clicking icons
instead of dull
hypertext links.

Shareware news by email

If you want to keep up with the latest shareware releases, hop over to
http://shareware.cnet.com, look for the Free Newsletters section of the page,
then type your email address into the box and click the button. Every week you'll receive an
email message listing the most popular downloads at Shareware.com and details of the latest
arrivals. You can also click the More Newsletters link for a choice of several dozen other
Internet and computing-related newsletters.

Downloading – Choose Your Folder

If you plan to download a lot of software, it helps to create a few folders first to keep things organised. So I'm going to pile straight in and make a suggestion that works well for me. First, create a new folder on your hard disk called **Internet**. Then open that folder, and create three subfolders called **Download**, **Temp** and **Store**. You might want to choose different names for the folders, but here's how they're used:

Internet   Simply a handy container for the other three folders.

Download   When you click a file to download in your browser and choose to save it to disk, the browser will ask you to choose a folder to save into. Choose this folder. When you've used this folder once, it will automatically be offered to you for future downloads.

Temp   Almost all of the programs you download will be in compressed archives (I'll explain those in a moment). In some cases, before you can start to install the software it has to be uncompressed, and the Temp folder provides somewhere to put those uncompressed files. As soon as the software has been installed you can delete the contents of the Temp folder.

Store   You may want to keep some of the compressed files you download, perhaps as safety copies or to give to someone else later. Move them from Download into this folder when you've finished uncompressing and installing them so that you'll know they've been dealt with.

If you download files by FTP, as discussed in Chapter 11, you can enter the path to the Download folder in FTP Explorer's **Initial Path** box when you create a new profile, saving you the need to click around in the left-hand Save dialog window before you start to download a file. The Store folder is a good place to keep Index files from FTP sites you expect to find useful in future.

What Are Compressed Archives?

If you wanted to send several small packages to someone through the post, you'd probably put them all in a box and send that for simplicity. An archive works in a similar way – it's a type of file that contains other files, making them easy to move around on the Internet. Most of the software you download will consist of several files, including the program itself, a Help file, text files that tell you how to register, and so on. Downloading a single archive that contains the whole package is far simpler than downloading a dozen separate files one at a time. Before you can use the files in the archive they have to be extracted from it.

Most archives are also *compressed*. Using clever software trickery, files can be squeezed into these archives so that they take up much less space – sometimes only a few per cent of their original size – which means that downloading an archive will be a vastly quicker job than downloading its constituent files individually. When you extract the files from the archive, they'll be automatically uncompressed at the same time.

There are a few different types of archive, but all are easy to handle, and you'll be able to recognise them by their icons, shown in the following screenshot.

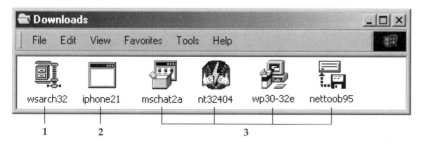

◀ Archive files are easy to recognise by their icons.

1 A ZIP archive – these files have the file extension **.zip**. You'll come across a lot of these, and they may contain just one file or many. You'll need a special program to extract the files from a ZIP archive, and the best of the lot is called WinZip (shown in the next screenshot). You'll find this on the CD-ROM accompanying this book, or you can download it yourself from **http://www.winzip.com** It's very easy to use, and includes good Help files, so I won't explain it all here. (If you have the Plus! 98 add-on to Windows 98, these archives will appear as **Compressed**

IT'S ON THE CD

Folders – a folder icon with a zipper down one side. You can simply double-click these to open them, just like any ordinary directory, rather than using a separate program.)

2 This is an MS-DOS self-extracting archive with the extension **.exe**. Copy this file into your Temp folder, double-click it, and its contents will be extracted automatically and placed in the same folder.

3 These are all types of self-extracting archive, also with the **.exe** extension, but they're even easier than **2**. Double-click the file's icon, and everything should happen automatically. The files will be extracted, the setup program will run to install the software, and the program should then delete the extracted files to clean up any mess it made.

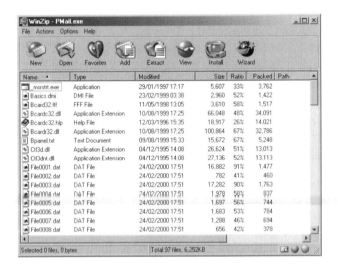

▶ View and extract the contents of an archive using WinZip.

What is a file extension?

GOOD QUESTION!

A group of three (or sometimes more) characters at the end of a filename, preceded by a dot. For the file **readme.txt** the extension is **.txt**. The extension tells you and your computer what type of file it is, which determines what type of program is needed to open that file.

There are several other types of archive, and they'll get a mention later in the chapter, but almost every piece of software you download will be either a **.zip** or an **.exe** archive. Archive files don't just contain programs, though – you might find a collection of pictures or icons gathered into an archive, or word processor documents, or sound and video clips – their portability and smaller size makes them the favourite way to transfer all types of file over the Internet.

Installing Your New Program

Before you start to install any software you've downloaded, your first job should be to check it for viruses, and we'll discuss those in a moment. What you do next depends upon the type of file you downloaded. If it's a ZIP file, use WinZip to extract its contents to your Temp folder; if it's an MS-DOS self-extracting file, copy or move it to your Temp folder and double-click it. Next, have a look in your Temp folder for a file called install.exe or setup.exe. If you see one of these, double-click it and follow any on-screen instructions to install the software. If you can't see one of these files, the software may not have an automatic setup program. Create a new folder somewhere, move the files into it, and create a shortcut to the program on your Start Menu or desktop for easy access. With the new program installed, you can delete all those extracted files in your Temp folder.

Close your programs first

Before you install any new software, it's a good idea to close any programs you're running (some setup programs remind you to do this). Sometimes the setup program needs to alter existing files on your computer while installing the software, and if another program is running it might not be able to do so.

The other types of self-extracting archive just need a double-click. Usually their setup program will run automatically and you can just follow the instructions to complete the installation. On occasions, though, you might find one of these that just extracts all the files and leaves you the job of finding the **install** or **setup** file, and of deleting the extracted files afterwards.

What if you don't like the software and want to uninstall it? If the software had its own setup program that installed it for you, the same program can usually uninstall it too – look in its directory for a file called **uninstall.exe** and double-click it. If there's isn't one, run the **install** or **setup** program again to see if there's a button marked Uninstall (if there isn't, click Cancel to escape). Failing that, Windows may be able to uninstall it for you. Open **Control Panel**, double-click **Add/Remove Programs** and see if this program is on the list; if it is, select it and click the **Add/Remove** button to uninstall it. If you simply created a new folder and copied the program files into it, you can delete the folder and its contents, and remove any shortcuts you added.

Scanning For Viruses

The risk from viruses on the Internet is pretty small, far less significant than some of the hysterical chatter would have you believe. And if you are unfortunate enough to get a virus on your computer, it won't necessarily be harmful – some viruses are jokey little things that do no more than make your computer go beep once a year. But there are others that can make a nasty mess of your system by trashing your files, swallowing your disk space, and filling your memory, and these are definitely best avoided. They're also easily avoided.

GOOD QUESTION!

What is a virus?

A virus is a small piece of code maliciously inserted into an ordinary program. When the program is run, the virus starts running too, and begins to do whatever it was programmed to do. Most viruses can replicate themselves and often invade other programs, or attach themselves to email messages and send copies of the message to everyone in your address book. Turn to Chapter 14 to find out what else you can do to reduce the risk from viruses.

There are two popular virus-checking programs in wide use, and both can be downloaded from the Internet. One is McAfee VirusScan, available from **http://www.mcafee.com**, and the other is Norton AntiVirus from **http://www.symantec.com** Which of these you choose doesn't really matter, but what does matter is that you update it every couple of months to make sure you're protected from the latest viruses.

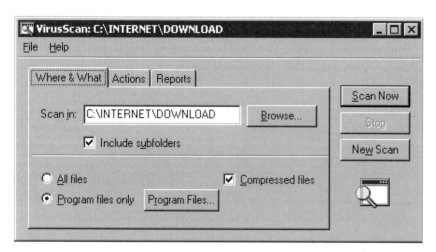

◀ McAfee VirusScan, a simple but effective virus checker.

So, what sort of files should you scan for viruses? Any file with an **.exe** extension, including self-extracting archives. After extracting files from a ZIP archive, always virus-check any .exe files it contained before you run them. You should also check any documents containing little 'macro' programs such as files created by Microsoft Word or Excel. Files that are simply displayed by a program (such as a picture, video, or plain text file) are safe. Virus-checking software will tell you if a file contains a virus, and can usually 'kill' any it finds at the click of a button. If you're unsure whether a particular file constitutes a risk, virus-check it – it only takes a few seconds.

What Are All Those File Types?

So far we've only looked at downloading programs from the Net, but you'll find many different types of file there – documents, sounds, videos, images, and a lot more. Clicking a link to any file will download it regardless of what type of file it is, and your browser will ask you whether you want to open it immediately or save it to disk to look at later (as we discussed in Chapter 6). But first you'll need to be able to recognise these different types of file by their extension and make sure you've got a program that can display them.

The list of computer file extensions is almost endless, and I'd be crazy to try to list all of them, but here's a brief description of the file extensions you're most likely to find on the Net. Some of these can be displayed or played by your browser itself, and many are compatible with programs included with Windows.

File extension	Description of file type
.arc, .arj	Two older types of compressed archive, similar to ZIP files.
.au, .aif, .aiff, .snd, .aifc	A type of sound file used by Apple Mac computers. Internet Explorer will play these files itself.
.avi	A Video for Windows file. Windows Media Player will play these once they're downloaded.
.bmp, .pcx	Bitmap files. View these in Windows Paint.
.doc	A Microsoft Word document. If you don't have Word you can use Windows 95's WordPad (although you may lose some of the document's formatting), or search **www.microsoft.com** for a viewer called WordView.
.flc, .fli, .aas	Animation files. Once downloaded, Windows Media Player should handle these.
.gif, .jpg, .jpeg, .jpe, .jfif	Image files often used on web pages, and displayed by your browser.
.gz, .gzip	Another less common type of compressed archive.
.htm, .html, .asp	World Wide Web documents (better known as 'pages').
.mid, .rmi	MIDI files, a type of compact sound file. Windows Media Player can play these after you've downloaded them.
.mov, .qt	A Quick Time movie file.
.mpg, .mpeg,	An MPEG video file, handled automatically by Windows Media Player.
.mp2	An MPEG audio file, also handled by Media Player.
.mp3	A near-CD-quality audio file handled by Media Player.
.pdf	Portable Document Format, a hypertext document similar to web pages that can be read only by Adobe Acrobat.
.ra, .ram	A RealAudio sound file.
.rtf	A Rich Text document that can be read in almost any Windows word processor.
.tar	Yet another type of compressed archive.
.txt, .text	A plain text file. Your browser should play these, or you can read them in Windows Notepad or any word processor.
.uue	A UUencoded file (see page 108).
.wav	A Windows wave audio sound. Your browser should play these automatically, or you can use Media Player or Sound Recorder.
.wri	A Windows Write document. Most Windows word processors will display these if you don't have a copy of Write.
.wrl	A VRML (virtual reality) 3D object. (We'll look at virtual reality in Chapter 21.)

You'll notice that some of these files have two slightly different extensions (such as **.htm** and **.html**, or **.jpg** and **.jpeg**). This is simply because MS-DOS and Windows 3.11 can't work with four-character extensions, so shorter versions are used instead. The file types are exactly the same, so don't worry if some of the files you download have a .jpg extension and others have **.jpeg**.

The Top 5 – Complete Your Software Arsenal!

A few of the file types listed in the table above can't be viewed or played by any program included with Windows – you'll need to find a separate program if you download files of these types. Without further ado, here are my Top 5 recommended accessories and viewers which, between them, will leave you ready for almost anything the Internet can throw at you.

▶ **WinZip** from **http://www.winzip.com** Apart from handling ZIP files, WinZip will extract files from almost any type of compressed archive, and can also decode UUencode or MIME attachments sometimes included in email messages and newsgroup articles. Don't even stop to think about it – you need this program as soon as you hit the Net!

▶ **LView Pro** from **http:// www.lview.com** A fast and easy image file viewer that supports all the popular file formats, as well as some of the not-so-popular ones. LView can also create contact sheets containing multiple images, or display them one at a time as a slideshow.

▶ **RealPlayer** from **http://www.real.com** RealAudio is a streaming audio format. Many websites now have RealAudio sound, and some radio stations use it to transmit live over the Internet. This type of program is known as a **plug-in** because it automatically 'plugs itself into' your browser and waits invisibly in the background until it's needed. You'll learn more about plug-ins in Chapter 21.

JARGON BUSTER

Streaming

You'll come across the terms 'streaming audio' and 'streaming video'. Streaming means that the file will start to play almost as soon as you click the link to it; you can watch or listen to it while it downloads instead of having to wait until the download has finished.

▶ **Net Toob** from **http://www.nettoob.com** A live streaming MPEG video player which you can also use to play MPEG videos you've already downloaded or found elsewhere. MPEG is the most popular video format on the Internet, and Net Toob handles it better than anything else around. As if that wasn't enough, it can also play most of the other video and sound formats mentioned in the table on page 198!

▶ **Acrobat Reader** from **http://www.adobe.com** PDF is a popular format for text-based documents such as help files, magazines, and research literature. Documents can include embedded images and fonts, together with hyperlinks to help you navigate long documents easily. The free Acrobat Reader is designed for viewing these documents only; to create them you'll need Adobe Acrobat, a retail product.

Some of the other types of file we've covered in this chapter can be played in a Windows program, but you have to wait for the file to download, and then find and double-click it, which rather spoils the surfing experience. In Chapter 21, we'll look at some of the other multimedia plug-ins and viewers you can download and install that will add the necessary capabilities to your browser itself.

SAFETY ON THE INTERNET

▶ **IN THIS CHAPTER**

Keep your kids safe on the Internet

The truth about credit card security on the Net

Active content on the World Wide Web

Are cookies really dangerous?

email – privacy and encryption

The virus threat: real or imagined?

Safety, or the lack of it, is a much-hyped area of Internet life. According to many press articles, as soon as you go online you're going to be faced with a barrage of pornography, your credit card number will be stolen, your personal email messages will be published far and wide, and your children will be at the mercy of paedophile rings.

Of course, articles like these make good news stories. Much more interesting than 'Child surfs Internet, sees no pornography', for example. In this chapter we'll sort out what the risks actually are, and what you can do to minimize them.

Will My Kids Be Safe On The Net?

The Internet has its fair share of sex and smut, just as it has motoring, cookery, sports, films, and so on. I'm not going to pretend that your kids can't come into contact with explicit images and language, but there are two important points to note. First, you're no more likely to stumble upon pornography while looking for a sports site than you are to stumble upon film reviews or recipes. If you want to find that sort of content, you have to go looking for it. Second, most of the sexually explicit sites on the World Wide Web are private – to get inside you need a credit card. Nevertheless, there are dangers on the Net, and given unrestricted freedom, your kids may come into contact with unsuitable material.

GOOD QUESTION!

What sort of material could my kids find?

On the Web, the front pages of those private sites are accessible to all, and some contain images and language designed to titillate, and to part you from some cash. The Web's search engines are another risk – enter the wrong keywords (or the right keywords, depending on your viewpoint) and you'll be presented with direct links to explicit sites accompanied by colourful descriptions.

However, these are not good reasons to deny children access to the Internet. Quite simply, the Internet is a fact of life that isn't going to go away, and will feature more strongly in our children's lives than it does in ours. More and more schools are recognising this, and promoting use of the Internet in homework and class projects. The wealth of websites created by and for children is a great indicator of their active participation in the growth of the Net. Rather than depriving children of this incredible resource, let's look at a few ground rules you should agree with your kids, and some simple measures you can take to make sure that their use of the Internet is both enjoyable and safe.

Establish Some Ground Rules

One way to protect your kids is to surf the Internet with them, or to make a point of discussing their online experiences, the services they use, and the websites they like to visit. Sometimes it's easier said than done of course – teenagers, for example, guard their privacy jealously, and parental interest and involvement can be regarded as 'prying'. The following rules were taken from the excellent kids' site, Yahooligans! (**http://www.yahooligans.com**). Read through these with your kids, and make sure they understand the importance of sticking to them.

▶ I will not give out personal information such as my address, telephone number, parents' work address/telephone number, or the name and location of my school without my parents' permission.

▶ I will tell my parents right away if I come across any information that makes me feel uncomfortable.

▶ I will never agree to get together with someone I 'meet' online without first checking with my parents. If my parents agree to the meeting, I will be sure that it is in a public place and bring my mother or father along.

▶ I will never send a person my picture or anything else without first checking with my parents.

▶ I will not respond to any messages that are mean or in any way make me feel uncomfortable. It is not my fault if I get a message like that. If I do I will tell my parents right away so that they can contact the service provider.

▶ I will talk with my parents so that we can set up rules for going online. We will decide upon the time of day that I can be online, the length of time I can be online, and appropriate areas for me to visit. I will not access other areas or break these rules without their permission.

More information for parents

You'll find the document from which these rules were taken at
http://www.yahooligans.com/docs/safety. For more information, and links to
other sites providing similar tips for parents, go to **http://www.safekids.com** or
http://www.larrysworld.com.

If you're ever concerned about the websites your children might be visiting,
remember that you can open Internet Explorer's History panel (or the
History subfolder of your Windows folder) to see a list of all recently-
accessed pages sorted chronologically by week and day. Similarly, if you go
to **Tools** | **Internet Options** and click the **Settings** button followed by the
View Files button you can also sort all recently-visited sites by time of day
by clicking the **Last Accessed** header bar.

Finally, there are two Internet services that are definitely not suitable places
for children to visit unsupervised: newsgroups and IRC chat channels.
Many service providers refuse to carry certain newsgroups, such as the
alt.sex and alt.binaries.pictures hierarchies, but articles in some quite
innocent newsgroups may contain views or language you wouldn't want
your kids to read. The same goes for IRC. As I mentioned in Chapter 10,
many chat channels are sexual in nature, and often in name too. But the
type of people trying to make contact with children through IRC won't limit
themselves to those channels. I'd simply suggest that if you have kids in the
house, you don't have an IRC program installed on your computer.

Is any type of chat safe for kids?

Online services' general chat rooms are moderated (controlled by a
representative of the service) to keep things friendly – I especially recommend
AOL in that department. If you access the Net through an ISP, give your children a copy of
Surf Monkey (**http://www.surfmonkey.com**), a free 'Rocketship' web browser that has
moderated cartoon-chat rooms.

Get A Little Extra Help

If all this seems a bit too much to handle on your own, don't worry! There are many software programs around that can take over some of the supervision for you. To balance maximum access with maximum security, you need a program that can identify the actual content about to be viewed, rather than the name of the page or site. There are many such programs available, but here's a short list of the most respected:

- ▶ **Net Nanny** from **http://www.netnanny.com**
- ▶ **CYBERsitter** from **http://www.cybersitter.com**
- ▶ **SurfWatch** from **http://www.surfwatch.com**
- ▶ **Cyber Patrol** from **http://www.cyberpatrol.com**

I'm going to stick my neck out on this one, and recommend Net Nanny. (Actually I'm not sticking it out too far – you can install the program from the CD-ROM, try it out for 30 days, and switch to another if you don't like it.) The power of this program lies in the fact that it doesn't work solely with Internet programs – it can bar access to documents viewed using any program on your computer. When your start your computer, Net Nanny runs invisibly in the background and watches for particular words or phrases. If they appear, Net Nanny instantly replaces them with X's, and threatens to shut down the program in 30 seconds unless you enter a valid password. The words in question may appear in email messages, web pages or chat rooms, they may be in files on floppy disks or CD-ROMs, or they may form the name of a file. You can add words, phrases, applications and websites to Net Nanny's list, and download regularly updated lists of restricted sites. For added parental reassurance, Net Nanny also keeps a note of any attempts to access restricted sites, as do many other programs.

Don't take these tools for granted

These 'babysitter' programs are useful tools, but a curious or technology-minded child might still find ways to override them. It isn't easy, but these are the same kids that remind us how to set the video recorder!

▶ Cyber Patrol
says No.

Is It Safe To Use My Credit Card On The Internet?

Another popular myth about the Internet is that credit card transactions are risky because your card number can be stolen. To put this in perspective, consider how you use your credit or debit card in the 'real world'. How many people get to see your card number during a normal week? How much time does your card spend out of your view when you use it? Do you always ask for the carbon paper after signing for a credit card purchase? The truth is, card numbers are *easy* to steal. It takes a lot more effort and technical know-how to steal numbers on the Internet, and a single card number isn't valuable enough to warrant the exertion.

Making the computer hacker's job more difficult in this department, modern browsers now encrypt the data they send, and most of the websites at which you can use your credit card run on **secure servers** that have their own built-in encryption. So when you visit one of these secure sites, enter your card number, and click the button to send it, your number will appear as meaningless gibberish to anyone managing to hack into the system. In fact, credit card companies actually regard online transactions as being the safest kind.

One final point about online credit card use though. Many 'adult' sites ask for your credit card details on the pretext that possession of a credit card indicates you're old enough to be allowed in. You'll also see claims that membership of the site is free. Don't be fooled: a credit card number has only one use, and if you can locate the small print on the site you'll find that's the use they've got planned for yours.

▶ *If you're ready for an online spending spree, skip ahead to Chapter 18 to find out how and where to shop on the World Wide Web.*

GOOD QUESTION!

How can I tell when I visit a secure website?

In Internet Explorer, look for a little padlock symbol in the lower right corner of the browser. In Netscape's lower left corner you'll see a similar padlock which will be 'locked' at secure sites and 'unlocked' at the rest. You'll also notice that the http:// prefix in the address bar changes to https://. More and more shopping sites are becoming secure all the time, and those that aren't usually offer alternative payment methods.

Protection From (Over) Active Web Pages

A new piece of jargon has recently been added to the language of the World Wide Web: **active content**. This is a term covering various types of small program that can be included in web pages to provide interactivity and animation. The results of active content are that the Web is better able to function as a productivity tool, and the ride is now so good you won't want to get off.

There are several programming languages used to create this active content, with names such as Java, JavaScript and Dynamic HTML. You can learn more about these in Chapter 22, and I'll point you towards some sites where you can sample them for yourself. The language we're interested in right now is called **ActiveX**. This is an extremely powerful and capable language, but its capability means that it can be used to write programs that get into mischief when they run on your computer. At present, ActiveX programs can run only in Internet Explorer, and Explorer also gives you all the options you need to be able to control what's going on.

Controls

ActiveX programs are usually referred to as *controls* by Internet Explorer, or sometimes, more vaguely, just as *objects*.

Explorer's default settings are going to be fine for most users, but I'll quickly tell you where they are and what they mean. Start Internet Explorer, click on **Tools | Internet Options** followed by the **Security** tab and you'll see the dialog shown in the screenshot below which lets you choose a security level. If you choose **High**, Explorer will not run any controls it doesn't recognise. The **Medium** setting will give you the choice of viewing or ignoring any unrecognised control. By choosing **Medium-low** you're taking a slightly bigger risk, but unrecognised ActiveX controls will still be avoided. Don't even consider selecting Low – however minimal a risk may be, there should never be a time in your life when you don't want protection from it!

▶ Drag the slider to choose how Internet Explorer handles active content in web pages.

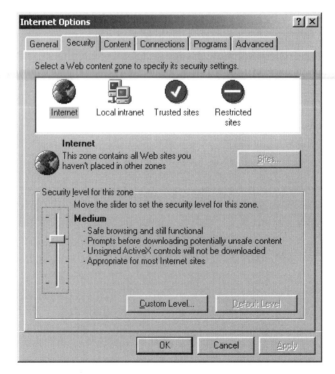

If you click the **Custom Level** button, a new dialog box will open with which you can choose your own security settings for a variety of active content types. However, unless you're worried about the possible effects of active content (and you really have no reason to be), it's best to stick with the Medium option.

So how does Explorer know when a control is 'safe'? It uses a system of **publisher certificates**. These certificates are granted to companies by particular authorities, and are automatically installed on your computer when you visit a certified site. When Explorer finds a control on a web page, it searches for an accompanying electronic 'certificate' that says the control is from a trustworthy company. If it doesn't find one, it will either not run the control, or it will notify you and ask whether or not you want to run it anyway (depending whether you selected **High** or **Medium** security). You can view details of the certificates you've accepted by going to **Tools | Internet Options | Content** and clicking the **Certificates...** button.

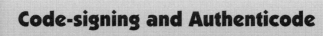

Code-signing and Authenticode

Code-signing is a term for the technology that makes this whole certification business work, allowing software writers to put a recognised 'signature' into their controls. Authenticode is a trademark for the same technology. It's all very similar to the digital signatures we were looking at on page 116.

Cookies – Are They Safe To Eat?

They sound cute and harmless, but what are they? Well, they're not particularly cute, but cookies are small text files that are stored on your computer's hard disk when you visit certain websites. To take a look at them, open your Windows folder, and then open the Cookies folder you find inside – you can double-click any of these cookies to read its contents in Notepad.

Cookies can serve several uses to the creator of a website, and some can even benefit visitors like you and me. A cookie might contain a unique code that identifies you, saving the need to enter a name and password when you visit, and perhaps allowing you to access restricted areas of a site. They're also often used by online shopping sites as a sort of 'supermarket trolley' that keeps track of the purchases you select until you're ready to pay and leave. Sites that rely heavily on displaying banner advertisements for their income might track 'click-throughs', keeping a log of the path you follow through the site and the pages you decide to visit. Knowing a bit about your interests in this way helps enable the site to target you with the type of adverts most likely to get your attention.

GOOD QUESTION!

Do all cookies have practical uses?

No. You may visit a personal site that asks you to enter your name which it then stores in a cookie. On every future visit, you'll see a message like *Hello Rob, you've visited this page 4 times.* It's pointless, but it's still harmless.

So, are they safe? Yes, they are. Cookies are often misunderstood – they can't be used to read any other data from your hard disk, to find out what software you've got installed, or to pass on personal information. When you visit a website, the page doesn't 'search' your hard disk for a cookie; instead, your browser sends the cookie containing the URL of the site as soon as you type in the address or click the link.

The wider question is whether you want anyone using your hard disk as a type of mini-database in this way – it's a point of principle rather than safety. If you want to join the anti-cookie ranks, Internet Explorer can help. Click on **Tools | Internet Options | Security**, select the **Custom Level** button and scroll down to the **Cookies** section. Here you can choose separate settings for cookies stored on your computer and cookies created temporarily while you surf. Pick **Prompt** to be given a choice of accepting or rejecting a cookie when a site tries to store one, or **Disable** if you want to take a tougher stand against them. Be warned though – some sites just won't let you in if you won't eat the cookie! A more practical method is just to delete the entire contents of your Cookies folder as soon as you've finished surfing for the day.

How Private Is My email?

The words 'email' and 'private' don't go together well. I'm not saying that the world and his dog are going to read every message you send, but email can get you into trouble (and people have got into very hot water from using email where a phone call or a quiet chat would have been wiser). If you're concerned about who could read it, don't write it.

The most obvious problem is that your 'private' messages can be easily forwarded or redirected, or the recipient might simply fail to delete an incriminating message after reading it. But apart from existing on your computer and the recipient's computer, however briefly, the message also spends time on your service provider's mail server and that of the recipient's service provider. Will the message really be deleted from both? And what if the administrator of one of these systems decides to run a backup while your message is waiting to be delivered?

If you really must use email to exchange sensitive material, you might want to safeguard it using **encryption**. The safest form of encryption is known as **public key encryption**, in which messages are encrypted and decrypted using two codes called **keys**. One is your private key, the other is a public key that you'd hand out to anyone who needed to use it, or perhaps publish on your website. If someone wanted to send you an encrypted message, they'd use your freely available public key to encrypt it, then post it off as usual. The message can only be decoded using your private key, and only you have access to that key. Likewise, if you wanted to send someone else a private message, you'd use his private key to encrypt it.

◀ Encrypt an email message with one click in Outlook Express.

I mentioned digital signatures on page 116, and the way they're used to prevent email forgery by binding the sender's digital identity into the messages he sends. These certificates use the same public key system, so if you have a digital signature you can use that to encrypt your messages. In Outlook Express, for example, just click the **Encrypt Message** button on the toolbar in the message window, as shown in the screenshot on the previous page.

Need more encryption information?

The most popular encryption program is called PGP (Pretty Good Privacy). Although unbreakable, it isn't easy to use and you might want an extra program that sits on top and puts a 'friendlier face' on it. Go to **http://www.gildea.com/pgp** and **http://www.hauert.net/pgpwins.html** to learn more about the system and the software available.

Am I At Risk From Viruses?

Viruses can't find their way on to your computer during ordinary Net-surfing – you're not taking a greater risk by surfing for two hours a day than only surfing for one. But, as I mentioned in Chapter 13, you might receive a virus-infected program on a floppy disk or CD-ROM, in an email message, or by downloading it from the Internet. In almost all cases, your computer can only become infected by that virus when you run the program, so always use a virus-checker to scan software received by one of these methods before running it. (Skip back to page 196 for details on finding virus-checker software.)

An increasingly popular type of virus is the so-called 'email virus'. An ordinary email message is just plain text, making it completely harmless, but you can receive programs as email attachments which definitely *could* be infected with a virus. Always save email attachments and virus-check them before opening them. Although you should always be suspicious of attachments from people you don't know, remember that viruses can come from friends and colleagues too: they may be unaware that their system is infected when they send you an attachment. Many recent types of virus automatically copy themselves to everyone in your email address book, so nowadays you're actually more likely to receive infected attachments from someone you know than from someone you don't!

A final type of virus risk comes from malicious scripts built into HTML email. Outlook Express supports this type of email, and with so many Outlook Express users out there it's an attractive target for virus writers. To guard against viruses in HTML email, follow these two steps:

1   In Outlook Express, go to **Tools | Options | Security**, select the option labelled **Restricted sites zone** (as shown in the next screenshot) and click **OK**.

◀ Protect yourself from malicious scripts built into HTML email messages.

2   In Control Panel, run the Internet Options applet, and choose the Security tab. Select the **Restricted sites** icon at the top of the page, drag the slider below up to **High** (if it's not there already), and click OK.

FAQ – INTERNET QUESTIONS & ANSWERS

▶ **IN THIS CHAPTER**

How to work with multiple service providers

Having trouble connecting to a website?

How you can keep your email address for life

Combat junk email

Remain anonymous as you surf the Net

Make money from your website

Shifting once again into 'quickfire' mode, this chapter contains a collection of answers to recurring questions, problem fixes, and pointers to more sites offering useful information.

Can I Sign Up With More Than One Service Provider?

Yes you can, and in these days of free access there's little reason not to. Most ISPs simply install a new icon in your Dial-Up Networking folder (located inside the My Computer folder), and add a new email account to Outlook Express and a new dial-up connection to Internet Explorer. You won't end up with multiple copies of Internet Explorer on your system, and (as long as it's a free account you're adding) there's no need to bother uninstalling or cancelling anything if you find you never use a particular ISP account.

Why would I want more than one ISP?

GOOD QUESTION!

A common reason is that service providers' services tend to vary in quality over time as their membership increases; some ISPs are busier than others at different times of day. If you're unable to connect to the Net using a particular ISP, or the connection is slow, you can hang up and dial in using a different ISP account.

I do have a few words of caution, though. First, some ISP accounts don't co-exist happily on a system that has an online service like AOL or CompuServe installed. Second, every time you add a new ISP account to your computer, it will be set as your default account – the account that's dialled whenever you want Internet access, and the primary email account. You can switch defaults easily, though: go to the **Tools | Internet Options | Connections** tab in Internet Explorer, and **Tools | Accounts | Mail** in Outlook Express.

▶ *Not sure how to create, add and remove connections and accounts in Windows? Skip ahead to Appendix G for step-by-step details.*

Why Is The Web So Slow Today?

There could be several answers to this one. To start with, it may be to do with the time you connect. The Internet is at its quietest (and therefore its speediest) while America is sleeping, and at varying degrees of 'busy' at all other times. Although it isn't a cheap time to connect, you'll normally get a faster response by going online in the morning than the evening. If you're having trouble with just one particular site, you can sometimes get things moving by clicking the link again, or, if the page started to download and then stopped, clicking the **Stop** button on the toolbar followed by the **Refresh** button. But if absolutely everything seems unusually slow, try logging off and then dialling up again – this often seems to result in a faster connection.

Why Can't I Open This URL?

When you click a link to a web page, type in a URL, or even select an entry on your Favorites list, you may see a page like the screenshot below (or a similar page containing more text and headed 'The page cannot be displayed'). Not what you were expecting at all. So what went wrong?

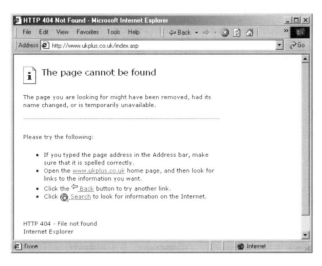

◀ It's a 404! The page has been moved, removed or renamed.

The page in the screenshot above is referring to an HTTP 404 error: the page you're trying to open can't be found by the server. In other words, either you've made a mistake in typing the URL or the page has been moved, deleted or renamed. There are several things you can do to try to locate the page:

▶ Try changing the file extension from .htm to .html (or vice versa).

▶ Try replacing uppercase letters in the URL with lowercase letters.

▶ Try deleting sections from the end of the URL (deleting back to the previous slash each time) and pressing Enter until you do find a document on that site – it may contain a link to the (now retitled) page you were looking for.

If you see a page headed 'The page cannot be displayed', with the more useful note 'Cannot find server' in the titlebar, things may be more serious. After ruling out a spelling mistake, either the web server is too busy to reply at the moment, it's not running, or the domain name you entered is no longer used by any server on the Net. Try pressing **Refresh** a few times to see if the situation changes after a few minutes, but if you can't get in when you try hours or days later, you've got to face the fact that this is an ex-website.

My Connection Crashed During A Download. Have I Lost The File?

A lot depends upon the server from which you're downloading the file, but you may be lucky. Restart your connection and Internet Explorer will usually pick up the download from where it left off. If it doesn't, or the 'Downloading File' dialog is no longer on your screen, click the same link to the file as if you were starting the download again from scratch. Internet Explorer may find the matching incomplete file in its cache directory and just grab the missing portion. For a little more certainty, a handy utility called GetRight from **http://www.headlightsw.com** and included on the CD-

ROM can manage your downloads for you and complete partial downloads. (Remember – you can minimise the chances of being disconnected by turning off Call Waiting!)

If I Leave My ISP, Will I Lose My email Address?

Yes you will, and it can be a real pain. If you use email a lot, it's worth hanging on to that first account for a while as you pass out your new email address to everyone and give things a chance to settle down. But there are a couple of things you can do to ensure that your email address will never change.

The first of these is quick, simple and free. Skip along to Bigfoot (the email lookup site mentioned in Chapter 8) at **http://uk.bigfoot.com/Profile/ Profile_join.htm** Type your current email address into the box and click on **Join**, then fill in your details and select a password. You can then choose a brand new email address which will have **@bigfoot.com** tagged on the end. From now on, give this new email address to everyone, and Bigfoot will automatically redirect your email to the address you entered. If you move to a different ISP, just return to Bigfoot, type in your password, and change the email address to which Bigfoot should send your email.

Another 'hot' email option

As an alternative to Bigfoot, visit Hotmail at **http://www.hotmail.com** Instead of transferring email to your email address, Hotmail actually gives you a free Web-based email account. As well as giving you an email address for life, this service could be ideal if you don't have a computer or permanent Internet access and you do all your surfing from cyber cafés or libraries: wherever you are, just log on to Hotmail and collect your email.

A more expensive, but flashier, way to go is to register your own domain name (such as *myname*.**co.uk** or *myname*.**com**). Visit **http://www.netnames. co.uk** to see if your chosen domain is available. If it is, shop around for a good deal by searching for 'domain registration' at a UK search engine. There's a lot of competition to sell domains, and a **.co.uk** domain could be yours for around £20 for the first two years. Many registration companies will throw in *redirection* for free: when somebody types your new domain into their browser they'll be taken straight to your website, wherever it is; if they send a message to your new email address it'll be passed to your current address. As with the Bigfoot option above, if you switch to a different ISP, just contact the registration company to change the redirection details.

Don't be a uk.com

There are companies offering unusual domains that mix a country suffix with **.com**. Don't pay for one of these – it may become very expensive, or simply cease to be recognised by the Internet at large. Stick to the standard top-level domains listed on page 10, or choose one of the new suffixes, **.firm, .store, .web, .arts, .rec, .info** and **.nom** when they become available.

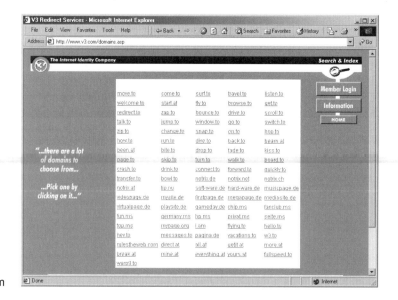

▶ Choose a permanent free URL for your website at http://www.v3.com

I Suppose My Website URL Will Change Too?

If you took advantage of your service provider's generous allocation of free web space to create your own site, you'll find that this generosity comes to a sudden halt if you cancel your account with them. You still have all the files that make up your site on your own hard disk, of course, so you can recreate this site quickly and easily by uploading them to your new ISP's computer. The problem is that your site's URL will change and your regular visitors won't know where to find it.

There are several options here, all of which should be treated as preventions rather than cures. One is to buy your own domain name, as mentioned above, which you can then carry with you from one provider to another. The second is to take advantage of free web space offers from companies such as GeoCities and FortuneCity (see page 364) instead of using the space provided by your ISP. A third option is to visit **http://www.v3.com**, a site that provides a free web forwarding service in much the same way that BigFoot provides email forwarding. You can choose a catchy URL such as **http://surf.to/MySite**, and everyone visiting this URL will be redirected to your website. Whenever you change your ISP or your site URL, you can return to the surf.to site and update your redirection details. If you don't like the 'surf.to' part, you can choose others such as **welcome.to**, **travel.to** or **start.at**.

How Can I Stop All This Junk email Arriving?

You mean you don't want to learn how to become a millionaire overnight simply by posting five letters? The trouble is, even when you've done it once and your bank account is so full you have to open another one, these wonderful offers keep arriving in your email inbox every day. In most cases you have to download them, which costs money, and you have to sift through to find the messages that matter, which takes valuable time. Pretty soon you'll be poor again, so it's best to nip this in the bud.

Here are two possible solutions, although neither is guaranteed to work:

▶ Send the company an email threatening to invoice them for your time and expense in retrieving their garbage.

▶ Send an email to the company's service provider explaining what's happening, and request that they enforce the small print in their contract with the company that prohibits this abuse of the email system.

The problem with both options is that it's not always easy to tell where the message came from – the sender's email address is often non-existent or temporary.

Another solution, again not guaranteed to work, comes from those useful folk at Bigfoot mentioned earlier in this chapter. After registering your email address with Bigfoot and receiving (almost) instant confirmation by email, go back and select the **Edit Profile** link. You'll see a simple page like the one shown in the next screenshot: just check the box, enter your email address, and click the button, and Bigfoot will send your details to the Direct Marketing Association asking for your address to be removed from their lists. And it's free!

Want to know more about junk email?

Stop *Junk Email* is an excellent site offering clear, practical advice, a wealth of useful information to help you avoid becoming a victim, and examples to help you fight back. Point your browser at **http://www.mcs.com/~jcr/junkemail.html**

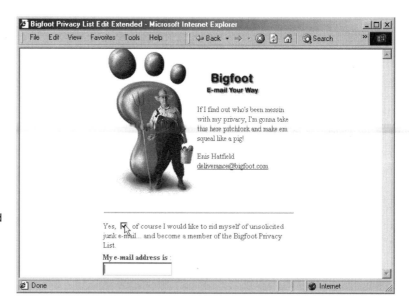

▶ Visit Bigfoot and take a large step towards ridding yourself of junk email.

If you're willing to accept something of a compromise, some email programs now have facilities to delete junk email on receipt without showing it to you. True, you'll still be downloading this mail, but you won't be constantly reminded of that by seeing piles of junk in your Inbox. One such program is Microsoft Outlook, included in the Office application suite and available separately, which filters out junk email according to certain words and phrases that typically appear in the subject lines and text of junk email. You can also add your own 'rules' to have all email from particular sources or containing particular subject lines deleted automatically. Outlook Express has similar 'message rules' options, and allows you to 'block' particular senders by choosing **Block Sender** from the Message menu.

Can I Be Anonymous On The Net?

There may be many non-criminal reasons why you'd want to surf the Internet in anonymity, and it isn't difficult to do. The best way to hide your identity completely is to take out an account with an ISP or online service using an account name (or *username*) that's nothing like your own. You'll also have to ask your ISP to turn off finger access for your account (we met Finger in Chapter 12). The only way someone could learn your true identity would be to persuade your service provider to disclose it.

If you want to send untraceable email messages and newsgroup articles, you can use an **anonymous remailer**. By following the instructions, you send your message to the remailer which will remove your personal details and send it on to its final destination. Any replies will come back to you via the remailer, but the sender won't know who you are. Although the job they do seems simple, remailers can be tricky to use – they all need their own brand of special commands. You can find out more about the remailers and their instructions at **http://www.stack.nl/~galactus/remailers**, along with details of email encryption. If you find it all a bit baffling, a program called Private Idaho (from **http://www.eskimo.com/~joelm/pi.html**) may be able to simplify things.

Anonymity not guaranteed!

Anonymous remailers are viewed with (understandable) suspicion by the police and other law-enforcement agencies. Faced with the threat of prosecution, as many have been, the remailer's administrator may elect to surrender his records.

Could Someone Be Forging My email?

Yes, they could. It doesn't happen often, but it does happen. It's easy to do, too. Every time you send an email message, your name and email address are attached to its header. When the recipient retrieves their email, these details are displayed so that he or she can see who the message is from. But how does your email program know what details to enter? When you installed your email software and filled in those little boxes on its options page, you told it! So, of course, if you go back to that options page and enter something different, those are the details that will go out with your email.

So it's entirely possible that someone could attach your name and email address to a message they send from their computer, and it would be difficult (although not impossible) to trace it back to them. Actually, it's a wonder that email forgery hasn't become a major pastime on the Net, because there's nothing you can do to prevent it happening other than to be careful what you say in chat rooms and newsgroups, and avoid riling anyone.

Which Of These Sites Should I Download From?

A major conundrum when you're about to download a large file, is that some websites are just too helpful! You arrive at the download page, and they offer you a dozen different links to the same file. Which one should you choose? Here's a couple of rules worth following. First, discount any links pointing to FTP sites if you can – your browser often takes longer to connect to them, and downloads tend to be slower and less reliable. Second, choose the HTTP link that's geographically closest to you, ideally marked as a UK or European site.

 Of course, there's no guarantee that you've found the best link using this method. And even if you have got a fast link, you'll still be sitting there wondering if a different one may have been quicker still! For times like this, here's a nifty little utility called Dipstick, from **http://www.klever.net/ kin/dipstick.html** and included on the CD-ROM, that's worth keeping handy. Drag the links into Dipstick's window and it will test the speed of each, and then tautomatically begin downloading from the site that gives the fastest response.

Can I Make Money From My Website?

In theory, yes you can. In practice, probably not – many people have tried and failed, and others are making money without turning a profit. If your site is popular enough, you may be able to sell advertising space to other companies – you can find some more information about this at the Internet Advertising Bureau (**http://www.iab.net**).

If you're thinking of selling products or services via your website, the golden rule is: You're not running an *Internet-based* business, you're running a business. Successful selling on the Net takes at least as much work and marketing savvy as selling anywhere else. Although the Internet is a global marketplace, you need to attract visitors to your site and keep them coming back, so your competition numbers in the millions.

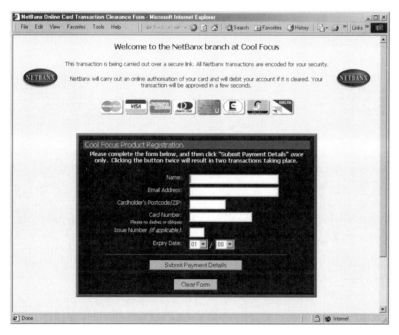

◀ NetBanx provides merchant services accounts and secure payment forms for your website.

When you have visitors that are ready to buy, you need to take their money of course – an Internet technology known as **e-commerce** (electronic commerce). Primarily you need to set up a merchant account so that customers can pay securely online by credit card. If this is an extension of an existing business, your bank may be able to provide this service. For a new business, however, the 'big four' banks won't touch you with a bargepole. In this case, a go-between company such as NetBanx (**http://www.netbanx.com**) may be able to help. NetBanx takes payments on your behalf (for a small percentage of turnover), and provides all you need to add secure payment facilities to your site.

Can I Surf The Web Using A WAP Phone?

In case you've somehow missed all the hoo-hah about these things, WAP is short for Wireless Application Protocol, a means of viewing certain types of computer content on the screens of mobile phones. This alone probably gives you a few clues about the answer to the question: those screens are currently about an inch square and greyscale, so they can't display the colours, graphics, animations, fonts or neat interactive controls that we've come to expect on the Web. Instead you'll see short text-based pages (with one or two simple pictures) designed especially for WAP devices, and you'll move from page to page by clicking buttons on the phone.

A site for sore fingers

Medical science has shown that children's index fingers are getting shorter and shorter, due to the amount of time they spend poking the keys of their mobile phones to send each other text messages (otherwise known as SMS, or Short Message Service, messages). Protect those fingers – send your kids to **http://www.lycos.co.uk/service/sms** or **http://www.community.co.uk/sms**, where they can send text messages to mobile phones from the Web instead!

◀ Surfing the Web, WAP-style. Disappointing? At the moment, yes, but the future is rosier.

Needless to say, the only sites worth 'WAPulizing' are sites that deal with text-based information already – news sites, reference sites, and e-commerce sites for people needing to make quick purchases or bookings on the move. You can also send and receive email using a WAP phone. It surely isn't the Web, or anything like it, but it offers a service some may find useful in a neat and compact unit, and it'll start to look a little prettier when the next generation of phones with colour screens arrives.

THE WEB – YOUR COMPLETE ENTERTAINMENT GUIDE

▶ **IN THIS CHAPTER**

Use electronic TV and radio guides

See the latest movies, and book theatre tickets online

Find out what's on in towns and cities around the UK

Book hotels, holidays, flights and cars

Check travel timetables & traffic conditions

Giggles, games and gambling online

It's a paper world. It doesn't matter what you want to do, nine times out of ten you have to consult a piece of paper before you can do it. Want to watch TV? Book a holiday? See what's on at your local cinema or theatre? Plan a trip or a day out? If you do any of those things, you've probably got a mountain of guides, catalogues, brochures and local newspapers, and many of them are probably out of date! So let's go paperless…

Use Online TV & Radio Listings

No more scrabbling around to see which of those 28 Sunday supplements contains the TV listings this week – just hit the Web instead! Visit the BBC's RT Guide at **http://www.rtguide.beeb.com**, click the **TV Section** link to arrive at the page shown in the screenshot below, and choose between a Quick Search (to find out what's on today) and a Mega Search (to find out what's on in the next two weeks). You can click any program title for more information about it, and of course you can save the list to your own disk to read offline by selecting **File | Save As**.

▶ Quick and easy TV listings from RT Guide.

If you'd prefer simple, at-a-glance listings instead, head for
http://www.sceneone.co.uk, click the **Television** link and choose the **Multi Channel** option (a good candidate for your Favorites menu when you get there). Satellite and digital channels are included, and you can even search for a particular programme by name.

Where can I get satellite TV listings?

The Sky TV site at **http://www.sky.com** has a TV Listings link taking you to a page which you can reach directly via **http://www.skynow.co.uk/tvguide/tv_channel.jsp** Most satellite and digital channels have their own websites, of course, such as **www.discovery.com**, **www.disneychannel.co.uk** and **www.cnn.com**

You'd expect Auntie Beeb to have her own website, and indeed she does. In fact she has two – point your browser at **http://www.beeb.com** for a magazine-style site of chat, features and current TV favourites, or visit **http://www.bbc.co.uk/a-z** for a massive site covering every aspect of the BBC you could imagine. Many of the most popular TV and radio shows also have their own mini-sites here, including *Tomorrow's World*, *Top Gear*, *Blue Peter* and *EastEnders*.

Need a few more TV and radio links?

▶ **http://www.itv.co.uk** A single searchable site for the entire ITV network with news, program listings and features.

▶ **http://www.ctw.org** Despite the less-than-inspiring title (Children's Television Workshop), this Sesame Street site brilliantly combines fun and education for young children, although a little parental help might be needed.

▶ **http://www.yahoo.co.uk/Regional/Countries/United_Kingdom/ News_and_Media/Radio/Stations** Links to the websites of over 80 local radio stations.

▶ **http://www.channel4.com** A well-designed and stylish site for Channel 4, complete with program listings and an easy-to-navigate set of buttons. And not to be outdone, you can find Channel 5 at **http://www.channel5.co.uk** (and you won't even need your browser retuned!)

Soap heaven

Need to catch up with your favourite UK soaps? Head for **http://www.geocities.com/TelevisionCity/2533** for the latest news and plot developments. You'll even find 'spoiler' pages of future plot lines here, but they're easily avoided if you prefer the suspense!

▶ *You don't necessarily need a radio to listen to the radio – this is the Internet after all, anything's possible. Skip ahead to page 310 to find out more.*

Want To Take In A Movie?

The Web can tell you just about everything you want to know about movies and cinemas except for the price of the popcorn, and the site to check out is MovieWeb at **http://movieweb.com** Here you'll find an alphabetical list of movies going back to 1995 with cast information and plot synopses, pictures and posters, and a lot more. MovieWeb gets previews of new movies long before they hit the cinema, and you can view these online in QuickTime format (you'll find out more about QuickTime in Chapter 21). And if you're not sure what's worth seeing, the weekly Top 25 box office charts should point you in the right direction.

Once you've chosen the movie you'd like to see, it's time to find the local cinema showing it. To do that, head off to Yell's site at **http://www.yell.com** and click the **Cinema** link. Or maybe you were looking for older movies to buy on video? If so, get your credit card details ready and visit TheZone at **http://www.thezone.co.uk** or Amazon at **http://www.amazon.co.uk** (If you haven't bought anything online before, skip ahead to Chapter 18 to see how it all works.)

If you're a real movie addict, it's worth visiting the UK Internet Movie Database at **http://uk.imdb.com/a2z** This site doesn't go in for previews, unlike MovieWeb, but it's one of the most-visited sites in the UK for the range of information it does cover, from up-to-the-minute news and reviews to lists of Oscar recipients, famous marriages and recent releases.

◀ Video previews of the latest movies at MovieWeb.

How About A Night At The Opera?

Well, not necessarily an opera. Perhaps a ballet, an ice show, a pantomime, a kids' show, or the latest Andrew Lloyd Webber musical. Make your way to What's On Stage at **http://www.whatsonstage.com** (shown in the next screenshot) and run a simple search for live entertainment in your area. You can select a single town or the whole of the UK, and choose one of 20 categories of stage show if you're looking for something in particular. You can even confine your search to particular dates, or use keywords.

Finding more culture

UK Calling (at **http://www.uk-calling.co.uk**) is a very attractive site with extensive listings in seven categories including Classical Music, Art Galleries, Dance, Theatre, and Museums. Or visit EventSelector at **http://www.eventselector.co.uk**, choose a category and enter the name of a show, venue or town to find out what's on.

When you've found a show you'd like to see, you can usually book tickets online. Click the **Tickets** icon, fill in the form, and you should receive email confirmation within three days.

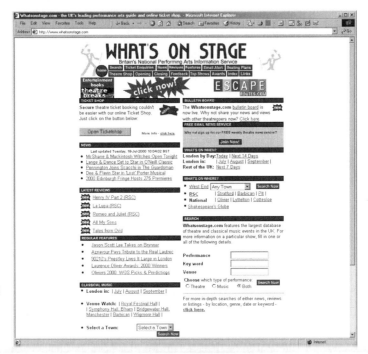

▶ Stage show news, reviews and easy ticket booking at What's On Stage.

Get Away For The Weekend

If you're going to book up to see a show, why not make a weekend of it? The first thing you'll want to do is to find somewhere to stay, so wander over to Expotel at **http://www.expotel.co.uk** By clicking the **Hotel Search** button, you can enter the name of a town anywhere in the world and Expotel will display prices and details of all hotels found. You can also select from a list of forthcoming events and conferences to find accommodation in the right area, and sort out travel tickets and car rental. Click the **Book Now** button to fill in the secure online booking form.

Capital letter

If you're looking for accommodation in London, take a visit to **http://www.london-hotels.co.uk** This free service divides the capital's hotels into four bands – Economy, Tourist, Business and Deluxe – and claims to offer discounts of 15 to 25 per cent over travel agents' prices.

If you can't find what you're looking for at Expotel, try the UK Hotel & Guest House Directory at **http://www.s-h-systems.co.uk/shs.html** This uses handy clickable maps to pinpoint a location (along with ordinary hypertext links for the geographically-challenged!), and gives all the important information about each hotel along with photographs. Booking isn't quite as nifty here – you send an email which is delivered to the hotel as a fax, and they should then get in touch with you to confirm the details – but this does have the advantage that you can use the Net to reach as yet un-Netted hotels. Or for something more exclusive, try Open World's Luxury Hotel Search Engine at **http://www.openworld.co.uk**

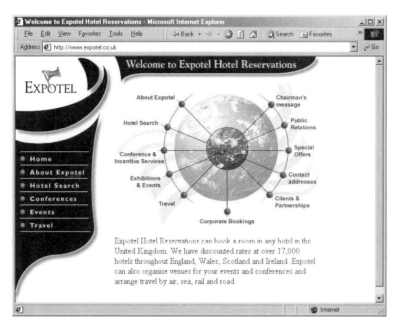

◀ Expotel can point you towards hotel rooms, conference venues and much more.

Where To Go, What To Do

So you've got tickets to a show, and booked a hotel, but what will you do with the rest of the weekend? Once again, the Web leaps in to help – try one of these sites:

▶ **Virgin Net Days Out**. Pick the type of activity you're looking for, the place you're going and when, and this handy site at **http://www.virgin.net/daysout** will provide a list of things to do.

▶ **Travel Britain**. A handy UK travel site covering car hire, hotel and rail booking, domestic and international flights, and a small amount of 'what's on' information. If you're looking for places to go in London, particularly, this site should be your first port of call. Head for **http://www.travelbritain.co.uk**

▶ **World Wide Events**. If you're going a little further afield, visit **http://www.wwevents.com** and find out what's going on in Europe, North America or Australasia while you're there.

And don't forget our old pal Yahoo! Point your browser at **http://www.yahoo.co.uk/Regional/Countries/United_Kingdom/Cities_ and_Towns** for a list of hundreds of cities, towns and villages. The entries for a particular town can be a bit of a mixed bag – all types of local information may be listed here, from tourist attractions and restaurants to butchers and council offices. If you're looking for something particular, such as a zoo or a theme park, visit Yahoo's front page (**http://www.yahoo.co.uk**) and use a keyword search.

Want to play a round?

What better way to relax than to hit a little ball very hard and then go looking for it? If you're tired of looking in all the usual places, visit **http://www.golfweb.com/europe** and try a change of course.

Getting From A To B

Finally, let's sort out those travel arrangements. For this, there's one magical website that handles the lot – the UK Online All-In-One page, at **http://www.ukonline.co.uk/content/Travel.html** From here, you can access dozens of European and international airlines and airports and check flight information; find the departure and arrival times of trains and National Express coaches; and book seats on planes, trains and buses. If that isn't enough, you can hire a car from one of four companies (or visit Hertz at **http://www.hertz.com**), check the latest news on motorways, London traffic and the tube, track down a taxi or look at the World Ski Report. And that's barely skimming the surface of this huge site!

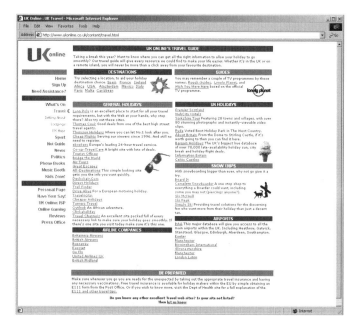

◀ A tiny slice of UK Online's incredible resource for travellers.

Book Your Holiday On The Web

If you want to journey farther afield, the Internet has to be the ideal place to start. With a few clicks you can book flights and accommodation, read city guides, swot up on culture and currency, and check local events. You might even find a few photos that don't have painted blue skies! Here's a tiny taste of some of the best sites:

▶ **American Express Travel** at **http://travel.americanexpress.com** A great travel resource for buying flights, finding last-minute offers, organising insurance and travellers cheques, tracking flights, checking weather reports and learning more about your chosen destination before you go.

▶ **World Travel Guide** at **http://www.wtg-online.com/navigate/world.asp** Find out anything you want to know about every country, region, city and airport in the world before you visit.

▶ **Thomas Cook** at **http://www.thomascook.co.uk** A mine of useful information including currency conversions, special offers, and links to other sites.

▶ **Eurostar** at **http://www.eurostar.com** Fare and timetable information for passenger services through the Channel Tunnel, as well as online reservations.

▶ **Internet Travel Solutions** at **http://www.itsnet.co.uk** Links to sites offering information about every aspect of travel you could imagine, including Health, Self-Catering, Insurance, Ferries, Cycling Holidays, Travel Agents… the list is almost endless.

To find general *What's On?* information in the major cities of the world, a couple of useful starting points are Excite's CityNet (**http://www.city.net**) and *Time Out* magazine (**http://www.timeout.com**).

Let's talk travel

Usenet is a useful source of travel information and real-life experiences. Check out the **alt.travel** and **rec.travel.marketplace** newsgroups, and take a look at the rest of the **rec.travel** hierarchy.

▶ *Need to find maps of towns and cities in the UK and elsewhere? Skip ahead to page 281.*

Amuse The Kids (And Yourself!) Online

Once you've discovered the Web, you've got a whole new world of entertainment at your fingertips. The effort that people put into creating some of these sites is stunning, and they do it for no particular reward. There's no 'license fee' to pay, and you won't get interrupted by advertisements every 15 minutes!

Entertainment Sites For Kids

The best children's sites are the ones that take a little education and add a sugar-coating of fun and interactivity, and America is leagues ahead of the UK in this department. In fact, UK kids' sites are thin on the ground, and good sites are probably still a year or two away. As long as you're not too concerned about the odd bit of weird spelling, point your kids at **http://www.yahooligans.com** for a mass of links to tried and trusted web pages.

Of course, you may not be convinced that the Internet is a safe or worthwhile place for kids. Prepare to be persuaded! Fire up your browser and visit **http://www.bonus.com**, shown in the following screenshot. As soon as you arrive, the 'worthwhile' element should be obvious: there are over 500 activities for kids, including games and puzzles, animations, interactive adventures, scientific explorations, and a whole lot more. The entire site is colourful, stylish, and easy to navigate. But apart from the incredible content you'll find here, this site illustrates the sense of responsibility found increasingly on the Web – your kids are locked in and they can't escape! Whenever you visit this site, a second browser window opens automatically, minus toolbars and menus, to display the pages; your children can move around this site to their hearts' content, but the only way to access a different site is to return to the original window and choose a Favorites item or type a URL into the address bar.

Another site that knows how to keep kids entertained, not surprisingly, is Disney at **http://www.disney.co.uk** Although the content here is clearly tilted towards the latest cinema and video releases, there's no big sell. Instead, you'll find games and activities that tie in cleverly with the films, with plenty of favourite cartoon characters, animated story books, and a very friendly, 'kids club' feel. You can also find out more about the various Disney resorts, and watch live camera broadcasts from Main Street.

▶ Bonus.com, one of the most absorbing sites on the Web. But give your kids a go too!

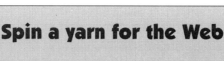

Spin a yarn for the Web

Do you have a budding novelist in the family? Point your kids at The Young Writers Club (**http://www.cs.bilkent.edu.tr/~david/derya/ywc.html**) where they can submit their own stories and read other children's creations online.

The sheer novelty value of surfing the Internet can be enough to keep kids amused for hours at a stretch (if your phone bill can stand it!), and a particular branch of web-based entertainment also makes a great starting point for learning how the Net works – the online scavenger hunt. Working from a set of clues, the goal is to track down pictures, pages and information on the Internet, like a treasure hunt at a kids' party. In fact, scavenger hunts are popular with adults too (especially the ones that pay cash prizes!), and often lead you to explore areas of the Internet that you'd studiously avoided, such as Gopher or Telnet. Yahoo's UK site keeps a list of current scavenger hunts, but its location seems to change periodically, so head off to **http://www.yahoo.co.uk** and enter the keywords 'scavenger hunts' to see where they're keeping it these days.

Play Online Games With Other Web-surfers

If you like computer games, the Web is exactly what you've been waiting for. Forget Minesweeper and Solitaire – Yahoo offers an incredible 45 different categories of online game at **http://dir.yahoo.com/Recreation/Games/ Internet_Games/Web_Games** Some of these are single-user games in which you play against the clock, solve a brain-teaser, or try to beat someone else's highest score; others are multi-user games in which you play against anyone else who happens to be visiting the same site at the same time.

Looking for single-user games?

Visit Karl Hörnell's site at **http://www.javaonthebrain.com/brain.html** for a collection of beautifully crafted games including Mastermind, IceBlox and RubikCube.

If you're stuck for somewhere to start, here are a few suggestions:

▶ **Gamesville** at **http://www.gamesville.com** This Lycos site proudly announces that it's been wasting your time since 1996, and it's obviously keen to go on doing it. There's poker, bingo, blackjack, pop quizzes, and links to many more types of games (including kids' games, puzzles and Pokemon games).

▶ **Interligence** at **http://www.interligence.com** Join Interligence (it's free) and play some stylish online games including Chess, Go, Reversi and Gomoku.

▶ **Casino Royale** at **http://www.funscape.com** If you like a gamble, visit this site and play poker, blackjack, roulette, slot machines and more. It really is a gamble, though – you can win real money, you can lose real money, and you'll have to pay a few dollars of real money to open an account before you start!

▶ **Tucows** at **http://tucows.mirror.ac.uk/window95.html** Tucows is an excellent source of Internet software, and the Entertainment section of this page will point you towards dozens of online games including shoot-'em-ups, board games, casinos and trivia quizzes.

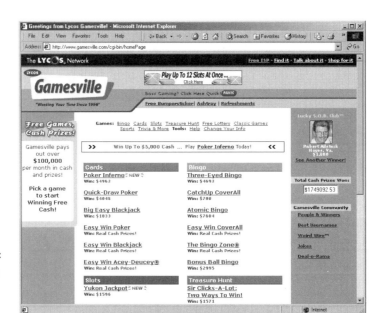

▶ Gamesville –
wasting your time
(and trying to do
the same with
your money!)

Gags & Giggles Galore

The World Wide Web has a seemingly endless store of joke pages,
cartoons, comic strips and comedy sites. For instance, go to the UK
Comedy Guide at **http://members.xoom.com/pammys/comedy** and
you'll find links and reviews for almost 400 British comedy sites. If
you're a fan of sci-fi fantasy writer Terry Pratchett, you can find a page
of hilarious quotes at **http://www.us.lspace.org**. For reams and reams of
jokes and humour links, try The Comedy Corner at
http://www.geocities.com/Eureka/2531 or the British Comedy Library
at **http://www.audiophile.com/BritCom**.

Yahoo strikes again

As usual, Yahoo can lead you to funnies of all descriptions. Just head for **http://dir.yahoo.com/Entertainment/Humor** Or visit UK Plus at **http://www.ukplus.co.uk**, choose the Entertainment category and click on Comedy.

If you're a cartoon fan, your first stop should be CartoonStock at **http://www.cartoonstock.com** Although the main aim of the site is to promote cartoon artists and sell their work, you'll find thousands of cartoons online in the Daily Cartoons, Free Cartoons and Artist Samples sections, and more still if you click the Search Library link and pick a category. For a taste of 'real life' humour from around the world, try Dumb Warnings at **http://www.dumbwarnings.com**, a collection of the silly warning labels included on product packaging (such as Nytol Sleep Aid's warning, 'May cause drowsiness', or the vital instructions on packs of American Airlines peanuts, 'Open packet, eat nuts'). While you're there, follow the links to Dumb Laws, Dumb Facts and Dumb Criminal Acts for more of the same.

Whatever flavour of humour you prefer, you'll find another generous helping on Usenet. A couple of self-explanatory newsgroups are **alt.binaries.pictures.cartoons** and **rec.arts.comics.strips**, and there are many more lurking in the **rec.humor**, **alt.humor** and **alt.jokes** hierarchies.

ONLINE NEWS & CURRENT AFFAIRS

Everybody in the world wants news of one sort or another. And, of course, there's plenty of it – it's being made all the time! But where traditional newspapers can print no more than two or three editions per day, Internet news services can be updated hour-by-hour, or even minute-by-minute. In this chapter you'll find some of the best sources of UK and world news, learn how to build your own tailor-made news service, and meet the revolutionary Internet technology that's about to make your paperboy redundant!

Read Your Newspaper On The Web

Unexpectedly, it's the broadsheets that have made it to the Internet first, and they've made a surprisingly good job of combining content, style and usability. If you find the paper versions of *The Times* and *The Daily Telegraph* a bit stuffy, their online versions are going to come as a revelation.

Not that the broadsheets are alone on the Net, by any means, but let's take *The Times* as an example. Go to **http://www.the-times.co.uk**, and as soon as you arrive at the site's front page you'll see clear links to the major sections of the paper (Britain, World, Business, Sports, and so on), plus summaries of the major stories in several categories with hypertext links to the related articles if you'd like more detail. In true newspaper style, you'll also find links to classified ads, crosswords, cartoons and puzzles.

▶ Click any hypertext headline at *The Times* to read the complete article.

So, it's all there, and it's easy to navigate. But what makes it better than an ordinary paper version? In a word – storage! *The Times* and all the other online newspapers are building ever-expanding databases of news articles. With a quick keyword search, you can retrace the path of a news story you missed, track down articles on a particular subject, or find out what made headline news on any particular day. And, of course, it's a lot easier to save and store useful articles on your own hard disk for future reference than it is to keep a stack of newspaper clippings!

Information swapping

Although access is usually free, when you first visit many online newspapers and magazines, you'll have to fill in one of those infamous registration forms, giving your name and address, and a few other details. Provided you're honest, this provides useful marketing information for the publishers which they regard as a fair exchange for the information they're giving you.

So where can you find your favourite paper online? Perhaps it's one of these:

Newspaper	URL
The Daily Telegraph	http://www.telegraph.co.uk
The Guardian	http://www.guardian.co.uk
The Independent	http://www.independent.co.uk
The Mirror	http://www.mirror.co.uk
The Sun	http://www.the-sun.co.uk
The Sunday People	http://www.people.co.uk

Let's Talk About The Weather

The weather is officially the most popular topic of conversation in the UK. Probably because we have so much of it. And the Internet has a solution to that centuries-old problem, *What can you do when there's no one around to listen?* Just start up your newsreader and head for **alt.talk.weather** or **uk.sci.weather**

To become a real authority on the subject, though, you need to know what the weather's going to do next. One option is to consult the online newspapers mentioned above, but here's a better one: head for **http://weather.yahoo.com/Regional/United_Kingdom.html** On this page you'll find a hypertext list of almost every town in the UK – click on the appropriate town to see a five-day local weather forecast. (You might want to add the forecast page to Internet Explorer's Favorites menu or create a shortcut to it on your desktop for quick access.)

For more detailed weather information, including shipping forecasts and meteorological data, visit the Met Office site at **http://www.met-office.gov.uk/sec3/sec3.html**

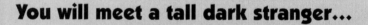

You will meet a tall dark stranger...

Yes, the Net has horoscopes too! One of the best known is Jonathon Cainer's Zodiac Forecasts at **http://stars.metawire.com** Or, for a more humorous approach, visit **http://www.xmission.com/~mustard/cosmo.html**

Play The Money Markets Online

There's little that can't be done on the Internet, but a few things cost money, and share dealing is one of them. Because the sort of information you're looking for is worth money, you'll have to whip out your credit card and cross palms with silver before you can trade. Nevertheless, there's no shortage of companies on the Internet holding their palms out expectantly, and one of the better known is E*TRADE at **http://www.etrade.co.uk** Alternatively, nip along to The Share Centre (**http://www.share.co.uk**) or Sharepeople (**http://www.sharepeople.com**), two easy-to-follow sites for new investors, offering plenty of straightforward help and explanations of the financial world.

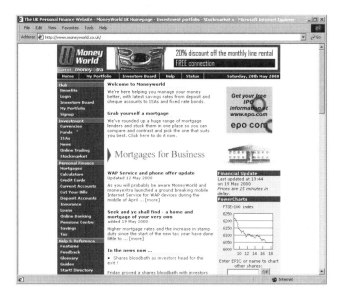

◀ MoneyWorld makes an excellent starting place for all things financial.

For information on more wide-ranging money matters, the place to be is MoneyWorld (**http://www.moneyworld.co.uk**). This is a huge and popular site covering every aspect of personal finance you can imagine – homebuying and mortgages, ISAs, unit and investment trusts, and company performance, to name but a few. You can read the London closing business report, check the FTSE 100 and 250, view regularly updated world prices, and consult the glossary to find out what everyone's talking about. And if MoneyWorld doesn't have the information you're looking for, you'll find links to other financial services and organisations in the UK and abroad.

Money talks

BY THE WAY

Usenet has several newsgroups for people wanting to give or receive a little financial advice. A good starting point is **uk.finance**. For more international input, try **misc.invest** and **misc.invest.stocks**, and have a look at the **clari.biz.stocks** hierarchy.

Online newspapers such as *The Times*, mentioned earlier in this chapter, also provide city news and prices just like their disposable counterparts, but if you need in-depth analysis, you can find the major finance publications on the Web too:

▶ *The Financial Times* at **http://www.ft.com**

▶ *The Wall Street Journal* at **http://www.wsj.com**

▶ *The Economist* at **http://www.economist.com**

Financial scandals

The financial world has caught a few hands in a few tills in recent years. To find out more about financial scandals and the owners of those unfortunate hands, hurry along to **http://www.ex.ac.uk/~RDavies/arian/scandals**

▶ *As a daily part of financial life, you can now run your bank account online, check account balances, and pay bills. Turn to page 268 to find out more.*

Create Your Own Custom News Page

You probably buy a newspaper every day, and perhaps a weekly or monthly trade journal of some sort. But do you actually read them all from cover to cover? The chances are that you glance at the headlines or the contents page, read the articles that interest you, and ignore the rest. Wouldn't it be great if there were one publication you could buy that gave you just the stories that appealed to you, and left out everything else? Well there is. In fact there are quite a few, and you don't even have to pay for them!

The 'personal page' is a recent arrival to the Web, but more and more online publications are building the option into their sites. If you find a trade journal that covers one of your hobbies or interests, take a look around the site to see if they offer the service, or send them an email to ask if it's in the pipeline.

One of the best non-specialist services is provided by Yahoo, the web-search chaps, and it takes only a couple of minutes to set it up. Point your browser at **http://edit.europe.yahoo.com/config/login**, and click the **Sign me up!** link. On the next page you'll have to fill in another of those registration forms – although this is a free service, Yahoo needs to assign you a unique username and password to personalise your page. When you come to choose these, make sure you pick something that's easy to remember; it doesn't matter if it's easy for someone else to guess, since there's no security issue at work here.

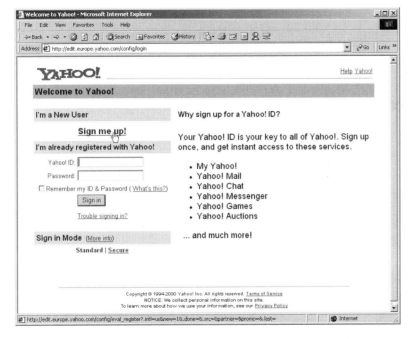

◄ Login at My Yahoo and read your own customised news pages.

As soon as you've filled in the registration form you can start to build your own page by checking boxes in all sorts of categories covering entertainment, news, sports, and leisure activities, and then click the button to confirm your choices. From now on, whenever you visit the main My Yahoo page at **http://my.yahoo.com** you'll see your personal page. Your browser should store and send your username and password to save you the bother of entering it every time, but make sure you keep a note of it somewhere, just in case!

▶ *After setting up a personal page at Yahoo or elsewhere, why not make it your Internet Explorer start-page? To find out how, skip back to page 60.*

All-in-one news and weather

If you prefer to find your news, weather and sports information all in one place, go to **http://www.uk.news.yahoo.com** and choose news headlines or summaries in several categories together with UK, Irish and worldwide weather forecasts.

Chart Hits & Bestsellers

Want to take a look at the UK albums and singles charts? The law of averages says you do – Dotmusic, at **http://www.dotmusic.co.uk**, is one of the most successful UK sites on the Web. Along with these charts and other information about the music scene, you'll find the Indie singles and albums charts; dance, R & B and club charts; and the US Airplay chart. While you're there, watch out for the little basket icons – if a CD you want to buy has one of these symbols beside it, you can click to add it to your 'shopping basket', and pay at the checkout when you're ready to leave.

Your bank account isn't running the same risks at the Publishers Weekly Bestseller Lists (**http://www.publishersweekly.com/bestsellersindex.asp**), but you'll find useful lists of the current bestsellers sorted by hardback and paperback fiction or non-fiction, children's, religious, computer, and audio books. For more general information and reviews, the main Bookwire site makes an ideal starting point – head for the homepage at **http://www.publishersweekly.com**

▶ *Skip ahead to the next chapter to discover the ins and outs of shopping online.*

Politics & Politicians On The Internet

Whether you want to explore 10 Downing Street, delve into government archives, read press releases and speeches, or check electoral and constituency information, the Internet has all the resources you need. But let's start with the obvious – if you're interested in politics, the first place you'll want to visit is your own party's website, so consult the table below and pay them a visit.

Political party	Website URL
Conservative Party	http://www.conservative-party.org.uk
Green Party	http://www.greenparty.org.uk
Labour Party	http://www.labour.org.uk
Liberal Democratic Party	http://www.libdems.org.uk
Plaid Cymru	http://www.plaidcymru.org
Scottish National Party	http://www.snp.org.uk

If you're more interested in the real workings of government, head for the Government Information Office at **http://www.open.gov.uk** This is a huge site containing thousands of documents and articles, but there are several different indexes to help you find your way through it. The easiest method is probably to click on Topic Index, pick a general category and 'drill down' through more specific categories. For a comprehensive hypertext listing of the government departments and organisations on the Web, click the Organisation Index link and use the alphabetical index to pick the initial letter of the organisation you want to visit.

Until recently, one of the few ways to get a look around 10 Downing Street was to become a politician – rather a high price to pay when one look is probably enough. Thanks to the wonders of the Web, you can tramp around to your heart's content at **http://www.number-10.gov.uk**, and read a selection of speeches, interviews and press releases while you're there. Or jump on a virtual bus to **http://www.parliament.uk** to tour the House of Commons and the House of Lords, and search through the parliamentary archives.

An Eye on the Net

You don't have to take politics entirely seriously, of course. For a more satirical view, try *Private Eye* at **http://www.cix.co.uk/~private-eye**

For all the government departments and official bodies on the Web, one of the most useful and informative sites I've come across is actually unofficial. The British Politics Pages (**http://www.ukpol.co.uk**), shown in the next screenshot, is a veritable goldmine that includes local and national electoral information, constituency lists and analyses, local government details, and a useful Basic Information section. There are even lists of MPs' personal web pages and email addresses!

Oil The Wheels Of Government Yourself!

Getting your voice heard in the crowd isn't easy, but if you can find a few people who share your views you can improve your chances. Or perhaps you'd like to let off a bit of steam, or get into a good old political scrap once in a while. The newsgroups provide one of the few resources available anywhere that allow you to discuss your political opinions with people from all over the world. Indeed, they could even act as a springboard for launching pressure groups and petitions, or organising online 'conferences' using programs like NetMeeting and PowWow. The three major political newsgroups in the UK are **alt.politics.british, alt.politics.europe.misc** and **uk.gov.local**, but you'll find many more under the **uk.politics** hierarchy. Or try filtering your list of groups by entering **politics** to find related groups in other Usenet hierarchies.

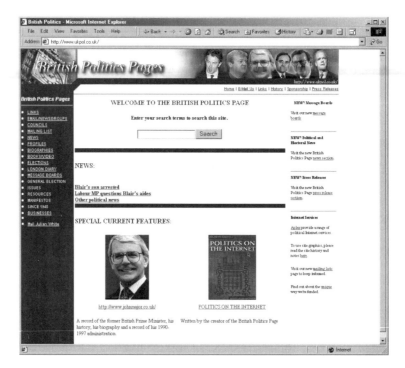

▶ A massive resource of local and national political data at the British Politics Page.

Why don't UK politicians answer questions?

They've probably learnt a lesson or two from US Senator Dan Quayle! As a dose of light relief from everyday politics, read The 'Wisdom' of Dan Quayle at
http://www.concentric.net/~salisar/quayle.html

STAY HOME & GO CYBER-SHOPPING

▶ **IN THIS CHAPTER**

Learn how to buy goods online

Visit shopping malls to find the big High Street names

Buy your groceries on the Web

Online banking, books, loans, wine and more

Cyber-romance – kisses, cards and flowers

Buying and selling at online auctions

The Internet connection is starting to look like the Swiss army knife of the 21st century. In the last few chapters we've seen how the Net has tools to replace the telephone, answerphone, radio, TV, newspapers and magazines, fax machine, and a fair bit more. Granted, there's no tool for getting stones out of horses' hooves, but they're probably working on it. And now, with the recent arrival of secure transmission on the Internet, you can use your credit card at thousands of online 'cyberstores' to buy anything from a car to a… well, a Swiss army knife. It's quick, it's easy, and in this chapter I'll show you how to do it, and point you towards some of the best stores in cyberspace.

Are These The Stores Of The Future?

So will we be doing all our shopping in cyberspace sometime in the future? Definitely not. Let's face it, shopping is fun! Online stores cover the Web, but they've been slow to really 'take off'. To a certain degree that's because of an imagined concern about the safety of using a credit card online, but it's also because people like their shopping the way it is. To buy an item without speaking to a cashier, or a voice on the end of a phone, is a curiously unsatisfying feeling.

That's bad news for the online stores, but its good news for humanity. The much-vaunted prophecy that we'll live our entire lives hunched in front of computer screens is obviously nonsense – there are comparatively few purchases you'd want to make without first seeing, touching and testing the goods. The main use of online shopping is for products like books, computers, videos and cars – the type of item you don't need to see before buying – and for 'impersonal' goods and services such as travel bookings, insurance or theatre tickets.

GOOD QUESTION!

Should I only buy from cyberstores in the UK?

If a store has a good, honest reputation, you could buy from them regardless of where they're situated. If you don't know anything about the company, it's easier to deal with any problems that arise if that company is based in the UK. Otherwise, there's no doubt that a lot of goods are far cheaper in the US than in the UK or Europe, and there's no reason not to buy from America or any other country. Always check the exchange rate so that you know how much you're spending, and look at the cost of packing and delivery. When buying from outside Europe, most goods valued at over £18 are subject to an import duty (imposed by our own Customs & Excise) which you'll have to pay when the goods arrive at your door.

And there's more good news: the cyberstores *know* they've got a fight on their hands! So you can bet your boots that they're putting a lot of effort into making their services as simple, reliable and quick as they possibly can.

How Do I Buy Stuff Online?

In almost any online store you visit, the routine will be pretty much the same. The layout will vary, of course, just as real stores all look different once you're inside, but most stores use a readily accepted 'supermarket' metaphor that involves placing items in an electronic shopping trolley and then going to the checkout to pay. As an example, follow me through a quick spending spree at Amazon (**http://www.amazon.co.uk**), one of the best-known UK cyberstores for CDs, videos and DVDs.

◀ Step one: choose a product to buy.

From Amazon's front page I chose the link to the Rock Music Chart page, arriving at the page shown in the screenshot above. Every item has an **Add to Shopping Basket** button beside it, so I click the button beside the CD I want to buy. At the top of the page there's a little basket icon – at any point in my shopping trip I could click that button to go and pay.

Clicking the **Add to Shopping Basket** button takes me to a **Shopping Basket** page which shows all the items I've placed in my 'basket' – just a single CD so far. I could change the quantity of any item by typing a new figure to replace the **1** shown, or remove an item from the basket by clicking the **Delete** button beside it if I've had a change of heart. I haven't, so I take a quick glance at what's in the basket so far and choose what to do next: should I buy more stuff, or **Proceed to checkout?** Throwing caution to the wind, I decide to buy more stuff, so I click the **Back** button to return to the music charts page.

▶ Step two: verify the item and quantity, and decide what to do next.

A few minutes later I'm back at the **Shopping Basket** page (shown in the screenshot above) after clicking the **Add to Shopping Basket** button beside another CD. My basket now boasts two items and I'm ready to pay up and leave, so this time I click the **Proceed to checkout** button.

From this point on, Amazon keeps me posted on my progress with a set of six icons across the top of the screen (shown in the next screenshot). As this is my first visit I have to enter all my contact information – name, address, phone number, and so on. (Notice Internet Explorer's padlock symbol in the lower right corner and the https://prefix in the address bar, both indicating that these pages are secure – see page 207.)

After one final check on the items in the basket and the total price including VAT and delivery, I arrive at the Pay stage (shown in the screenshot for step four) where I enter my credit card details and choose a password I'll be able to remember on future visits to save retyping all the same details again. In

◀ Step three: enter your contact and delivery details.

the final step, which commits me to the transaction, all these details are passed to Amazon. I click on **File | Save As** in the browser to save the order-confirmation web page to my own disk in case I want to refer to it later, and an emailed confirmation of my order arrives a few minutes later. Exhausted, I search for their cafeteria, but they don't seem to have one.

◀ Step four: enter your credit card details and confirm your purchase.

Worried about the security aspects of shopping online? It's actually the safest way to use your credit card – turn to page 206 to find out more.

What do *you* think?

Your opinions are worth money to a lot of companies (that's why you have to fill in forms to access some of the online shops and services). If you head off to **http://www.questions.net** and fill in their questionnaire you can receive entries in a sweepstake and points that you can trade for online goods, or donate to charity.

Take A Tour Of The Shopping Malls

Where do you go when you want to find the biggest selection of stores and merchandise quickly and easily? A shopping centre, of course! The theory behind shopping malls in your local town translates perfectly to the Internet – not only are all your favourite stores within easy reach, but while you're there you might be tempted to do a spot of 'window shopping'.

You've probably guessed, from the generic name shopping 'malls', that many of these centres are American. Elsewhere in cyberspace it makes little difference which part of the world you're looking at, but online shopping tends to be different. You may not be at ease working in dollars, for instance, or you may not want to wait so much longer for transatlantic delivery. So, for this section, I'm going to stick to just UK malls and stores.

Shopping all over the world

If you can't get what you want from the sites in this chapter, the trusty Yahoo! has a mammoth page of UK shopping sites at **http://uk.shopping.yahoo.com**, or worldwide sites at **http://shopping.yahoo.com**

Actually, these days it's not too difficult to stick to UK malls. Not only are
there a lot more of them now than there were a couple of years ago, but the
quality and choice has improved dramatically. A good example is the UK
Shopping City at **http://www.ukshops.co.uk**, shown in the next screenshot.
Pick a 'zone' from a choice of 11 including Travel, Property, AutoPark,
Technology, or Shopping. Among these zones you'll find simple links to some
well-known stores such as WH Smith, Marks & Spencer, Lunn Poly, and the
RAC, along with a bundle of not-so-well-known but nicely varied sites.

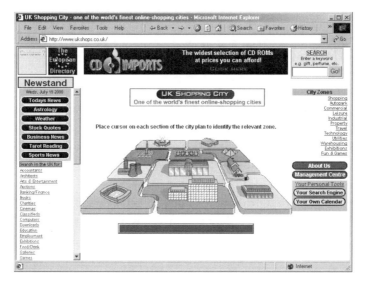

◀ UK Shopping
City – a virtual
retail park with 11
shopping zones.

UK Shopping City is slightly unusual in that it shows store names up front rather
than *types* of product. In some cases this is ideal, but if you'd like to find stores
by selecting product categories or searching by keyword, here are some more
malls worth a visit:

▶ **Shops On The Net** at **http://www.shopsonthenet.com** Browse directory style
through 34 categories of shopping site (with useful indicators of the number
of links in each category) or search by keyword for a shop or a product.

▶ **British Shopping Links** at **http://www.british-shopping.com** A deceptively
simple site with almost 100 categories of store, descriptions of every store
listed, and icons to indicate if secure payment can be made at each site.

▶ **Safe Street** at **http://www.safestreet.co.uk** A small but growing mall that
hosts sites for small (but, hopefully, also growing) shops around the UK.
This is a good place to find something a little out of the ordinary.

Search for a Store

Some items are hard to find wherever you go. If you need to find a particular product, such as a cricket bat, try using your favourite search engine, entering something like **+cricket+shopping online** (substituting the word **shopping** with **buy** if that doesn't yield results).

Groceries In Cyberspace

When you've been on the Net a short while, you get so used to electronic shopping trolleys that the idea of pushing one of those wire things around a supermarket loses all its appeal! No problem – head for Tesco at **http://www.tesco.com** to see if you can do your grocery shopping online too. Click the **Groceries Online** link and you'll be taken to the Register page where you can find out if the service is available in your area. If it is, follow the registration process (it's free and takes about five minutes), and you'll be able to fill your trolley with goodies, pay by credit card, and arrange delivery for a time that suits you.

▶ Tesco's technically advanced, but easy to use, online supermarket.

If your area isn't covered by the Tesco service, try Sainsbury's at **http://www.sainsburys.co.uk** Here, participating stores let you order over the Internet or by phone or fax, and you can wheel a virtual trolley around **http://orderline.sainsburys.co.uk** to get a feel for online grocery shopping before you order anything. Or you may prefer to order your groceries from Iceland (the store, not the country) by visiting **http://www.iceland-shop.co.uk**

Have A Wander Down The High Street

Away from the organised aisles of supermarkets and shopping malls, the Internet has thousands of individual shops gamely vying for your attention. So let's grab a carrier bag and venture out into the fresh air of the global village to see what's about.

How about a new car? If you're nervous about spending so much money online, maybe you'll be tempted by the prospect of saving up to 30 per cent of the purchase price: Carbusters (**http://www.carbusters.com**) is a Consumer Association site which aims to end what it calls 'the Great British Car Rip-Off' by importing new cars for you; Tins (**http://www.tins.co.uk**) aims to do much the same thing, but also allows trade-ins and can find you a used car if you prefer; Virgin Cars (**http://www.virgincars.com**) offers typical savings of over 20 per cent along with a unique '24-hour test drive' service. Of the more traditional car sales sites, CarSource (**http://www.carsource.co.uk**) has a huge database of used motors. If you can't find what you want, submit your details and they'll try to track it down for you.

◀ Carbusters brings you new UK cars at European prices.

Perhaps you need a loan to buy your dream machine. If so, the Abbey National (**http://www.abbeynational.co.uk**) should give you the information you need, and you can use their handy loan calculator to work out what it's going to cost. Finally you'll need car insurance, and EasyCover might be able to help you out: visit **http://www.easycover.co.uk**, fill in the details, and EasyCover will submit them to ten major (and not-so-major) insurance companies on your behalf. While you're there you can get quotes for home and travel insurance too. One of the popular insurance companies that doesn't appear on EasyCover's list is Direct Line at **http://www.directline.co.uk**, which also offers an email quotation service and loan calculator.

Next, a brief stop at Wine Cellar. You can find this wonderful, friendly site at **http://www.winecellar.co.uk**, browse through tempting categories such as Wine, Champagne, Beer and Cider, and top up with soft drinks and cigars. Not content with simply selling, the Wine Cellar offers some nice extras. Click the **Magazine** icon, for example, and you'll find a range of interesting recipes with suggested accompanying wines. And for real wine aficionados there's a newsgroup-style message centre in the **Arena** where you can follow discussions, ask questions, and receive (possibly rather slurred) answers.

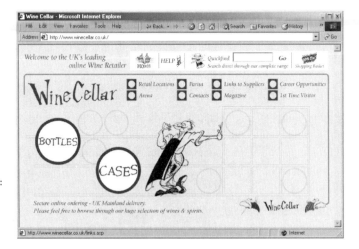

▶ The Wine Cellar: so good you can almost smell the feet.

Are there any shopping newsgroups?

Not shopping, exactly, but there are certainly small ads and trading groups. You'll find the most useful groups in the **uk.adverts** hierarchy and the extensive **biz** hierarchy. If that's not enough, you should find a few extras by filtering your newsgroup list with the word **marketplace**.

After a nice meal and a crate of Beaujolais, you'll probably want to settle down with a good book. Visit Waterstones at **http://www.waterstones.co.uk** or The Internet Bookshop at **http://www.bookshop.co.uk** and search by title, author or ISBN. Better still, go to BookBrain at **http://www.bookbrain.co.uk**: BookBrain doesn't sell books itself, it searches over a dozen other bookshops to find the best price on the book you want. On a slightly different tack, try Online Originals (**http://www.onlineoriginals.com**), a site which publishes original works in email form only. Read synopses and samples on the website, and if you find something you like, you can pay around £4 to have the complete text sent to you by email.

Classic literature online

If your reading tastes include authors like Somerset Maugham, Daniel Defoe, Oscar Wilde and Arthur Conan Doyle, visit Project Gutenberg at **http://www.promo.net/pg**, a site that publishes out-of-copyright works in electronic format.

If you prefer to browse through a lot of different items without too much trudging around, you need a department store. Head for BigSave at **http://www.bigsave.com**, shown in the next screenshot, run a quick search, or pick the department that takes your fancy. In a similar vein there's ShopSmart at **http://uk.shopsmart.com** Here the departments actually consist of different stores, giving the added benefit of price comparisons to help you find the best deal.

▶ BigSave.com,
the online
department store

After all this spending, it's probably about time to check your bank balance and settle your credit card bill. No, don't get up – you can do that online too! Many of the UK's biggest banks, including Barclays (**http://www.barclays.co.uk**) and NatWest (**http://www.natwest.co.uk**), offer their account-holders online banking, allowing you to transfer funds, pay bills, and check balances at any hour of the day or night. If you're a Barclaycard holder, register at **http://www.barclaycard.co.uk** and settle your account online using your bank debit card.

It Must Be Love...

Here's a branch of Internet shopping that romantics won't be able to resist – show someone how much you care by filling their email box with virtual kisses, cards and poetry. For more romance than you can shake a stick at, visit The Seduction Palace at **http://www.seductionpalace.com** Kisses are in the form of WAV (audio) files, and cards use graphics, so it pays to choose carefully if the love of your life has a slow Internet connection. You can also order chocolates, take a tour of the 3D Virtual Palace, and test your romance quotient by taking the online quiz. And if that cyber-kiss hits the spot, why not follow it up with a virtual proposal?

◀ The Seduction Palace, the ultimate romance site for lovers with fast connections.

Virtual cards are all the rage on the Internet as more and more people take to email as an alternative to the post. A couple of free 'all-purpose' card shops are E-greetings at **http://www.egreetings.com** and Awesome Cyber-Cards at **http://www.marlo.com/card.htm** You can also send customised digital postcards with pictures, music and web links from **http://www.all-yours.net/postcard/dp.html**

Online lunar-cy

Have you ever promised someone the moon? Now you can put your money where your mouth is. Visit the MoonShop at **http://www.moonshop.com**, hand over about 30 dollars to the official Lunar Embassy, and you'll receive documentary title to your lunar property and its mineral rights. Getting planning permission for it might be more tricky, of course...

In the time-honoured traditions of romance, you won't be taken seriously if you don't send flowers. Head for Interflora at **http://www.interflora.co.uk**, browse through the catalogue, and place your order online complete with accompanying message.

But it isn't always possible to 'say it with flowers' – the average bouquet has a limited vocabulary. For those sentiments that only a hand-crafted voodoo doll can truly express, Virtual Design has the answer at **http://www.virtual-design.com/v2/onlinedemos/voodoodoll/voodoo.htm** To the sound of jungle drums, you can use pins, a candle and a machete to mutilate the doll to your own requirements – inducing yelps and screams as you do so – and then enter the email address of your intended recipient. You'll also have to enter your own email address so that you can receive any response that may be coming to you. This site definitely demands a weird sense of humour, but if you have that, you won't be able to keep away!

▶ 'Say it with pins' – the Virtual Design Voodoo Doll.

To finish on a more positive note, let's assume those virtual kisses and proposals did the trick, and a wedding is imminent. Head along to Wedding Bells at **http://www.weddingbells.com** to find out what's involved. This is an American site, so you might prefer not to buy goods here (you can visit the UK's Wedding Day Guide at **http://www.wedding-day.co.uk** to find bridalware, cars, cakes and so on) but the other resources are valuable and free: you'll find an Idea Pool, wedding facts and figures, a selection of toasts for worried speech-makers, gift suggestions, wedding etiquette and style advice, and a whole lot more to make a successful day virtually guaranteed.

e-commerce

The 'e-' before any recognisable word is short for 'electronic', and has somehow come to mean 'taking place on the Internet'. So e-commerce means commerce or trading that takes place on the Net. Other similar words are 'e-business' and the wonderfully silly 'e-tailing' (electronic retailing).

Selling Online – Auctions, Swaps & Classifieds

Nowadays there's a lot more to e-commerce than just 'buying stuff from stores'. One of the first variations on the online store theme was the online auction, and it was an immediate hit. Two of the biggest auction sites are eBay (**http://www.ebay.co.uk**) and QXL (**http://www.qxl.com**), and both provide clear information about how to sell an item or bid for one. Bidding is a doddle, of course – just check the current highest bid, decide how much more you're willing to pay, then keep an eye on the daily email messages that tell you whether you've been outbid. If you have, you can nip back and enter a higher bid. Selling isn't much more complicated: set up a free account, fill in a few online forms describing the item you're selling and the price you want for it, then sit back and wait. As with 'real' auctions, sales at online auctions are legally binding and auction sites have a number of security systems in place to protect both buyer and seller.

Online auctions have opened the floodgates for other person-to-person trading methods. One is the straight swap, offered by Swopworld (**http://www.swopworld.com**) and Webswappers (**http://www.webswappers.com**), which is as simple as you'd expect: fill in a form telling the world what you've got and what you want in return, then wait for the world to respond. If what you want in return is money, though, you'd be better off using a classified ad, and two of the biggest names in classifieds are online: Loot at **http://www.loot.com** (which has the great benefit of being a free service) and Exchange And Mart at **http://www.exchangeandmart.co.uk**. And, in case you're still wondering whether that whole 'online auctions' idea is just a flash in the pan, both of these sites can auction your item for you instead of simply advertising it for sale.

▶ QXL – put unwanted items under the hammer.

19

RESEARCH & WORK ON THE INTERNET

▶ **IN THIS CHAPTER**

Use online dictionaries, encyclopaedias, thesauruses and more

Locate online maps, atlases and city guides

Find pictures, videos & information about the entire universe

Online schools, universities and study tools

How the Internet can help you find a job

Whatever you do in your daily life, the Internet can help. It can provide you with vital reference and research materials; supply information about complementary or competing companies; enable you to work or study from home; and put you in touch with other users working in a similar field. And if your daily life leaves you too much time for aimless surfing, the Internet can even help you find a job!

Look It Up Online

I'm not going to pretend that you'll be using 'lookup' references on the Internet a great deal. In the UK, where a local phone call still costs money, going online every time you need to check the spelling of a word or find a synonym is hardly an economical pastime. More than likely, your word processor has a built-in spellchecker and thesaurus; you may have a CD-ROM-based multimedia encyclopaedia too. But it's a safe bet that the Internet outweighs your book and CD-ROM collections, so here are some of the resources you can call on when you need to.

Material gains

If you need more reference materials than those given here and on the CD-ROM, point your browser at **http://uk.dir.yahoo.com/reference** for the characteristically comprehensive set of categories.

Encyclopaedias

The words 'online encyclopaedia' sound a bit odd. After all, the Internet itself is the ultimate encyclopaedia, so why would you search its contents for a smaller version? A search engine will provide a greater number and variety of links to information than any encyclopaedia. So the only time you're likely to want an online encyclopaedia is when you need concise, comprehensive information on a subject fast, and, as in 'real life', the only contender is the *Encyclopaedia Britannica*'s online incarnation at **http://www.eb.com**

◀ Encarta – the other well-known encyclopaedia, now online and free.

The Britannica site itself is excellent – you'll find an Image Tour, a word game, Random Article feature, news and current events articles, Birthday Lookup, and masses more. As for the reason you visited in the first place, the search facilities are fast and powerful: you can enter a keyword or phrase, or even type a question in standard English. The search engine will then give you the information intelligently – if it believes it's answered your question, it will display the relevant article, or the portion of an article that seems to contain the answer. As with keyword searches, you'll also find more links to related articles to help you dig deeper.

Being unique, Britannica is a subscription service. Fortunately, like many Internet services, it's getting cheaper all the time and currently costs $5 per month (roughly £3). You can sign up for a free trial by clicking the **Free for 30 Days** link, but be prepared for a rather convoluted signup process. The other big name in encyclopaedias (although for different reasons) is Microsoft's CD-ROM-based Encarta, which has recently made the transition from CD-ROM to Net. You can use Encarta's online edition free at **http://encarta.msn.com**

Encyclopaedia for the kids

Kids and teenagers can find a good reference site at
http://www.letsfindout.com This encyclopaedia allows keyword searches,
browsing through its nine categories, or a trawl through its entire list of entries. Although it's a
US site with an obviously American slant, the information is well-presented and might make
all the difference to school projects or homework.

Dictionaries

I don't know who has the time or energy to put them there, but dictionaries
of all types abound on the Internet. One of the best spelling and definition
lookups is *Webster's* (subtly retitled *WWWebster's* for the Web) at
http://www.m-w.com/netdict.htm As usual, enter a keyword, and its
pronunciation and definition will appear. If you're not sure of the spelling,
just get as close as you can – WWWebster's will suggest some alternatives if
it doesn't recognise your word. A great all-rounder is the OneLook
Dictionaries site at **http://www.onelook.com** This handy resource can search
through 626 dictionaries simultaneously, or you can restrict your search to a
particular area such as medical, computer-related, or religious dictionaries.
Both WWWebster's and OneLook support the use of wildcards, allowing
you to find multiple words or hedge your bets on the spelling.

Wildcards

Wildcards are characters used to represent unknown characters in a word. The
asterisk replaces multiple letters (so you could enter **demo*** to find
'democracy' and 'demographic'); the question mark replaces a single letter (so **te?t?** would
find 'tests' and 'teeth').

Of course, neither of the above sites can help you much when you receive an email from your Hungarian penpal. For that you need a dual-language dictionary, and Dictionaries On The Web (**http://www.iki.fi/hezu/dict.html**) is the place to find one. This page contains links to a huge number of translating dictionaries including Russian, Estonian, Czech, Latin and German, most of which translate to or from English.

If you prefer to start with a less demanding language, here's a couple of oddball sites you might like. The Aussie Slang & Phrase Dictionary (**http://members.tripod.com/~thisthat/slang.html**) is a real ripper worth a burl. BritSpeak is a site that introduces English as a second language for Americans (although it also has an American–English version). It's intended to be tongue-in-cheek, but some of its humour is quite unintentional, though they'll probably call me a bounder for saying so. You can find BritSpeak at **http://pages.prodigy.com/NY/NYC/britspk**

◀ 2 440 427 different words. It makes you feel guilty asking for just one, doesn't it?

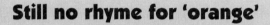

Still no rhyme for 'orange'

The word 'orange' continues to look an unlikely candidate for your latest love poem, as confirmed by the Rhyming Dictionary at **http://www.rhymezone.com** This keyword search lets you choose between perfect and partial rhymes, or homophones (such as there/their/they're).

Thesauruses

The most pristine book in my collection is *Roget's Thesaurus*. To look at it, you'd think I care for it deeply. I don't – I find it very unfriendly (hostile, antagonistic and, indeed, adverse). Fortunately, Roget's online version, at **http://web.cs.city.ac.uk/text/roget/thesaurus.html**, uses the now-traditional keyword search. Just type in a word, and then choose the desired meaning from the resulting list to see its synonyms.

Quotations

'The Internet is a great way to get on the Net.' So sayeth US Senator Bob Dole, and it takes a brave man to disagree. Another good way is to say something sufficiently wise, amusing or obtuse that people will include it in their online quotation pages. Everyone from Shakespeare to Stallone has said something quotable, and the best place to find it is **http://www.geocities.com/Athens/Forum/1327/quotearc.html** This page gives an immense hypertext list of words from 'Ability' to 'Zest' – just click a likely word to open a page of related quotes.

Alternatively, visit Bartleby at **http://www.bartleby.com/99** to read quotes by choosing an author from the list, or by running a keyword search. The quotes are limited to classical literature (no Oscar Wildes or George Bernard Shaws here), and the search engine responds best to a single-word entry.

ASCII art

If you're looking for quotes and one-liners to use as an email signature, hop along to **http://huizen.dds.nl/~mwpieter/sigs** Along with the gags, poems and opinions, you'll find a huge collection of ASCII art – pictures created using ordinary ASCII characters.

If you're in the market for the humorous quotations, try the Random Quotes page at **http://www.tomkoinc.com/random_quote.html**, or the Insulting Sarcasm (Put-Downs from Famous People) at **http://www.corsinet.com/braincandy/getinsulted.html**

And Lots More Besides...

Need to find the meaning of some of those acronyms and abbreviations that seem to crop up so often in modern life? Head off to the Acronym Lookup at **http://www.ucc.ie/cgi-bin/acronym** This simple service consists of just a text-box (nope, no button!) Type in your acronym, and press Enter to see the results.

Another often-needed reference is a weights and measures converter. For a straightforward list of units and their conversion factors, visit **http://www.soton.ac.uk/~scp93ch/refer/convfact.html** The list is comprehensive, and appears on a single page, so you could even save the page to your own disk for easy use. But if you'd prefer to avoid the brain exercise of doing the maths yourself, the Measurement Converter at **http://www.ur.ru/~sg/transl** has the answer. Choose one of the nine categories (such as Weight, Speed, Pressure or Area), type a figure in the appropriate box, and press the Tab key to see the equivalent value instantly displayed for all the other unit types.

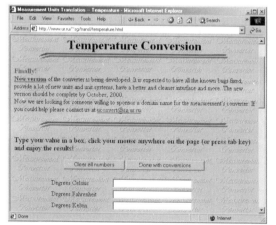

◀ The Measurement Converter gives nine categories of unit type, and immediate results.

Along similar lines, you'll find a useful currency converter at **http://www.xe.net/currency/** Type an amount into the text-box, select your Convert From and Convert To currencies from the dropdown lists, and click the button to see the result based on the latest exchange rates.

The writer's bible

Confused by the comma? Perplexed by the apostrophe? You need *The Elements of Style* by Strunk and White. In fact, if you write anything more adventurous than a shopping list, this captivating little book is a must-have. But don't take my word for it – read it online at **http://www.bartleby.com/people/Strunk-W.html**

Finally, a little bit of everything on one unusual site: Research-It! at **http://www.itools.com/research-it/research-it.html** On this single well-organised page you'll find a choice of dictionaries and thesauri, a translator (with a range of options such as a verb conjugator and an anagram creator), biographical lookup, biblical lookup, maps, CIA factbook, currency converter, stock quotes, and even more.

Language problems?

For quick and easy language translation, head for **http://babelfish.altavista.digital.com** Type text into the box, select a language and click the Translate button. This handy service can also translate a foreign-language web page, given the URL. Although the translation of individual words is accurate, the sense can go wonderfully awry. For a few minutes' entertainment, try translating English sentences to Portuguese and then back again.

The Earth Unearthed

The world is generally accepted to be a pretty big place, and most calculations indicate that the universe is bigger still, so the potential for acquiring knowledge is inexhaustible. Whether you're looking for fact, conjecture or opinion, the Internet can help you find a street map of Dallas, the best restaurant in Prague, a video of a lunar eclipse, or several answers to the mystery of crop circles.

Discover The World

There's no single, comprehensive site for maps and atlases, so if you want something particular you'll have to be prepared for a bit of traipsing around. A good place to start, though, is Streetmap.com at (you guessed it) **http://www.streetmap.com** Although the USA is disproportionately well-served, you'll also find maps of cities elsewhere in the world, atlases and historical maps, plus a few links to interactive and virtual reality map sites.

If you want some local information to go with your maps, try visiting the Excite search engine's Travel site at **http://www.excite.com/travel/maps** You can type the name of a country, region or city to run a keyword search, or (more enjoyably) click your way through the interactive maps to home in on the area you want. Once again, American cities are plotted and detailed to the last manhole cover at the expense of other countries, but it still manages to be a smart and informative site. If you like these clickable maps, you'll enjoy a visit to Magellan Geographix (**http://www.maps.com/cgi-bin/magellan/Maps**) – you'll find a few extra UK cities here, and superb graphics.

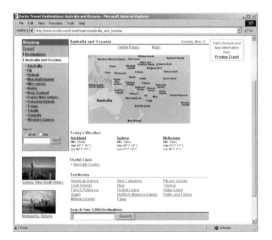

◀ Excite's interactive maps lead to photos, local maps, and background information.

For historical maps, check out the Oxford University Map Room at **http://rsl.ox.ac.uk/nnj** You'll get an even better selection by visiting the room itself, but of course that entails a trip to Oxford! You can also visit the Ordnance Survey online at two sites: **http://www.ordnancesurvey.co.uk** is the official government site, while **http://www.mapzone.co.uk** is a strange site that initially appears to be aimed at children, but currently sends you to the far less friendly government site when you click any link – hopefully this is a work in progress.

Flying colours

Looking for flags of the world? Visit **http://www.fotw.net/flags** and search for a flag by clicking interactive maps or entering keywords. The flags can be downloaded as GIF image files, and each is accompanied by a page of fascinating historical background.

Zooming out for a global view, there's a mass of information available. If you need to check up on a time zone in a hurry, head along to **http://tycho.usno. navy.mil/tzones.html** a US Navy site, and click the initial letter of the country you're interested in. For a slower, but stylishly interactive, way of reaching similar information, the WorldTime site at **http://www.worldtime.com** will keep you clicking around in fascination for ages as you zoom in and out, and switch between night and day.

The world in pictures

For the best images and movies of the Earth, visit PlanetScape's Earth page at **http://planetscapes.com/solar/eng/earth.htm** There's also a list of Earth Science links covering Clouds From Space, Terrestrial Impact Craters and Volcanoes, plus animations and statistics. If you like this sort of thing, check out the main page at **http://planetscapes.com** for similar views of other planets, asteroids, comets and more.

Understand The World

Why do we have seasons? What causes volcanoes and tornadoes? What is a rainbow? Even those of us who've been living on it for several decades still have questions about the Earth. As usual, the Web is the place to turn to find the answers, and it has one huge benefit over any encyclopaedia – if you can't find the explanation you're looking for, you can just ask!

One of the best and largest science-related sites, with over 50 000 articles, is SciCentral at **http://www.scicentral.com** Pick one of its eight categories and you'll find links to more specific categories, speciality sections, journals, and more. Better still, as you move around the site you'll find links to discussion groups covering each topic, so if you can't find the answer you're looking for you can just pick a discussion group and ask.

A similar site, aimed more at children, is The Why Files at **http://whyfiles.news.wisc.edu**, shown in the screenshot below. Although there's no option to submit your own questions at the moment, the subjects covered are well chosen, with plenty of pictures, tasty facts you can impress your friends with, and a light-hearted approach.

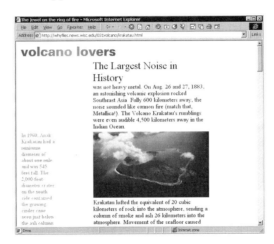

◀ The Why Files – an easy and light-hearted collection of scientific answers.

New horizons, old horizons

The BBC's popular series, *Horizon*, has a useful site at **http://www.bbc.co.uk/horizon** As well as details of forthcoming programmes, an Archive section collects many past documentaries into eight categories, with summaries of each. You can even download complete programme transcripts.

One of the most popular questions, of course, is How did it all start?, and the Cosmic Web Site at **http://www.geocities.com/CapeCanaveral/Lab/2048** sets out to explain the popular Big Bang Theory for the creation of the universe. (Big Bang theorists haven't got the field to themselves though – maybe there was nothing there to go Bang in the first place, a point put forward by The Theory of Nothing at **http://www.aambury.freeserve.co.uk/NOTHIN~1.HTM)**

For general science-related features and articles, two of the best-known names are *New Scientist* magazine (**http://www.newscientist.com**) and the BBC's *Tomorrow's World* (**http://www.bbc.co.uk/tw**). Both sites change regularly and hold large archives of past features, making them well worth visiting for general interest or for serious research.

But if you prefer your science to be a little on the 'weird' side, head for **http://www.eskimo.com/~billb/weird/wpage.html** This links page will take you to stories about science hoaxes, jokes, unusual theories and much more in a similar vein, along with 'The Official Truth', a great collection of science-related quotations such as 'I think there is a world market for maybe five computers' from a past president of IBM.

▶ *New Scientist* online: in-depth stories, a huge archive and easy searching.

Change The World

There is a number of pressure groups and organisations dedicated to educating and improving the world, and you'll find many of them online. If you know the name of a particular organisation or society, try entering it into your favourite search engine; if you don't, enter descriptive keywords such as **wildlife protection**. Here are a few organisations you might want to visit:

Organisation	Website URL
Amnesty International	http://www.amnesty.org.uk
Crime Prevention Initiative	http://www.crime-prevention.org.uk
Friends Of The Earth	http://www.foe.co.uk
Greenpeace International	http://www.greenpeace.org
Save The Children	http://www.oneworld.org/scf

The Universe... And Beyond!

If you need information about the rest of our solar system, the obvious starting point is NASA. In fact, the primary NASA site at **http://spaceflight.nasa.gov** is so immense it's hard to believe you'll ever need another site! Alongside image and movie galleries, there are sound files, details of new and current missions, information about the types of technology involved, the history of space travel, and the NASA organisation itself.

If you want to find undiluted Shuttle information, go to **http://spaceflight.nasa.gov** This is an in-depth, but friendly, NASA site about Shuttle life, with videos of the craft taken from both inside and out, latest news about the Shuttle program, and a wealth of fascinating background that you won't find anywhere else.

To boldly go where no man has gone before, head for the Royal Greenwich Observatory at **http://www.ast.cam.ac.uk** The site itself is uninspiring, but its links can lead you to pictures from the Hubble Space Telescope, and many more observatories around the world (some of which provide live camera feeds to the Web from their telescopes).

More solar system links

For more on our solar system, **http://astronomy-mall.com/hotlinks/solar.htm**
is a simple list of links to all manner of resources – eclipses, meteors, a Mars
atlas, moon maps, you name it.

▶ Visit NASA,
and you'll
probably never
be seen again!

A popular topic of discussion on the Internet, as elsewhere, concerns the
existence of little green men (and women, presumably) from outer space,
and many websites and newsgroups have sprung up to present, discuss,
and dispute the evidence for UFOs. The best of these is Mystical Universe at
http://mysticaluniverse.com, which also covers crop circles, ancient civilizations,
paranormal phenomena, and many more mysteries and unanswered questions.
Confirmed UFO addicts will want to check out these sites too:

▶ Bufora, the British UFO Research Association, at **http://www.bufora.org.uk**

▶ UFO Magazine at **http://www.ufomag.co.uk**

▶ Alien-UK at **http://www.cwd.co.uk/alien-uk**

▶ SETI Institute at **http://www.seti-inst.edu**

Usenet, as usual, can put you in touch with other people around the world interested in the known and unknown universe. Take a look at the **sci.space** and **sci.astro** hierarchies, or drop in at **alt.sci.planetary** You'll also find an alt.paranormal hierarchy, and there's a scattering of UFO-related groups that you can track down by filtering the list with **ufo**.

Education On The Internet

Education is at an interesting stage in its online development. Although universities and colleges were among the first sites to appear on the Net, online classes are still few and far between. The technology is there: conferencing programs like NetMeeting (see page 156) can link students to classes using video and sound; course-work can be sent back and forth by email; and reference materials can be downloaded by FTP or read from the World Wide Web.

One of the few UK organisations that can provide courses over the Internet, unsurprisingly, is the Open University. Their site, at **http://www.open.ac.uk**, explains how the system works, and they'll even provide you with the software you need (you'll have to find your own computer, though!) There are details of all the available courses here, and you can apply for a place on a course by email

Schools on the Web

EduWeb (at **http://www.rmplc.co.uk**) is a site dedicated to UK schools on the Internet, with national curriculum information, a noticeboard, and a penpals page. You'll also find a list of email addresses and web page links for thousands of schools nationwide.

The tradition for universities and colleges to have a presence on the Internet hasn't abated, and you can track them all down easily from the clickable maps at **http://scitsc.wlv.ac.uk/ukinfo/uk.map.html** This page shows universities, and two links at the top of the page open similar maps for UK colleges and research establishments – click on any location and you'll be whisked straight to its web page. The links to research venues, especially, are many and varied, including museums, libraries and observatories, and make excellent resources for your own online research. The university sites have an extra value you might not think of straight away – many of them include a fund of local information such as bus and train timetables, maps, and places of interest.

For GCSE, SAT and A level students useful websites have been slow to appear, but they're here at last. Among the best is the BBC's Schools Online site at **http://www.bbc.co.uk/education/revision**, shown in the next screenshot. Along with areas for parents, and primary and secondary school children, you can choose from a range of subjects in the dropdown lists according to the grade you're studying. If you get stuck, the 'Ask a Teacher' service may be able to provide an answer.

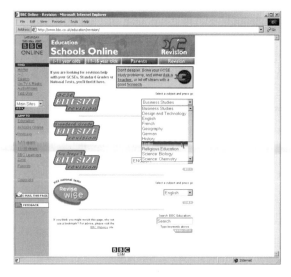

▶ The BBC's Schools Online site provides an excellent resource for students of all ages.

Here are a few more education and revision sites worth a look:

- ▶ **LineOne Reference Project** at **http://lineone.net/gcse/rev16** offers practise exams for GCSE English students and an Agony Aunt to help you through exam-related agonies.

- ▶ **GCSE Answers** at **http://www.gcse.com** covers GCSE Mathematics, English and English Literature, with downloadable revision notes and plenty of exam tips and techniques.

▶ **a-levels.co.uk** at (you guessed it) **http://www.a-levels.co.uk** has a vast collection of links for students of Biology, Maths, Chemistry, French, Psychology and other subjects, with more on their way.

▶ **Homework High** at **http://www.homeworkhigh.com** is a Channel 4 site covering English, Maths, Science, History and Geography using a question-and-answer format: search the 'library' for an answer to your question and, if it hasn't been answered, send it in to the experts.

▶ **UK Schools Resources Page** at **http://www.liv.ac.uk/~evansjon** provides ready-sorted links to best sites for humanities, sciences, arts and general reference.

▶ **UniSurf** at **http://www.unisurf.co.uk** is a site by and for university students, with links to all UK universities, financial and housing advice, and more.

Find A Job Online

We all get involved in the employment market at some time in our lives, and it's usually a frustrating, hit-and-miss ordeal. Although the Internet can't give you any firm guarantees, it can give you access to resources that your 'unwired' competitors don't have, and it puts all these right on your computer desktop to take some of the drudgery out of job-searching and self-promotion.

If you're looking for (or offering) full- or part-time work, two UK sites are head and shoulders above the rest, between them offering many thousands of vacancies. PeopleBank, at **http://www.peoplebank.com**, gives its services free to jobseekers. Just fill in the online registration form, and you can then submit your résumé or browse through the database of job vacancies. JobSearch UK (**http://www.jobsearch.co.uk**) offers a free mailing list of vacancies, and (like StepStone at **http://www.stepstone.co.uk**) allows searching by keyword or job category and submission of your CV to their database.

Where can I learn to write a résumé?

Go to **http://www.yahoo.co.uk** and run a keyword search for **résumé**. You'll see a list of Yahoo employment categories that have a Resumes subcategory (click on **Next 20** to view more of the list). Pick a link that matches the type of work you're involved in, and browse through some of the résumés written by others to pick up a few ideas.

▶ Search for job vacancies or prospective employees by keyword at JobSearch UK.

If there's a particular company you'd like to work for, it's worth visiting their website. Many companies list their job vacancies online (although it sometimes takes a bit of clicking around to find the right page), and you can usually submit an application and CV by email. If you don't know the company's web address, use your favourite search engine to search for the company name, or try **www.*company-name*.co.uk** or **www.*company-name*.com**.

Scan the professional journals

Yahoo lists 15 categories of trade and professional journals such as Science, Culture, Computers and Arts. Visit **http://uk.dir.yahoo.com/News_and_Media/Journals**, pick a suitable category and choose a journal to read online.

If you want to be even more enterprising, why not publish your résumé on the World Wide Web for all to see? If your line of work involves something that can be demonstrated on a computer, such as graphic design, journalism, or music, you could even include examples on your website. Most ISPs and online services provide free web space, and in Chapters 23 to 25 you'll learn how to go about creating and publicising your pages.

Newsgroups provide valuable methods of 'meeting' potential employers, employees, collaborators and customers. If you filter your newsgroup list with the word **job** you'll see a number of useful groups, including **alt.jobs**, **alt.jobs.overseas**, and an entire **uk.jobs** hierarchy that includes **uk.jobs.offered** and **uk.jobs.wanted**. It's well worth looking for newsgroups catering for your particular profession or vocation too: sometimes the only way to learn of a job opportunity is to be on 'speaking terms' with the type of people who can point you in the right direction.

Jobs by mail

It doesn't get much easier than having job vacancies delivered to your mailbox automatically does it? Head for **http://paml.net/subjects/employment.html** and look for a promising mailing list. Clicking the list name will give you details about subscribing to the list.

PURSUE YOUR
HOBBIES & INTERESTS

▶ **IN THIS CHAPTER**

Read leisure and specialist magazines online

Find other Internet users who share your hobbies

Where to seek advice and support on the Net

Find friendship (or even love!) in cyberspace

Follow your favourite sports, teams and players online

See the sights of the world without leaving home

However solitary a pursuit your hobby is, it probably isn't something you like to follow completely alone. Whether you like gardening, fishing, stamp collecting, or origami, part of the enjoyment is being able to talk about it with other enthusiasts, and share knowledge and skills. The Internet can help in this department, of course, but far from just being a place to air your origami anecdotes, it can teach you more about your hobby, give you advice and support on a range of issues, and help you to organise your own clubs and societies.

Read Your Favourite Magazines Online

The chances are good (and getting better all the time) that your favourite magazine has an online edition in the form of a website. If so, the URL will probably be listed somewhere in the magazine itself, but if you don't see it it's worth visiting a search engine and typing its name into a keyword search. If that doesn't work, it's a racing certainty that there's an online magazine somewhere that fits the bill, so try a search in the form **magazine** *your hobby*.

To point you in the right direction, two of the UK's biggest magazine publishers have sites containing all their magazines in online form. Head along to MAG.net (home of VNU Publications) at **http://www.vnu.co.uk**, or FutureNet (Future Publishing's site) at **http://www.futurenet.co.uk**, and fill in the registration forms to get free access to dozens of major magazines. But, in case that's not enough, here's a few more:

Magazine	Website URL
Cosmopolitan	http://www.cosmomag.com
Esquire	http://www.esquireb2b.com
Gourmet World	http://www.gourmetworld.co.uk
Hello!	http://www.hello-magazine.co.uk
Q Magazine	http://www.qonline.co.uk
Reader's Digest	http://www.readersdigest.co.uk
Empire	http://www.empireonline.co.uk
What Car?	http://www.whatcar.co.uk

Still not found the magazine you're looking for? Yahoo lists a full 44 categories of magazine at **http://uk.dir.yahoo.com/Regional/Countries/ United_Kingdom/News_and_Media/Magazines**

Pros and cons of online magazines

Online versions of magazines are usually free, but you pay a price of sorts. Often the online version will be 'published' a week or two later than the paper version, and it may not be a complete copy. In their favour, though, you can save a small fortune if you normally buy several magazines every month, and you can store interesting articles on disk rather than snipping out pages!

◀ *Cosmopolitan* online – at last Internet geeks can wear designer anoraks!

Get In Touch With Other Enthusiasts

The most obvious way to make contact with others that share your hobby is through Usenet. The **rec.** and **talk.** hierarchies cover a vast number of interests between them, but if yours isn't there, use your newsreader's filter option to find it – if a group like **alt.macdonalds.ketchup** can exist, there must be something there for you!

A better method still might be to subscribe to a related mailing list. Mailing lists greatly outnumber newsgroups, but there's no sure-fire way to find out what's available. You'll find a good selection of lists at the Publicly Accessible Mailing Lists site (**http://www.paml.net**), but a more reliable method, paradoxically, might be to join a newsgroup and find out which mailing lists the other subscribers belong to.

Share it on the Web

The majority of websites are created by personal users like you and me who want to share their interests, so why not join them? As well as being a satisfying achievement, it adds another opportunity for meeting people (as long as you give them an email link to click).

There are bound to be sites on the World Wide Web relating to your hobby, and a keyword search in your favourite search engine should find them. It's a safe bet that anyone creating a website on a particular topic is an enthusiast, so why not check the site for an email address and get in touch?

Support & Advice At Your Fingertips

The Internet is the ideal place to find advice and support groups for any issue imaginable. In some cases, the Net is the only way you could ever access these services – if they exist in the 'real world' at all, they may be based on a different continent! If you know the name of an established organisation or group, you might be able to find it on the Web using a search engine. Otherwise, use a descriptive keyword search such as **advice legal** or **support disability**. Here's a brief taste of some of the help available – as usual, you'll find links to many more sites on the accompanying CD-ROM.

▶ Law Lounge is a complete one-stop free legal advice centre that can also point you to UK solicitors and barristers, law schools, and a range of other services. Visit **http://www.lawlounge.com**

Laugh away your problems

It's not always easy to smile through adversity. Unless it's someone else's adversity, of course – then you can laugh like a drain. Visit Other People's Problems at **http://www2.paramount.com/opp/index.html**, chortle sympathetically, and offer your own advice.

▶ For consumer advice, go to **http://www.oft.gov.uk/html/consume/ consume.htm** at the Office of Fair Trading. The site is split into categories including Credit & Debt, Holiday Problems, How To Complain, and General Consumer Rights.

▶ If you're looking for some straightforward health tips, head for CyberDiet at **http://www.cyberdiet.com** Despite its name, the site covers all aspects of healthy living and provides copious tips.

◀ Let CyberDiet tell you if you've exceeded your daily cheeseburger ration.

Passively reading a web page may give you the information you need, but in some cases you'll want to draw on the experiences of others. In one recent case, after being told that nothing could be done for her child, a mother appealed for help in a support newsgroup and learned of a potentially life-saving operation in South America. There are many such newsgroups available – either filter your list with the word **support**, or take a look at the extensive **alt.support** hierarchy.

Share Your Interests With A Penpal

This is really one for the kids – after all, grown-ups have Usenet largely to themselves, don't they? There's quite a range of sites that can put you in touch with an email penpal, and you can find a good selection of them at **http://uk.dir.yahoo.com/Social_Science/Communications/Writing/ Correspondence/Pen_Pals/Children** Two of the best, though, are KeyPals at **http://www.mightymedia.com/keypals** and AusPals at **http://www.virtualaustralia.com.au/auspals** (shown in the screenshot on page 299). KeyPals has the benefit of being secure, making it a good choice for young children. It's also searchable, so once you've registered you can look for your perfect penpal based on age, location and interests.

AusPals, as you've probably guessed, was originally built for Australian kids, although there's now an OsPals area (short for 'OverSeas'). It's a lot more free and easy than KeyPals, requiring no registration and offering no protective measures, and penpal seekers are sorted into simple lists by age: 5–9 years, 10–15 years and 16–18 years. Pick someone who sounds interesting and click the email link to get in touch.

For a wider choice of penpals, and some casual online chat into the bargain, take a look at the newsgroups. By far the most popular is **soc.penpals**, but you'll also find plenty of movement going on in **alt.kids-talk.penpals** and **alt.teens.penpals**

GOOD QUESTION!

How do my kids know that their penpals really are kids?

They don't, necessarily, so a little parental involvement would be wise in the early stages. Nevertheless, it's unlikely that an adult would register an identity with a penpal site as a means of getting into contact with children, so your kids are probably safest if they initiate a contact themselves.

◀ Find penpals
from all over the
world at
AusPals/OsPals.

Try Some Real Computer Dating!

No, I'm not suggesting you should take your Pentium out to dinner. By 'real' computer dating, I mean that you can finally use your own computer to search a database of people waiting anxiously to meet you. Visit Dateline at **http://www.dateline.uk.com** and give the service a trial-run by checking off the attributes your perfect partner should possess and then searching the database.

Before you can even think of meeting anyone, however, you'll have to register with the service and part with some cash. After you've spent a little time on the Net, the idea of actually paying for a service starts to seem like an unnecessary extravagance – why not just search a little harder for a free service instead? In the dating game, unfortunately, there's very little option: although free dating services do exist, most seem to have databases of about five people, all of whom live in a different hemisphere from you.

Keep Up With Your Favourite Sport

Whatever your sport, you'll find it on the Net in abundance – team websites, sporting facts and figures, fan pages, fantasy games, and much more. The search engines are your key to finding these sites, as usual, by entering the name of your sport, team or player. Here's a mixed bag of links to get you started, and you'll find another bundle on the CD-ROM.

Sports site	Web address
Adidas Webzine	http://www.adidas.com
Athletics World Records	http://www.hkkk.fi/~niininen/athl.html
Formula 1	http://www.f1-live.com/GB
GolfWeb Europe	http://www.golfweb.com/europe
SoccerNet	http://soccernet.com
Paralympic Games	http://www.paralympic.org
Rugby Leaguer	http://www.rugbyleaguer.co.uk
Tennis	http://www.tennis.com

If you're a football fan, don't waste your time tracking down separate sites at the search engines, head straight for Planet Football at **http://www.soccercity.com** instead. Here you'll find soccer news from all over the world, links to team and fan sites, statistics, league tables, you name it! For tennis fans, the place to be is **http://www.wimbledon.org** During the Wimbledon championships this site is truly 'live', with up-to-the-minute news and scores, plus live camera views of Centre Court during play. For the rest of the year, it still promises to be one of the most comprehensive tennis sites in the UK.

For almost any sports fan, the *Sporting Life* online edition (**http://www.sporting-life.com**) is a good candidate for your Favorites menu, covering soccer, rugby, racing, golf, cricket, and more, together with the latest sports news and a messages centre. You'll also find some of the most popular sporting magazines at Future Publishing's site (see page 294).

◀ The *Sporting Life* site should be a regular port of call for all sports fans.

Track Down Your Favourite Celebrity

Everyone wants to know what their favourite film star, band or singer is up to, and you'll find at least one website devoted to every celebrity you've ever heard of (and quite a few that you haven't). Visits to some of these sites can turn up biographies, interviews, photos, movie clips, and the latest reviews and news. You can use a search engine to track down these pages by entering the celebrity's name, but it's helpful to know how your chosen engine works before you do so. If it allows you to, enclose the name in quote signs (such as **"Jennifer Aniston"**) so that you'll only see pages in which both names appear. Alternatively, prefix each name with a plus sign (**+Jennifer +Aniston**).

If all that seems a little complicated, start by visiting Yahoo. You'll find a massive list of links to movie star pages at **http://www.yahoo.co.uk/ Entertainment/Actors_and_Actresses**, and a similar list of musical artists at **http://www.yahoo.co.uk/Entertainment/Music/Artists**. Both lists are so long that they've been grouped into separate alphabetical pages: click an initial letter at the top of the page corresponding to the name of the band or the surname of the celebrity you're looking for. Most fan pages contain links to other fan pages, so when you've found your way to one you'll probably have easy access to the best sites around.

For news and chat, celebrities have a similar level of coverage in the newsgroups as they do on the Web. There are large **alt.fan** and **alt.music** hierarchies with groups dedicated to specific artists such as **alt.music.paul-simon** and **alt.fan.jen-aniston** (okay, I admit it, I'm a fan), plus more general groups like **alt.music.midi** and **alt.music.bluegrass**.

The sounds of the stars

If you're looking for interviews with the stars, visit Yahoo! Broadcast at **http://www.broadcast.com/music/interviews** armed with your Windows Media Player (see Chapter 21). There are also video chats, concerts and music channels that you can reach by removing the **/interviews** directory from the URL above.

▶ *Want to find your favourite celebrity's email address? Take a look at the sidebar on page 120 for a method that might turn up trumps.*

Take A Cyber-sightseeing Tour

One interest that most of us share is an ambition to 'see the world' – that vague term that encompasses natural and architectural wonders, famous works of art, and the ruins of ancient kingdoms. The trouble is, unless you're extremely wealthy and have no pressing engagements for the next few years, it's a difficult ambition to realise.

Fortunately, the sights that we'd happily travel for days to see are just a few clicks away on the Internet, and can usually be found with a keyword search. Many of these websites include background information too, but if you need a little more depth you might be able to find a 'travelogue' site created by someone who's actually visited that country – try a search for **travelogue** *country*. To save you a little searching time, here's a few of the sights you're probably itching to see:

Sight	Web address
Golden Gate Bridge	http://www.goldengate.org
Grand Canyon	http://www.kaibab.org
Great Barrier Reef	http://www.greatbarrierreef.com
Leaning Tower of Pisa	http://ww2.webcomp.com/virtuale/us/pisa/opera.htm
Le Louvre	http://mistral.culture.fr/louvre/louvrea.htm
Mount Rushmore	http://www.state.sd.us/tourism/parks/rushmore
Niagara Falls	http://www.niagarafallslive.com
Seven Wonders of the Ancient World	http://ce.eng.usf.edu/pharos/wonders
Yellowstone National Park	http://www.yellowstone-natl-park.com

Sightseeing Closer To Home

Of course, the United Kingdom can boast its own places of interest, and you don't have to travel for days to see them. Many now have websites that can tell you how to get there, when to visit, and what you'll have to pay to get in. Better still, you'll find enough information on some of these sites that you don't even have to set foot outside!

A good example is HMS Belfast, which you'll find on the River Thames at Tower Bridge, and on the Web at **http://www.hmsbelfast.org.uk** Along with fascinating historical information, you can take a full photographic guided tour, find out what fo'c'sle, messdeck and grog are all about, and link to live camera views of HMS Belfast and other sights of the Thames.

When you've finished kicking around the quarterdeck, how about a look at the Imperial War Museum (**http://www.iwm.org.uk**) which also incorporates Whitehall's Cabinet War Rooms and the Duxford Airfield. In fact, if you're a keen museum-goer, you'll find plenty to keep you busy on the Web. The National Museum of Science and Industry at **http://www.nmsi.ac.uk** includes the London Science Museum, The National Railway Museum at York, and Bradford's Museum of Photography, Film & Television. Want to try a few more?

Museum	Web address
Beaulieu National Motor Museum	http://www.beaulieu.co.uk/main/museum/index.asp
British Museum	http://www.thebritishmuseum.ac.uk
Dickens House Museum	http://www.rmplc.co.uk/orgs/dickens/DHM/DHM2
Natural History Museum	http://www.nhm.ac.uk
Victoria & Albert Museum	http://www.vam.ac.uk

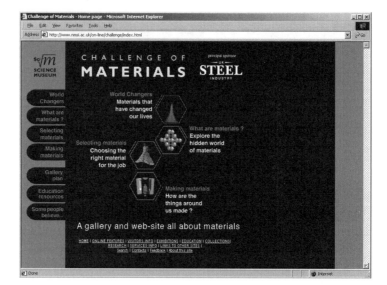

▶ One of the many online exhibitions at the London Science Museum.

So much for the great indoors. Perhaps you're more interested in the natural world. If so, an ideal starting point is Naturenet at **http://www.naturenet.net** This site gathers links to all manner of UK nature-related sites from environmental and political issues to county-by-county listings of country parks and nature reserves (many of which have websites of their own) and organisations such as The National Trust, The Woodland Trust, Plantlife and The Countryside Commission.

▶ Naturenet's comprehensive links make this ideal starting point for nature lovers.

4

THE WEB – ACTIVE & INTERACTIVE

▶ **IN THIS PART**

THE MULTIMEDIA EXPERIENCE

▶ IN THIS CHAPTER

Getting the best out of the Web's multimedia elements

Listen to music and live radio with RealAudio

View and download clips of your favourite movies

Visit animated multimedia-intense web pages

Virtual reality – fly through 3D online worlds

If you've trundled through Part Three, you've got a pretty good idea of how much you can accomplish using your Internet connection. Without a doubt, the sheer scope of its content, together with its convenience, helps to explain the Net's popularity. But that's not all of it. After all, the Net has been reasonably convenient and varied for thirty-something years. No, the main reason for this popularity surge is that it's now *fun to use* – today's World Wide Web launches an all-out assault on your senses with animation, sound and video to give you a true multimedia experience.

In this chapter, you'll learn about the different multimedia elements used on the Web, the software needed to make the most of them, and some of the unashamedly 'cool' sites you can visit to chew some of this cyber-bubblegum. But first, a more pressing question…

Do I Need A Better Computer For Multimedia?

Multimedia is a sort of ex-buzzword. A few years ago, the 'multimedia computer' was the all-singing, all-dancing machine that had all the trimmings and cost a lot more than everything else in the shop. Today every computer has a soundcard, a CD-ROM or DVD-ROM drive, and a high-quality graphics card, which are the essentials of multimedia. In fact, if you bought your computer any time in the last three years or so, its hardware can certainly handle whatever the Web throws at it. But here's a quick hardware rundown for *good* multimedia:

▶ If your graphics card has 8Mb or more memory fitted, letting you set your monitor to a fairly high resolution and the High Colour (16-bit) setting, visual elements like images, videos and 3D objects will be clearer, smoother and generally more appealing.

▶ Some of the larger virtual reality models and worlds can take their toll on both processor and memory. A good graphics card with 3D support will help a lot, and, of course, there's no such thing as too much RAM!

▶ The modem matters most. If you connect at less than 56Kbps you'll just find the whole experience frustratingly slow. Movies and virtual reality objects, in particular, can be huge files, so use the fastest method of connecting to the Net you have available when you're on a multimedia hunt.

Do I Need A Lot Of Extra Software?

There are literally hundreds of plug-ins and viewers out there for different types of multimedia file, and you certainly don't want them all! Some, of course, cover the same types of file as others and you can simply choose the one you like best. Others are proprietary programs that let you view a type of file created by one particular company – if this format isn't in wide use on the Web you might prefer not to bother installing the software for it.

GOOD QUESTION!

What's the difference between a plug-in and a viewer?

A plug-in is a program that displays a file in your browser's own window by adding capabilities to your browser that it doesn't have already. A viewer is an entirely separate program that opens its own window to display or play a file you've downloaded.

Let me make two suggestions to simplify things. First, start with the software I've included on the free CD-ROM that accompanies this book – not only are these some of the best programs of their kind, but you don't have to download them either! Second, go and buy an uninstall utility such as Quarterdeck's CleanSweep: these utilities monitor every change and addition made to your system when a new program is installed so that you can remove all trace of it later if you decide you don't like it.

Finally, if you're using Windows Me, Windows 98 SE, Windows 2000 or Internet Explorer 5.5 (included on the free CD in the back of this book) you may not need any new software at all. A much-improved Windows Media Player is included with each of these, capable of handling most of the popular multimedia formats in use on the Net. You can download the latest version of the Media Player from **http://www.microsoft.com/windows/windowsmedia**

RealAudio – The Sound Of Cyberspace

You won't travel far on the Web before arriving at a site that uses RealAudio for music, speech, or a mixture of the two. RealAudio is a streaming format that plays as the file is being transferred, with none of that tedious waiting around for the sound file to download first. As soon as you click a RealAudio link, your RealAudio Player or Windows Media Player opens (as in the next screenshot), grabs the first few seconds of the transmission to help it to stay one jump ahead and ensure smooth playback, and then starts to play. You can pause or stop playback by clicking the appropriate buttons, or (if you were playing a single short sound-clip), replay the entire clip which will now be residing in Internet Explorer's cache folder (see page 70). If you're using Windows 98 or you've installed Internet Explorer from the CD-ROM you

 don't need to do anything more – RealAudio support is built in. If you're using a different browser, you'll have to visit **http://www.real.com** to download and install the player software.

▶ A live RealAudio broadcast from Virgin Radio.

So, where do you have to go to get some RealAudio action? As with all multimedia plug-ins and viewers, your first stop should be the website of the people who wrote the program – you'll always find plenty of samples and links to let you play with your new toy once you've installed it. In this case, then, skip off to **http://www.real.com**

▶ Why not tune in to Virgin Radio at **http://www.virginradio.co.uk** to hear the wireless come down the wires?

▶ Want to hear the latest pop music releases? Visit London's Capital FM at **http://www.capitalfm.com,** click the **New Releases** link and click the **Listen** button beside the song you'd like to hear. Better still, click on **Charts** and you'll be able to hear clips from the Top 40 singles chart or the Top 20 albums.

▶ Visit The UK Tuner at **http://urn.su.nottingham.ac.uk/tuner** for a useful directory of RealAudio and RealVideo radio and TV stations in the UK.

Surfing sounds

Internet Explorer 5 has a built-in Radio Stations toolbar that you can switch on from **View** I **Toolbars** I **Radio**. Click the **Radio Stations** button to add stations from the Station Guide and select a station to listen to, then click the **Play** button for some musical accompaniment while you surf.

Replace Your CDs With MP3s

Well, maybe not. The MP3 format is a new innovation that claims to pack near-CD-quality music into comparatively small files (a typical song weighs in at between 1 and 2Mb). Whether the quality is *near enough* to a CD to be listenable for long periods is a matter of taste, but these files have been the 'big thing' on the Net for the last couple of years and hundreds of websites have sprung up offering free MP3 copies of chart hits and albums. Just as quickly, dozens of MP3 players have appeared (both the hardware and software varieties), some of which are able to create MP3 files from CD tracks, known as 'ripping'. One of the most popular MP3 players is Winamp from **http://www.winamp.com**, which can also play CDs and other audio formats. Both the RealPlayer and Windows Media Player also have MP3 playback capability.

Another aspect of MP3 is that of copyright infringement. There's been a lot of anxiety among record companies who've seen whole CDs uploaded to the Web in MP3 format for anyone to download, and they've issued a lot of writs against a lot of sites. The result now is that you're not likely to find files by artists you've actually heard of just yet (at least, not legal files), but you *will* find plenty of free music by new artists who've unexpectedly got the field to themselves for a while and are making the most of it! Here are a few places to look:

▶ The popular and hugely stylish Winamp MP3 player.

▶ Visit **http://www.mp3now.com** for the best 'MP3-everything guide' around.

▶ MP3 Sound, at **http://www.mp3sound.com**, carries the chart Top 10 from several countries, several MP3 archives, and even some legal MP3s!

▶MP3.com has reams of information about the MP3 format, software, hardware and files, all at **http://www.mp3.com**

More Music With MIDI

MIDI is a different type of sound format from RealAudio and .wav files. Instead of being a recording of sounds, a MIDI file uses the sounds already built into your soundcard and just contains enough information to tell your soundcard what notes to play and when, making them much smaller by comparison. A MIDI file will usually have the extension **.mid** (although you might occasionally see the **.rmi** extension used).

The best plug-in for MIDI files is Crescendo from **http://www.liveupdate.com**, which comes in two flavours. The free plug-in will play the MIDI file when it's finished downloading. Crescendo Max, which can be yours for a few dollars, will begin to stream playback almost as soon as you click the link to the MIDI file, just as the RealAudio player does with its own brand of audio.

There are two shortcomings to playback of MIDI. First, the Crescendo console may replace the page you were viewing, so you'll need to hit the Back button after listening to the file. Second, the file repeats endlessly, so if you chose to open a second browser window and continue surfing with a musical backing, it would soon drive you up the wall! Fortunately, many MIDI sites embed a Crescendo console into their pages to prevent this happening. (Your other option is to right-click the link to the MIDI file, choose **Save As…** and play the file later using Windows' own Media Player.)

Duly armed with your Crescendo plug-in, here's a few sites worth a visit:

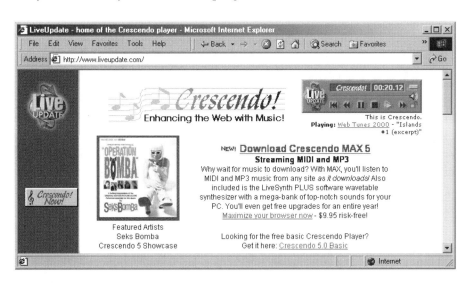

◀ The Crescendo console playing a MIDI file.

▶ The makers of Crescendo, Live Update, list some of the best MIDI pages at **http://www.liveupdate.com/streamsites.html**

▶ Check out the MIDI Farm at **http://www.midifarm.com** for MIDI files, the best MIDI links, and yet more plug-ins.

The good, the bad and the ugly

Anyone with an ounce of musical talent and a MIDI sequencing program can create a MIDI file. The trouble is, many do, and an ounce isn't really enough. You'll find that some MIDI files sound superb while others sound as if a five-year-old just sat on a piano.

If you don't have a good wavetable soundcard, don't despair! You can still sample the delights of crystal clear MIDI sound on the Web using a sort of software soundcard. Head off to **http://www.edirol.com** to download Roland's Virtual SoundCanvas, or **http://www.yamaha.co.uk** for Yamaha's MidPlug. Sadly you'll have to register and pay up if you want to make full use of these, though. And talking of paying for stuff, if you want to learn more about MIDI as a method of making music, check out my book, *The MIDI Files*, also published by Prentice Hall.

It's Movie Time... Soon!

First things first. Video files are big! A one-minute movie will be roughly 2.5 megabytes, and in some cases you'll have to wait for the whole thing to download before you can watch it. With a 56Kbps modem, that means ten minutes' boredom for your one minute of entertainment. All the same, as with most multimedia elements, it pays to have the software installed just in case you come across something that really seems worth the wait!

The three most common types of movie file on the Web are MPEG (which will have **.mpeg**, **.mpg** or **.mpe** extensions), QuickTime (**.mov** or **.qt**), and Video For Windows (**.avi**). If you've installed Internet Explorer 5 (or you're using Windows 98 SE, Windows Me or Windows 2000) you should already have the enhanced Media Player which can usually play each of these types. For all its capabilities, though, it doesn't always handle MPEG videos correctly and it isn't completely compatible with QuickTime. Here are two other programs well worth adding to your collection:

- ▶ **QuickTime Player**. There are various types of QuickTime file, including audio and Virtual Reality, and this program was built to handle them all. Grab it from **http://www.apple.com/quicktime**

- ▶ **Net Toob**. An all-purpose plug-in that handles just about every video and audio file you'll come across. It can also stream some types of MPEG movie to prevent that agonizing wait. You can install Net Toob straight from the CD-ROM and visit its website at **http://www.nettoob.com** to register your copy.

Ready to watch some videos? To make the most of your QuickTime Player, head for **http://www.apple.com/quicktime/hotpicks** where you'll find links to movies, music and QuickTime virtual reality. Or visit QuickTime TV at **http://www.apple.com/quicktime/qtv** and pick a channel. The MPEG format is used mostly for animations nowadays, and you can find a great collection at **http://wwwzenger.informatik.tu-muenchen.de/persons/paula/mpeg**.

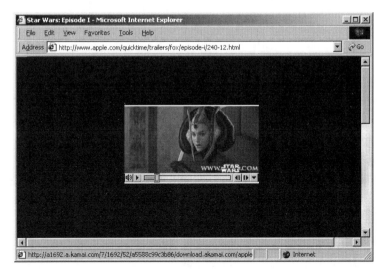

◀ Saturday Night at the Movies (but I started downloading on Tuesday).

The Hot Topic – Cool Animation

The word 'animation' doesn't sound cool – it probably reminds you of Bugs Bunny – but it's a major multimedia craze on the Internet. Where images and text have always been fixed on the page, they can now move around and react to the mouse passing over them. Part of this popularity lies in the fact that animations are easier for the average user to create than videos, and they take no more time to download than an image.

It gets better! The two hottest types of animation are Macromedia's ShockWave and Flash, both of which you can view in Internet Explorer without adding anything else to your software mountain. If you're not using Explorer, though, you'll have to head off to **http://www. macromedia.com** to download the necessary plug-ins.

How can I add these animations to my own web pages?

Flash animations are reasonably simple to create using Macromedia's Flash software. You can download a trial version from **http://www.macromedia.com**, but be prepared to spend some serious money if you decide to continue using it!

The list of good animation sites is almost endless – you'll keep bumping into them wherever you go on the Web. Unless, of course, you're actually looking for one: that's how the world works, isn't it? So here's a few to let you see what all the fuss is about:

▶ Visit Macromedia's Flash Gallery at **http://www.shockwave.com/shockzone/edge/flash** for links to some of the Flash-iest sites on the Web.

▶ Choose from several dozen Shockwave games at **http://onlinemediagroup.com/goldrake/shock.shtml**, and more still at **http://clevermedia.com/arcade**

▶ Visit H. Smackett's Claustrophobic Universe at **http://www.o-matic.com/happy** for a bit of (sometimes slightly weird) interactivity.

▶ For a bit of overkill in the Flash department, visit Spooky and the Bandit at **http://www.spookyandthebandit.com**

◀ The Spooky and the Bandit page – if it holds still, click it!

Explore Virtual 3D Worlds

Virtual reality is something that's either going to grab you immediately and not let go, or leave you wondering why anyone would bother. Using on-screen controls (often combined with right mouse-button menus), you can select angles from which to view the scene, walk or fly through it, zoom in and out, and interact with objects you find. True VRML files have the extension .wrl (although they're often accompanied by a collection of GIF images that form various elements of the world), and you'll need to install a plug-in before you can start exploring.

JARGON BUSTER

VRML

An abbreviation of Virtual Reality Modelling Language, the programming language used to build these graphical 'worlds'. The original version of the language was 1.0; the latest version, 2.0, adds new features such as the ability to pick up and move virtual objects.

In fact, there are many companies also producing proprietary plug-ins for their own brands of 3D world, but I suggest you pause awhile and see if

Virtual reality is your cup of tea. Most plug-ins are pretty big programs, and the worlds themselves can be slow to download and slow-moving once you start to explore – you'll definitely benefit from a fast Internet connection and a fast processor! That being said, VRML is a whole new experience you've got to try at least once, so grab one of these **.wrl** plug-ins:

▶ **Superscape Viscape** from **http://www.superscape.com/ services** You'll find a world full of more virtual worlds hosted by Superscape at **http://vwww.com**

▶ **Contact** by Blaxxun at **http://www.blaxxun.com**, where you'll find links to several virtual worlds.

▶ **Microsoft VRML 2.0 Viewer** is built into Internet Explorer 5 (included on the free CD-ROM in the back of this book), so for many VR sites you may not need to install any extra software.

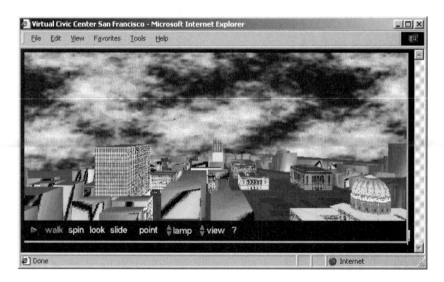

▶ A virtual flight through San Fransciso.

If you've followed the links from these sites and you still need more, visit Planet 9 at **http://www.planet9.com** to cruise through virtual American cities, or **http://nowtv.com/vrml/index.htm** to play 3-dimensional online games with other visitors to the site. If you fancy something that loads a little quicker, Protozoa's weird collection of 3D interactive creatures at **http://www.protozoa.com/vrml_scenes** fits the bill nicely, downloading in not much more than 30 seconds.

Where can I find other plug-ins?

You'll find the best selection at Tucows, a great site for Internet-related software. Head for **http://tucows.mirror.ac.uk/window95.html** and click the Streaming Applications link in the Browsers & Accessories section.

ROBOTS, CAMERAS &
OTHER ODDITIES

▶ **IN THIS CHAPTER**

Watch live camera feeds from all over the world

Command Internet linked robots by remote control

Bizarre, pointless, but amusing, interactive websites

Say hello to JavaScript, Java and ActiveX programs

People are weird – and if you need proof of that, the Web is the perfect place to look. After all, it's built by people, and very few constraints are placed upon them. At one end of the weirdness spectrum is the page that says *Hi. My name's Nigel. I like Cluedo. Here's a picture of my ca*t. You'll find a lot of pages built by people who have nothing of interest to offer, but feel the need to demonstrate that in public. (Okay, psychologists, perhaps that's interesting in itself?)

This chapter, fortunately, focuses on the other end of the Weirdometer – people who are brimming over with unusual ideas, and put vast amounts of time, effort, and even money into getting them on to the Web for the rest of us to share. These sites may be as absurd, pointless and unnecessary as anything created by Nigel and his cat, but it's this special brand of unabashed, entertaining weirdness that makes the Web the unique place it's become.

Catch The Action With Live Cam

I still find this one hard to believe. People who probably seem outwardly quite sane spend their hard-earned money on a special type of camera, rig it up to the Web via some complicated programming and a (usually) permanent Internet connection, and then point it at a street corner, or their desk, or a fish-bowl…

But what's really hard to believe is the reaction of someone visiting those sites, and I'm as guilty of this as anyone else. Try it, and you'll see what I mean. Point your browser at Edinburgh's Cyberia (**http://www.cybersurf.co.uk/spy**), and refresh the image every few seconds. You'll see vehicles passing, people moving in and out of shot… and it's entertaining! The longer you have to wait for something to actually move, the more rewarding it is when it happens.

Push or pull?

Some live-cam sites use something called 'server push' to *push* an updated camera view down the wires to your computer automatically *every few seconds or minutes*. At many sites, though, you'll have to *pull* instead – in other words, to view a newer picture, click Internet Explorer's **Refresh** button or press **F5**.

Okay, maybe I'm just too weird, but I can't be alone – there are thousands of web cameras running all over the world, and they can't all be there just for my amusement! Here's a taste of a few more:

▶ Visit **http://www.nj.com/dinercam/live.html** to see the New Jersey Diner Cam, the New York City Skyline Cam and the Shore Cam.

▶ Try the interactive webcam at Pacific Bell Park, home of the San Francisco Giants at **http://216.33.70.166/ignite/pacbell/camera.jsp** You might even catch a game!

▶ Take a look inside Jason's office at **http://george.lbl.gov/cgi-bin/jason/cave-cam**

▶ Visit the Almost Amazing Turtlecam at **http://www.campusware.com/turtles**

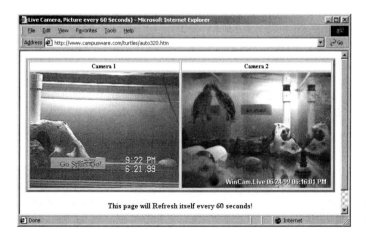

◀ The mesmerising TurtleCam.

Robots In Cyberspace

Venturing even deeper into Weirdsville, you'll find robots hooked up to the World Wide Web too. Some have cameras trained on them so that you can see what they're doing; others are actually mobile, with cameras attached to act as 'eyes'. The technology involved here is pretty staggering, so there are relatively few robot sites on the Web, and you might have to wait some time before you can take a turn controlling a robot yourself. At most sites you'll be assigned control for only a few minutes – make sure you read the instructions while you're waiting so that you'll know how the controls work when your turn comes around.

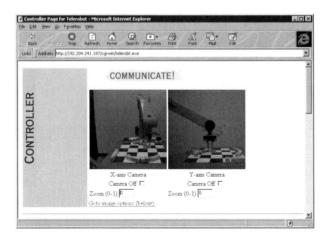

▶ Tell Telerobot where to put its building blocks.

A great place to start is Telerobot at **http://192.204.241.187/cgi-win/ telerobt.exe**, where your task is to arrange building blocks into satisfying shapes. Not only are the controls easy to understand, but the images are unusually clear and in colour. Another enjoyable robot is Xavier (**http://www.cs.cmu.edu/People/Xavier**) who roams through an office building according to your commands. Xavier's a popular guy, though, and he keeps US business hours, so he can be a little hard to reach.

For a more calming use of cyber-robotics, visit the Telegarden at **http://telegarden.aec.at/index.html** By clicking **Guest Entrance** (followed by **Enter Garden** on the next page), you can watch this horticultural robot at work. Alternatively, if you register as a member, you can water the garden and plant seeds by remote control, and leave messages online for other members.

And There's More...

Perhaps there are exceptions to the 'weirdness rule' – after all, there are many web authors out there selflessly providing a much-needed service from a sense of civic duty. Keep these URLs handy; you never know when you'll need them next:

▶ Visit the Net-connected house – doorbell, fridge, dustbin, toilet and more – at **http://www.icepick.com**

▶ Any news from Paul's refrigerator? Find out at **http://hamjudo.com/cgi-bin/refrigerator**

▶ I suppose all the laundry machines at **http://spleen.mit.edu/ LAUNDRY/laundry_java.html** are still busy?

If you're in the mood to send a few messages, and you're tired of email, try these instead. Visit **http://www.yikes.com/printer**, type a message to Eric, and it'll be printed out on his trusty ImageWriter printer. Or will it? For a more immediate result, send a message to the folk who work at a company called Geocast. Head for **http://www.weissman.org/sign** and type a short message into the box. The message will appear on the wall above their heads, and by clicking the link beside the textbox you can see it happening via a live cam link. (Click on **Refresh**, or press **F5**, every few seconds to continually update the image.)

Got a minute? Write an opera!

Visit **http://brainop.media.mit.edu** and take part in an interactive opera by playing graphical portrayals of real instruments. There are many instruments to choose from, and plenty of weird and wonderful places to explore on this site.

Try Some Interactive Graphics

While some people rush around connecting cameras, robots and hot tubs to the Internet, others take a far more relaxed, sophisticated approach to the whole thing. They sit down quietly to build into their web pages the type of challenging, constructive programs that people really want. Programs like…

…the Mr Showbiz Plastic Surgery Lab! You'll find this indispensable resource at **http://mrshowbiz.go.com/features/phantommenace/lab.html** Pick a set of celebrities to work with, choose features to combine from each, and then click the button to carry out the 'operation'. One of Mr Showbiz's previous clients is shown in the next screenshot.

Food is one of the few things that doesn't travel well on the Internet. Modern telephone lines are too narrow even for spaghetti. Curiously, though, pizza is an exception to the rule – you can find out for yourself by

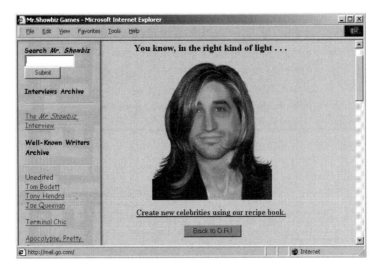

▶ Jennifer Aniston (and a few of her Friends) after plastic surgery.

visiting the Pizza Server at **http://www2.ecst.csuchico.edu/~pizza** Click on **Order and view a pizza over the Web**, halfway down the page, and then choose your toppings (salami, red pepper and golfball is particularly good). Finally, click the button to place your order – you'll see it displayed on the next page. Although you can download the result, it'll be in the rather chewy GIF format.

Simple fun...

Here's a neat (if slightly tasteless) Shockwave game to try. Visit Shoot The Singer at **http://www.joecartoon.com/reddot/singer.html** and, um, shoot the singer. No one said it was difficult.

For more artistic interactivity, check out The Fractory at **http://tqd.advanced.org/3288/myo.html** By choosing zoom ratios and colour palettes, and clicking on various points of an image, you can create and explore the infinite variations of fractal art. And if you produce a result that's too good to leave behind, fill in the form to send it to any email address.

Visit Web Pages That Talk Back!

Some of the weirdest stuff on the Net – the pages that make you ask *Why bother?* – are also the simplest. None will keep you entertained for hours at a stretch, but you'll get a few minutes' amusement from each of them. Here's about 20 minutes' worth to get you started:

▶ The Random Recipe Generator at **http://bobo.link.cs.cmu.edu/cgi-bin/dougb/recipe** This produces daft recipes such as '51-Minute Water' (which has a list of ingredients as long as your arm). Click on **Refresh**, or press **F5**, to see another one.

▶ Kevin's Fridge Magnets at **http://www.savetz.com/fridge/fridge.cgl** (shown in the next screenshot). Click the link to put your own message on the page, and you'll be returned to this main page to see it displayed. The next visitor to the page will see it too, and it will be added to the list of previous messages further down the page.

▶ The Surrealist Compliment Generator at **http://www.madsci.org/cgi-bin/cgiwrap/~lynn/jardin/SCG** does just what it says: you'll receive a random compliment such as *Your mother once had eyes that shone like the legs of Mae West*. If that made your heart skip a beat, click **Refresh** or press **F5** for another.

▶ As an antidote to all those compliments, your next port of call should be the Abuse-A-Tron at **http://www.upstart.xe.com/abuse** You might like to scribble these down for use in casual conversation; there's no arguing with *You chase cars and bark at them, you hairy, pustule licking, lewd harbinger of an itinerant somnambulist*.

◀ Add your own heading to Kevin's 'fridge' for all to see.

Where can I find more of this weird stuff?

Try Pretty Strange at **http://www.zdnet.com/yil/filter/strange**, or Weird, Bizzare, Funny & Engrossing at **http://now2000.com/weird/index.shtml**

Meet The Multilingual Web

After visiting some of the sites I've mentioned in this chapter, you might have realised that there's something funny going on – web pages aren't supposed to do this! A web page is just plain text with a few extra little codes added to set colours, fonts, and layouts, insert pictures, and other simple stuff. (More about that in the coming chapters.) Surely there's more happening here than just plain text? After all, nothing like this ever happens in Notepad!

This is yet another example of how much the World Wide Web has changed in the last couple of years: there are now several different languages that can be used to write programs that will run on (or from) a web page – any program that you can run on your computer's own operating system can now be inserted into a page. Sounds dead useful, doesn't it? And it is, except that the main use of these languages to date has been in the creation of Web-based entertainments and page-enhancements. True usefulness probably won't appear widely for another year or two. I'm not going to try to teach you how to use these languages, but here's a brief introduction to the ones that are used the most.

▶ **JavaScript**. The simplest of the four to learn and use, constructed specifically for use on the Web. This is a *scripting* language – it's written in plain text (although it looks very technical), and slots straight into the page with no extra files needed. This way, the script can run as soon as the page arrives at your browser, making it an ideal language for flashy effects (one of its main uses). To see some JavaScript pages in action, head for **http://javascript.internet.com/toc.html** and follow the links you find there.

▶ **Dynamic HTML** and **CSS**. CSS is short for Cascading Style Sheets, an extension to the Web's own HTML language that gives website designers a bit more control over how their pages are displayed. Combining HTML with JavaScript and adding a dash of CSS gives 'Dynamic HTML' (or DHTML) – a web page in which items can move or react to the user. To see some Dynamic HTML pages, go to **http://www.dynamicdrive.com** and follow categories and links that take your fancy.

▶ **Java**. This is related to JavaScript, but Java programs can run on any computer and aren't restricted to the Web. Java can be used to write full-blown applications such as word processors and databases, though its main use is still in creating interesting ornaments for web pages, which are referred to as **applets**. Java programs have to download to your computer before they can run, which they do automatically when you arrive at the page. The program files have the extension **.class**. Look at some of the applets created by Sun, the designers of Java, at **http://www.javasoft.com/applets**, or check out one of my own sites at **http://www.coolfocus.com**

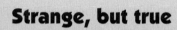

Strange, but true

Java? Strange name. The basics of this programming language were thrashed out during many long sessions in a coffee house in Silicon Valley, so the language was christened with the American slang for coffee.

▶ **ActiveX**. This is a Microsoft language known, until recently, as OLE. ActiveX programs are known as **controls**, and are normally downloaded to your system when you visit pages that contain them. Once there, they remain in place so that any other pages you visit containing the same control can be viewed instantly without waiting for the same components to be installed again. To see some of these controls in action, visit The ActiveX Gallery at **http://awdsites.com/x_amples**

YOUR OWN WEBSITE – THE BASICS

▶ **IN THIS CHAPTER**

The web page language – it's all tags

Helpful software you can use (if you really want to)

A simple web page: title, heading and paragraphs

Formatting text with bold and italic type

Inserting links to other pages and websites

Up to this point in the book, you've learnt how to use just about every area of the Internet – the major (and not-so-major) services, the search engines, plug-ins and multimedia, interactive pages, shopping, the whole shebang – but it's still everyone else's Internet you're using! Sooner or later you'll want to grab a little corner of it and make it your own.

 The mechanics of creating a website are simple enough, and over the next three chapters I'll show you how to do it. Of course, whole books have been written on this subject so this isn't an exhaustive reference, but you'll find many more examples, tips, and links to more information on the CD-ROM, plus a HTML quick-reference glossary in Appendix E. For best results, treat these chapters as a tutorial – work through them and experiment with the examples yourself, and in a few days this will all seem very simple stuff!

HTML – The Language Of The Web

Pages on the World Wide Web are written in a language called HTML (HyperText Markup Language). So what's that all about? Well, we've met hypertext already – those underlined, clickable links that make the Web so easy to navigate. A *markup language* is a set of codes or signs added to plain text to indicate how it should be presented to the reader, noting bold or italic text, typefaces to be used, paragraph breaks, and so on. When you type any document into your word processor, it adds these codes for you, but tactfully hides them from view: if you wanted bold text, for example, it *shows* you bold text instead of those codes. In HTML, however, you have to type in the codes yourself along with the text, and your browser puts the whole lot together before displaying it.

These codes are known as **tags**, and they consist of ordinary text placed between less-than and greater-than signs. Let's take an example:

```
<B>Welcome to my homepage.</B> Glad you could make it!
```

The first tag, <B>, means 'turn on bold type'. Halfway through the line, the same tag is used again, but with a forward-slash inserted straight after the less-than sign: this means 'turn off bold type'. If you displayed a page containing this line in your browser, it would look like this:

Welcome to my homepage. Glad you could make it!

Of course, there's more to a web page than bold text, so clearly there must be many more of these tags. But don't let that worry you – you don't have to learn all of them! There's a small bundle that you'll use a lot, and you'll get to know those very quickly. Others will begin to sink in once you've used them a few times, but until they do, just turn to page 407 to look them up!

Do I Need Special Software?

Believe it or not, creating a website is something you can do for free (once you've bought a computer that is). Because HTML is entirely text-based, you can write your pages in Windows' Notepad, and throughout these chapters I'm going to assume that's what you're doing. Indeed you can use any other word processor you want to, but you'll have to remember to save your files as plain text when you've finished. But there are other options, so let's quickly run through them.

WYSIWYG

JARGON BUSTER

A delightful acronym (pronounced 'wizzywig') for 'What you see is what you get'. This is used to describe many different types of software that can show you on the screen exactly what something will look like when you print it on paper or view it in your web browser.

WYSIWYG Editors

In theory, WYSIWYG editors are the perfect way of working: instead of looking at plain text with HTML tags dotted around it, you see your web page itself gradually taking shape, with images, colours and formatting displayed. There are a couple of drawbacks, though. First, WYSIWYG editors cost serious money compared to most other types of Internet software. Second, they probably won't help you avoid learning something about HTML. Once in a while the editor won't do what you want it to do, and you'll have to switch to its text-editing mode to juggle the tags yourself. More often, you'll see something clever on someone else's page and want to find out how it was done: if you don't understand the language, you might remain envious forever!

How do I see how someone else's page was put together?

In Internet Explorer, either click on the **View** menu and choose **Source**, or right-click on the page and choose **View Source**. Notepad will open the HTML code for that page.

My early experience with HTML was that it's far easier to learn the language itself than it is to learn how the WYSIWYG software works, but if you'd like to give the WYSIWYG method a shot, here are three of the most popular:

▶ **Microsoft FrontPage**. You can find out more about this at **http://www.microsoft.com/frontpage**, but you'll have to take trip into town to buy a copy. FrontPage is also included with Microsoft Office 2000 Premium edition.

▶ **Microsoft FrontPage Express**. A cut-down version of FrontPage included with Windows 98 and Internet Explorer 5.0 (which you'll find on the CD-ROM that accompanies this book).

▶ **NetObjects Fusion**. A stylish program with a huge number of high-quality page templates, available from **http://www.netobjects.com**

Markup Editors

Using a markup editor is rather like using Notepad – you see all the HTML code on the page in front of you. But instead of having to type in tags yourself, a markup editor will insert them for you at the click of a button or the press of a hotkey, in the same way that you use your word processor. You might still choose to type in some of the simple tags yourself, such as the tag for bold text mentioned earlier, but for more complicated elements such as a table with a lot of cells, this automation is a great time and sanity saver.

Markup editors are also ideal for newcomers to HTML. If you don't know one tag from another, just click the appropriate buttons on the toolbar to insert them: once you've seen them appear on the page a few times, you'll soon start to remember what's what!

Here are three of the most popular and feature-packed markup editors. You'll need to register these if you want to use them beyond the trial period, but I wholeheartedly recommend picking one of these to start you off:

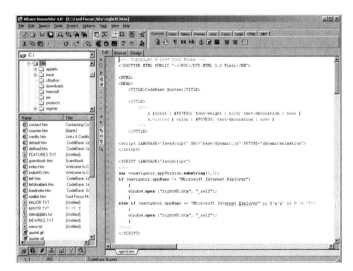

◀ Colour-coding and one-click tag insertion in HomeSite.

▶ **HomeSite** from **http://www.allaire.com**

▶ **HTMLed** from **http://www.ist.ca**

▶ **HoTMetaL Pro** from **http://www.sq.com**

Text Converters

Some modern word processors like Lotus WordPro and Microsoft Word have begun to include features to turn your documents into web pages. At their simplest, they'll let you create an ordinary word processed document and then choose a **Save as Web Page** option from the **File** menu to convert it into a web page. The result won't be as effective as other pages on the

Web, but it's an ideal way to convert a long document when the only other option is to add all the tags yourself!

You can also create web pages from scratch in these programs. For example, Microsoft Word has its own Web Page Wizard that can set you up with a ready-to-edit template like the one shown in the next screenshot. To start it up, go to **File | New...**, then click the **Web Pages** tab and double-click **Web Page Wizard**. You can add and delete elements on the page, and use the standard drawing and editing toolbars to slot in anything else you need.

Using Office on the Web

If you use Microsoft Office, the web authoring features don't stop at Word. Excel allows you to save a worksheet in HTML format, and PowerPoint helps you create multimedia pages by converting slides to web format. You'll also find a media library of pictures, sounds and animations that you can include in your pages, however you choose to create them.

▶ Creating a web page from a Microsoft Word template.

Let's Get Started

There are a few bits and pieces that will appear in almost every HTML document you write, so let's start by making a template file you can use every time you want to create a new page. Start Notepad, and type the text below (without worrying about the exact number of spaces or carriage returns). Save this file using any name you like, but make sure you give it the extension **.htm** or **.html**. Every web page you write must be saved with one of these extensions – it doesn't matter which you choose, but you'll find life a lot easier if you stick to the same one each time!

```
<!DOCTYPE HTML PUBLIC "-//W3C//DTD HTML 4.0//EN">

<HTML>

<HEAD>

                <TITLE>Untitled</TITLE>

</HEAD>

<BODY>


</BODY>

</HTML>
```

None of those tags does anything exciting by itself, but it's worth knowing what they're for. The first line is a piece of technical nonsense that tells a browser that the document is written in the latest version of the HTML language. The rest of the document is placed between the <HTML> and </HTML> tags, and falls into two separate chunks: the head (the section between <HEAD> and </HEAD>) and the body (between <BODY> and </BODY>).

The document's head is pretty dull: all it contains is the title of the document, inserted between the <TITLE> and </TITLE> tags. There are other bits and pieces that can be slotted in here, and you'll meet some of those in Chapter 25, but the title is the only element that must be there.

337

Do I have to type these tags in capitals?

No, browsers don't care about the case of the tags. If you prefer `<title>`, or `<Title>`, or even `<tItLe>`, it's all the same to your browser. But typing tags in capitals makes them stand out from the rest of your text, which can be useful at times.

The body section is the one that matters. Between these two tags you'll type all the text that should appear on your page, and put in the tags you need to display images, set colours, insert hyperlinks to other pages and sites, and anything else you want your page to contain.

Now that you've created a basic template, let's start adding to it to build up a respectable-looking page. Make a copy of the file (so that you keep this template unchanged for creating more web pages later) and open the copy in Notepad or your HTML editor.

Add A Title & Text

The first thing to do is to replace the word **Untitled** with a sensible title for the document, such as **Links To The Best Multimedia Sites** or **My EastEnders HomePage**. Pick something that describes what the page will be about, but keep it fairly short: the text between the `<TITLE>` and `</TITLE>` tags will appear in the title-bar at the very top of most browsers, and if your entry is too long to fit, it'll just get chopped off!

Choose your title carefully

The title is more important than it might seem. First, some search engines will list the title of your page (see Chapter 25). Second, if someone likes your page enough to add it to their Favorites or Bookmarks list, this is the title they'll see in the list when they open it.

Now we'll add some text to the page. Either type the same as I've entered below, or replace my first and second paragraph entries with whole paragraphs if you prefer. When you've done that, save the file as **links.htm** or **links.html**, but don't close Notepad yet.

```
<!DOCTYPE HTML PUBLIC "-//W3C//DTD HTML 4.0//EN">

<HTML>

<HEAD>

<TITLE>Links To The Best Multimedia Sites</TITLE>

</HEAD>

<BODY>
<H1>Welcome To My Homepage!</H1>
Here's the first paragraph.
<P>And here's the second paragraph.

</BODY>

</HTML>
```

Now take a look at your masterpiece in your browser. There are several ways you can do this: find the file you just saved and double-click it, or open your browser and type the path to the file in the address bar, or choose **File** | **Open** in your browser and click on **Browse**. When your browser displays it, it should look just like the next screenshot.

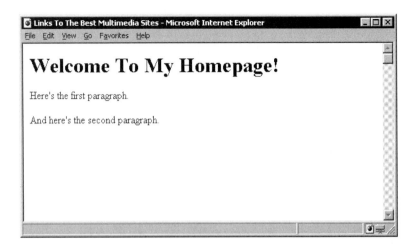

So what are those new tags all about? Let's take the `<P>` tag first. This tells your browser to present the following text as a new paragraph, which automatically inserts a blank line before it. And this raises an important point about HTML: you can't insert blank lines just by pressing Enter or Return. Although you can see blank lines in Notepad when you do that, your browser will just ignore them, which is why you need to start a new paragraph by entering `<P>`. (Notice that you don't have to put in a closing `</P>` at the end of a paragraph – the act of starting a new paragraph isn't an ongoing effect that has to be turned off again.)

How do I start a new line without starting a new paragraph?

Another tag, `<BR>`, will give you a 'line break'. In other words, the text that follows that tag will start at the beginning of the next line with no empty line inserted before it.

The other pair of tags that cropped up was `<H1>` and `</H1>` which format a line of text as a heading. You can choose from six sizes: H1 is the largest, followed by `<H2>` and `</H2>` down to the smallest, `<H6>` and `</H6>`. In one nifty little manoeuvre, these tags change the size of the text you place between them and make it bold. They also automatically start a new paragraph for the heading (so you don't need to place a `<P>` tag at the start of the line) and start a new paragraph for whatever follows the heading. Try changing the size of the heading by altering those tags to see the different effects, re-saving the file, and clicking your browser's **Refresh** button to update it.

Be Bold (Or Be Italic...)

The tags for bold and italic text are easy to remember: `<B>` for bold, and `<I>` for italic. As both of these are ongoing effects, you'll have to enter closing tags (`</B>` or `</I>`) when you want the effect to stop. And, just as in your word processor, you can combine these tags, so if your document contained this:

```
This is <I>italic</I>. This is <B>bold</B>. This is
<B><I>bold & italic</I></ B>.
```

the result would look like this in your browser:

This is *italic*. This is **bold**. This is ***bold & italic***.

Lesser-used text formatting tags that might come in handy one day are superscript (`<SUP>` and `</SUP>`) and subscript (`<SUB>` and `</SUB>`). If you really feel the urge, you can underline text using another memorable pair of tags, `<U>` and `</U>`, but be careful how you use underlining: most people surfing the Web expect underlined text to be a hyperlink, and might find your gratuitous use of these tags confusing.

Spaces in HTML

Just as browsers ignore your use of the Enter or Return key when you create your web pages, they have a similar attitude to the Spacebar. However many spaces you enter in a row, only the first will be recognised – the rest are ignored. If you really need more than one space, either type in the code ** ** for each space you need (so **   ** would give you three spaces), or use the <PRE> tag explained on page 360.

Insert Links To Other Sites

It's an unwritten rule of the Internet that a website should contain links to other websites. After all, the entire Web works by being interconnected, and if people surf their way to your site and have to retrace their steps before they can continue surfing, they'll steer clear in future! So let's put in another `<P>` tag to start a new paragraph, and add that sorely needed link as shown below:

```
<P>Visit Macromedia's snazzy <A
HREF="http://www.shockwave.com">Shockwave</A> site.
```

This is a more complicated tag, so let's look at it bit by bit. Although we call these 'links', in HTML they're called **anchors**, and that's where the A comes from after the first < sign. An anchor usually begins with the <A HREF= tag. Following that comes the URL of the page you want to link to, always enclosed in double quotes, and the > sign to finish the opening anchor tag.

Immediately after the opening anchor tag, type the text you want visitors to your page to click on. This might be a single word, a sentence, or even a whole paragraph, but don't forget to put *something* here, or there'll be nothing to click on to reach that site! Finally, type the closing anchor tag, </A>.

Get it central

You can place elements centrally on the page by placing them between <CENTER> and </CENTER> tags (note the American spelling, though!). This applies to headings, paragraphs of text, images, and almost anything else you might want to include.

Links To Other Pages On Your Own Site

The link we just added used something called an **absolute URL**. In fact, that's the only type of URL you've seen so far: an absolute URL gives the whole path to the page you want to open, including the http:// bit and the name of the computer. When you want to create links to other pages on your own site you can use a different, simpler method.

Create a new HTML document, and save it to the folder where the other is stored. Let's assume you've called it **morelinks.html**. Now, in your first document, you can create a link to this new page by typing this anchor:

```
<A HREF="morelinks.html">Here's a few more links.</A>
```

Yes, it's just a filename. This is called a **relative URL**. It tells your browser to look for a file called **morelinks.html** and display it. Since a browser doesn't know where else to look, it searches the folder containing the document it's displaying at that moment. As long as **morelinks.html** really is in that same folder, the browser will find it and open it.

What's so great about relative URLs?

First, less typing. That also lessens the chances of mistakes. But best of all, you can click these links in your browser while you're designing your site to check that they work. If you click a link to an absolute URL, your browser will have to connect to your ISP first to find that computer, costing you money and time.

You can make a browser look somewhere different for a file in a similar way. Open the folder containing these two documents, create a subfolder called **pages**, and move the **morelinks.html** file into it. The link we just added now needs to be changed to the following:

```
<A HREF="pages/morelinks.html">Here's a few more links.</A>
```

The browser now looks in the current folder for another folder called **pages**, and looks inside that for **morelinks.html**

Finally, let's open **morelinks.html** and create a link back to our original document (which we called **links.html**) so that you can click your way to and fro between the two. To do this, we need to tell the browser to look in the parent folder of **pages** to find this file. If you're familiar with using MS-DOS, you'll recognise this straight away: to move up one level in the directory tree, just type two dots:

```
<A HREF="../links.html">Here's my first links page.</A>
```

Case-sensitive filenames

When you refer to a page or file in your document, the case is vital. If you type in a link to **Index.html** and the file is actually called **index.html** or **Index.HTML**, the page won't be found. Most web authors save all their files with lower-case names to remove any uncertainty. Similarly, although you can use long filenames, they mustn't include any spaces.

So far we've looked at linking to other web pages, but a hyperlink needn't necessarily point to a **.html** document. If you have a movie file, a text file, a sound file, or whatever, create the link in exactly the same way entering the location and name of this file between the double quotes. If the file is particularly large, though, it's good practice to mention its size somewhere nearby so that people can choose whether or not to click that link.

email Links

Another type of anchor allows a visitor to your page to click a link which opens their email message window, with your email address already inserted, ready for them to send you a message. This is a lot like any other anchor, with the URL replaced by your email address. The only difference is that the word **mailto:** must be inserted immediately after that first quote sign. Here's an example – just replace the dummy email address with your own:

```
<A HREF="mailto:joe.bloggs@virgin.net">Click here to
send me an email</A>
```

COLOURS, IMAGES & WEB PAGE LAYOUT

▶ **IN THIS CHAPTER**

Choose page and text colours, and add a wallpaper image

Select and change fonts, sizes and colours

Divide the page into sections with horizontal rules

Use images to add sparkle or act as links

Create your own animations for your pages

In the last chapter you created a basic web page consisting of headlines, text (with a little style and paragraph formatting), and hyperlinks. As it stands it won't win any awards, but what matters most is that you've worked with a few HTML tags and seen the effect they have on a page when your browser displays it. Armed with this experience, let's improve the look of the page by adding colours, choosing images and fonts, and applying a few more formatting and design touches.

You Too Can Have A <BODY> Like Mine!

So far, in our example web page, everything looks a bit dull. The background is white, the text is black, the hyperlinks are blue – these are the default colours set up by Internet Explorer, and it's using them because we haven't told it to use anything different. All of this is easily changed, though, by typing our preferences into that opening <BODY> tag.

This brings us to a new area of HTML. A tag like <B> is self-contained – it simply turns on bold text, with no complications. Other tags need to contain a little more information about what you want to do. A good example is the <FONT> tag, which we'll look at more closely later in this chapter. By itself, it isn't saying anything useful: which font? what size? what colour? You provide this information by adding **attributes** to the tag such as SIZE=3, FACE=Arial, and so on, so a complete font tag might be: <FONT SIZE=3 FACE=Arial>.

Attributes

JARGON BUSTER

These are additional pieces of information slotted into a tag. Each attribute is separated by a space, and needs an equals sign between the attribute itself and the setting to be used for it. It doesn't matter what order the attributes appear in, and you don't need to include a particular attribute if you don't want to change its setting.

The <BODY> tag doesn't have to contain attributes, but browsers will use their own default settings for anything you haven't specified, and different browsers use different defaults. Most web authors like to keep as much control as possible over how their pages will be displayed, and make their own settings for the body attributes. There are six attributes you can use in the <BODY> tag:

This attribute...	...has this effect
BGCOLOR=	sets the background colour of the web page
TEXT=	sets the colour of text on the page
LINK=	sets the colour of the clickable hyperlinks
VLINK=	sets the colour of a link to a previously visited page
ALINK=	sets the colour of a link between the time it's clicked and the new page opening
BACKGROUND=	specifies an image to use as the page's 'wallpaper'

Without further ado, open the original **links.html** document you created in the last chapter, and change the <BODY> tag so that it looks like this:

```
<BODY BGCOLOR=MAROON TEXT=WHITE LINK=YELLOW VLINK=OLIVE
ALINK=LIME>
```

 Save the file, and take a look at it in your browser. Okay, the colour scheme may not be to your taste, but it's starting to resemble a 'real' web page! Try swapping colours around to find a scheme you prefer. There are 140 colours to choose from, so skip ahead to Appendix F and pick a few from the list, or take a look at the Colour Chart on the CD-ROM that accompanies this book.

The other attribute is BACKGROUND=, which places a GIF or JPEG image on the web page, and tiles it to fill the entire area. Let's assume you want to use an image file called **hoops.gif** which is in the same folder as the current document. Inside the body tag, add: BACKGROUND="hoops.gif" (not forgetting the double quotes). Your whole <BODY> tag might now look like this:

```
<BODY BACKGROUND="hoops.gif" BGCOLOR=MAROON TEXT=WHITE
LINK=YELLOW VLINK=OLIVE ALINK=LIME>
```

There are a few things worth bearing in mind if you choose to use a background image. First, make sure the image file isn't too large. If someone arrives at your page and sees a 50Kb background image starting to download, they'll probably rush away again without waiting to find out what else is on your page! Second, make sure you choose a text colour that will be easy to read over the background image (or an image that isn't too garish). Third, pick a BGCOLOR= colour that will allow your text to show up clearly – that way, if the background image is taking a while to download, visitors will still be able to read your page comfortably.

Set Up Your Font Options

At the moment you're also stuck with a single font (probably Times New Roman). Once again, this is set up by your browser by default, and, of course, different browsers might use different default fonts. Fortunately, the <FONT> tag leaps to your rescue, allowing you to choose and change the font face, size and colour whenever you need to. Here's an example of a <FONT> tag using all three attributes:

```
<FONT FACE="Verdana,Arial,Helvetica" SIZE=4
COLOR=RED>...</FONT>
```

Let's take these one at a time. The FACE attribute is the name of the font you want to use. Obviously this must be a font on your own system, but the same font needs to be on the system of anyone visiting your page too: if it isn't, their browser will revert to their default font. You can keep a bit of extra control by listing more than one font (separated by commas) as in the example above. If the first font isn't available, the browser will try the second, and so on.

Which font faces should I use?

GOOD QUESTION!

Most visitors to your site will have MS Serif, MS Sans Serif and Courier on their systems. TrueType fonts are better, and the safest are Arial and Times New Roman. Microsoft supplies a pack of fonts for the Web which many web authors now use, which includes Comic Sans MS, Verdana, Impact and Georgia. You can download any of these you don't already have from **http://www.microsoft.com/truetype**

Font sizes in HTML work differently than in your word processor. There are seven sizes numbered (unsurprisingly) from 1 to 7, where 1 is smallest. The default size for text is 3, so if you want to make your text slightly larger, use SIZE=4. The SIZE attribute doesn't affect the headings we covered in the previous chapter, so if you've used one of these somewhere between your <FONT> and </FONT> tags, it will still be formatted as a heading.

The colour of the text has already been set in the <BODY> tag, but you might want to slip in an occasional <FONT COLOR=PURPLE>...</FONT> to change the colour of a certain word, paragraph or heading. After the closing </FONT> tag, the colour will revert to that set in the <BODY> tag.

Big text, small text

If you find it hard to keep track of the font size you're currently using, don't bother trying! Instead, you can use <BIG> and </BIG> to make text one step larger, or <SMALL> and </SMALL> to make it one step smaller.

With the earlier changes to the <BODY> tag, and the addition of a couple of </FONT> tags, here's what the body of our document might look like now:

```
<BODY BGCOLOR=MAROON TEXT=WHITE LINK=YELLOW VLINK=OLIVE
ALINK=LIME>

<FONT FACE="Comic Sans MS" COLOR=YELLOW>
<H1>Welcome To My Homepage!</H1>
</FONT>

<FONT FACE="Arial">
Here's the first paragraph.
<P>And here's the second paragraph.
<P>Visit Macromedia's snazzy <A
HREF="http://www.shockwave.com">Shockwave</A> site.

</FONT>
</BODY>
</HTML>
```

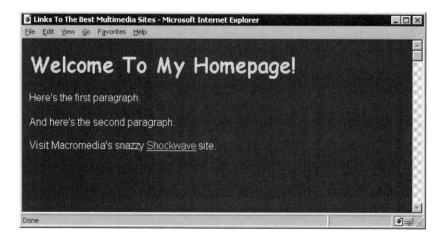

Horizontal Rules (Okay)

Horizontal rules are straight lines that divide a page into sections. For the simplest type of rule, the only tag you need is <HR>. This automatically puts a horizontal rule across the full width of the page, on a new line, and any text that follows it will form a new paragraph. Because the rule isn't something that needs to be turned off again, there's no closing tag.

If you want to, you can get clever with rules by adding some (or all!) of the following attributes:

Use this attribute...	...for this result
ALIGN=	Use LEFT or RIGHT to place the rule on the left or right of the page. If you leave this out, the rule will be centred.
SIZE=	Enter any number to set the height of the rule in pixels. The default setting is 2.
WIDTH=	Enter a number to specify the width of the line in pixels, or as a percentage of the page (such as WIDTH=70%).
NOSHADE	This removes the 3D effect from the rule. There's no equals sign, and nothing more to add.
COLOR=	Enter the name of a colour. The default setting depends upon the background colour. Only Internet Explorer supports this attribute – other browsers will ignore it.

It's worth playing with the <HR> tag and its attributes to see what unusual effects you can create. For example, the following piece of code places a square bullet in the centre of the page which makes a smart, 'minimalist' divider:

```
<HR SIZE=10 WIDTH=10 COLOR=LIME NOSHADE>
```

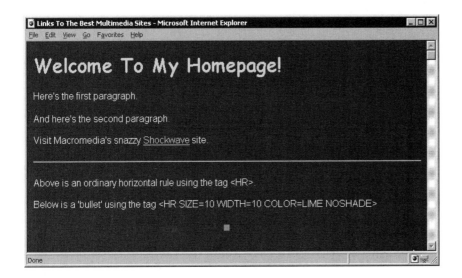

Add Spice With An Image

The horizontal rule is the simplest type of graphical content you can include on a page, but it's hardly exciting. To liven up a dull page, you can't go far wrong with a well-chosen image. Images on the Web are usually in either of two formats:

▶ **JPEG**. This format usually has a **.jpg** or **.jpeg** extension. The images are saved with 16 million colours, making them ideal for photographs but this format may create unnecessarily large files for pictures you create yourself.

▶ **GIF**. These images have a **.gif** extension, and save images in up to 256 colours. This gives pretty lousy results for photographs, but it's often the ideal format for anything else. Using the latest version of the GIF format (GIF89a), you can opt to make one of the colours in the image **transparent**, so that when it appears on your page you'll be able to see the page's background colour (or BACKGROUND= image) in place of that colour.

Make your GIFs smaller

When you create a GIF image, try reducing its number of colours to 16 before you save it. In most cases you won't notice any difference in quality, but the size of the file will be much smaller, making it download a lot faster.

If you're unsure about which format to choose, create your images in 16 million colours and save them in JPEG format. Then reduce the number of colours to 256 and save again in GIF format. You can then compare the file sizes and picture qualities to decide which you want to stick with.

Once you've chosen the image you want to use, the <IMG> tag will slot it on to the page. This tag works rather like the <FONT> tag – by itself it's meaningless, with all the information being supplied by adding attributes. Let's assume you want to insert an image called **splash.gif**, and the image file is in the same directory as your current HTML document:

```
<IMG SRC="splash.gif">
```

This is the <IMG> tag at its most basic: the SRC attribute (which is short for 'source') tells the browser where to find the image file you want to display, following exactly the same rules as those for relative URLs which we looked at in the previous chapter. Unless you preceded this tag with <P> or <BR>, the image will be placed immediately after the last piece of text you entered. If you enclose the entire tag between <CENTER> and </CENTER> tags, the image will be placed below the previous line of text, centred on the page. You do get a little more choice than that about where the image should be, though, by adding the ALIGN attribute:

This attribute...	Does this...
ALIGN=TOP	Aligns the top of the image with the top of the text on the same line.
ALIGN=MIDDLE	Aligns the middle of the image with the text on that line.
ALIGN=BOTTOM	Aligns the bottom of the image with the bottom of the line of text.
ALIGN=LEFT	Places the image on a new line, and against the left margin.
ALIGN=RIGHT	Places the image on a new line, and against the right margin.

Using these attributes, then, you can place the image roughly where you want it on the page. What's still needed is a bit of fine tuning: after all, if you use `ALIGN=MIDDLE`, the image will be butted right up against the text on the same line. The answer comes in the form of two more attributes which add some blank space around an image: `HSPACE=` inserts space either side of the image (horizontally), and `VSPACE=` adds space above and below it (vertically). Just enter a number in pixels after the equals sign. As usual with attributes, if you need to use only one of these, there's no need to include the other. So far, then, an image might be inserted with a tag that looks like this:

```
<IMG SRC="splash.gif" ALIGN=MIDDLE HSPACE=30 VSPACE=6>
```

How do I create a GIF or JPEG image?

There are many good graphics programs around that can handle these formats, but the most popular by far is Paint Shop Pro. You can download a trial version from **http://www.jasc.com** or install it from the CD-ROM. The latest versions also have built-in effects and filters that help the artistically-challenged create some very arty images.

Enter The Image's Width & Height

Two of the most important `<IMG>` attributes are `WIDTH=` and `HEIGHT=`, with which you specify the size of the image. If you've experimented with the tags above, you'll have noticed that your browser displays the image properly without these tags, so you're probably wondering why on earth you'd bother to do this.

At the moment, you're looking at pages and images that are already on your own system – there's no downloading involved yet. When your page is on the Web and someone visits it, things work a little differently. When the browser arrives at an `<IMG>` tag with no width or height attributes, it has to download the image and display it before it can work out where to put the other parts of the page, such as text. However, if the browser already knows how much space is needed for the image, it can hold it in reserve and display just an empty box until the image downloads, with the text correctly positioned around it. Another reason is that some people surf the Web with the option to display images turned off: if you don't enter the dimensions of your images, they'll simply see a tiny placeholder icon instead of a full-size box, which might upset your carefully planned layout!

Enter an alternative

It's common practice to enter some alternative text in place of an image. This displays in the placeholder box until the image is downloaded and displayed, and also appears in a tooltip when the mouse moves onto the image. Add the attribute `ALT=""` and place a description of the image between the quotes, such as `ALT="A picture of my cat"`.

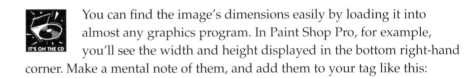

You can find the image's dimensions easily by loading it into almost any graphics program. In Paint Shop Pro, for example, you'll see the width and height displayed in the bottom right-hand corner. Make a mental note of them, and add them to your tag like this:

```
<IMG SRC="splash.gif" ALIGN=MIDDLE HSPACE=30 VSPACE=6
WIDTH=84 HEIGHT=81>
```

Bear in mind that if you enter the dimensions of an image like this, the browser will take your word for it! In other words, the browser will scale the image to these proportions regardless of what the original image looked like. This can be useful to increase or decrease the size of an image without creating a new version of it (or to create weird effects), but it's also a prime opportunity to screw things up!

Reuse your images!

Try to reuse images on different pages if you can. After an image has been displayed once, it will be reloaded from the browser's cache rather than downloaded, making your site a more immediate and pleasing experience for your visitors.

Use An Image As An Anchor

In the last chapter you learnt how to create hypertext links, or anchors, to a web page or file using the tag <A HREF="URL"> clickable text</A>. But the clickable section that appears on the page doesn't have to be text: you can use an image instead, or both image and text. For example, if you slot the whole image tag given above into the anchor tag, the image will appear exactly as it did before, but will now act as a clickable link:

```
<A HREF="morelinks.html"><IMG SRC="splash.gif"
ALIGN=MIDDLE HSPACE=30 VSPACE=6 WIDTH=84 HEIGHT=81
BORDER=0></A>Click this image to open my other links page.
```

If you want to make both the text and the image clickable, add some text before or after the <IMG> tag like this:

```
<A HREF="morelinks.html">Click this image to open my
other links page.<IMG SRC="splash.gif" ALIGN=MIDDLE
HSPACE=30 VSPACE=6 WIDTH=84 HEIGHT=81 BORDER=0></A>
```

Here's what those two methods look like when displayed in your browser:

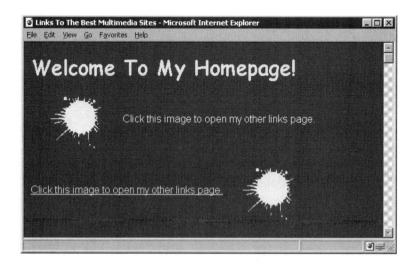

Turn off the image border

When you use an image as a link, a border will appear around it. You can alter the thickness of the border by adding `BORDER=` to the `<IMG>` tag followed by a number in pixels. If you'd prefer to have no border, enter `BORDER=0`, but make sure it's obvious that the image is clickable to avoid confusing visitors to your page. The border attribute can be added to any image, whether it's acting as a link or not.

How About A Little Animation?

The GIF image format has another little trick up its sleeve that can add sparkle to a page – you can use it to create animations. These are known by the simple enough name, **animated GIFs**, but you'll need special software to build the finished article. First, though, you need to create a series of images, each one slightly different from the others, like a cartoon, and save each with a different name and the **.gif** extension. Then you need to load these into the special software that can string them together in the order you choose, set the length of time that each frame of the animation should remain on the screen, and save them as a single animation (still with the extension **.gif**). The animation is placed on your page using exactly the same `<IMG>` tag and attributes as we looked at earlier. Two popular and easy-to-use animators are:

- ▶ Ulead GIF Animator from **http://www.ulead.com**
- ▶ Microsoft GIF Animator from **http://www.microsoft.com/ imagecomposer/gifanimator/gifanin.htm**

Although the process is easy, try to keep the number of images in your animation to a minimum to prevent the file becoming too big – a five-frame animation will take almost as long to download as five separate images. Those Ulead people make a neat utility called SmartSaver (also on the CD-ROM) that can reduce an animation's size by up to 90 per cent: the trial version won't actually convert your images, but it will tell you how much smaller you can make them if you register your copy.

Useful HTML Extras

 We haven't by any means exhausted the supply of HTML tags, but we have covered most of those you'll be using regularly, and you should have enough ammunition here to make a good start on your own site. You'll find more in Appendix E, and plenty of examples on the CD-ROM accompanying this book, but let's shift into 'quickfire' mode to look at a last little bundle of tags to keep handy.

Comments

You can enclose anything on your page between `<!--` and `-->` tags, and your browser will ignore them. The intention of these comment tags is that you can put little notes in your document to help you edit it later, such as `<!--The next bit of code inserts the image-->`, but they can be usefully inserted around a piece of code that you want to remove from the page, but don't want to actually delete in case you need to reinstate it sometime.

Marquee

A marquee is a piece of text that scrolls across the page. Only Internet Explorer supports this tag at the moment, so it's best not to use it for any text that really matters, but it makes a neat effect. Begin by adding the following code:

```
<MARQUEE ALIGN=Middle HEIGHT=10 WIDTH=80% BGCOLOR=Maroon
SCROLLAMOUNT=3 BEHAVIOR=Scroll SCROLLDELAY=3
DIRECTION=Left HSPACE=0 VSPACE=0 LOOP=INFINITE>This text
is scrolling</MARQUEE>
```

All the possible attributes are included above, and you'll recognise some of them, such as HSPACE and VSPACE. Height can be specified as a percentage of the page or (more usefully) as a number in pixels. Width is best set as a percentage. You can choose a BGCOLOR setting to blend the marquee into your page, or make it stand out, and the text will be displayed according to your last use of the <FONT> tag (or the TEXT attribute in the <BODY> tag). You can experiment with the SCROLLAMOUNT and SCROLLDELAY settings to achieve a comfortable speed, and change the BEHAVIOR setting to Slide or Alternate.

Paragraph Alignment

We met the <P> tag in the previous chapter. By itself, it inserts a blank line and places the following text on the next line. But the <P> tag also has an optional attribute, ALIGN=, that can be used with the settings LEFT, CENTER or RIGHT. The first two aren't particularly useful: by default, all paragraphs are left-aligned anyway, and it's easier to use the plain old <CENTER>...</ CENTER> tags to centre elements on a page. But if you ever want to align a paragraph of text with the right margin, surround it with these tags:

```
<P ALIGN=RIGHT>This text is right-aligned.</P>
```

Note that you have to use a closing </P> tag if you add an attribute to this tag, otherwise all the remaining text on your page will be aligned the same way!

Lists

HTML gives you built in ways of making bulleted or numbered lists easily with the addition of just a couple of tags. To create a list, just insert the tag <LI> at the beginning of each line. No paragraph or line-break tags are needed, so the following code would create a list containing three items, each on its own line:

```
<LI>Here's item one.<LI>Here's a second item.<LI>And
here's a third.
```

Now decide whether you want a bulleted or a numbered list. For a numbered list, enclose the entire code between <OL> and </OL> tags (which stands for 'ordered list'); for a bulleted list, use <UL> and </UL> tags (meaning 'unordered list'), as shown in the next screenshot.

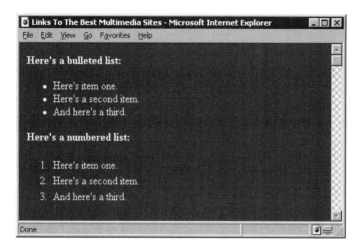

Make the editing easier

Since browsers ignore the use of carriage returns, use them liberally to space out your code. For example, although you can enter list entries all on one line, your code will be easier to understand and edit later if you place each on its own line.

If you use a numbered list, you can add the TYPE= attribute to the <OL> tag to choose which numbering system you'd like to apply. The default is Arabic numbers. To use capital letters, enter TYPE=A. For small letters, TYPE=a. You can also use large Roman numerals (TYPE=I) or small Roman numerals (TYPE=i). So your complete tag might look like this:

```
<OL TYPE=I><LI>Here's item one.<LI>Here's a second
item.<LI>And here's a third.</OL>
```

Pre-formatted Text

If you're having trouble laying out a piece of text exactly as you want it, enclose it between <PRE> and </PRE> tags. This way, all the spaces and carriage returns you type into that portion of your document will be displayed in exactly the same way in the browser with no need to muck about with <P> or <BR> tags. The ability to use the space bar also gives you an easy way to indent a line of text.

Make This Your Internet Explorer Home Page

In Chapter 6 you learnt how to change your Home Page in Internet Explorer. Your choices were to use a blank document (so that Explorer didn't try to dial up every time you started it) or to use any other page on the Web. But now you know how to build your own pages, why not create your own start page instead, perhaps containing links to some of your favourite sites?

When the page looks okay loaded into Explorer, click your way to **Tools | Internet Options | General**. In the Home Page section at the top of the dialog, click the button marked **Use Current**. Provided you don't move, rename or delete the HTML document you created (or any other files linked to it, such as images) this page will be displayed every time you run Internet Explorer, or click its **Home** toolbar button.

FROM DRAWING BOARD TO WEB

▶ **IN THIS CHAPTER**

Planning and preparing to build your site

Find free web space, graphics, animations & more

Upload and test your website

Publicise your site for maximum exposure

Add a 'hit counter' and submit your site to be judged

Now that you know something about HTML, it's time to put on your hard hat and start building. But there's more to constructing a good website than a knowledge of HTML. How should the site be laid out? What about page design? Where do you find graphics files? How does your site get on to the Web? And how will everyone else know it's there? Looks like you've come to the right chapter…

Think First, Write Later!

A little planning never goes amiss, so try to do all your thinking before you start designing anything – especially graphics. I once spent ages designing a fabulous set of textual buttons for a page, and realised when I'd finished that no one but me would understand where they were linking to unless I put an explanatory paragraph beside each one! I had to junk the lot and start again. Remember that you'll know how to navigate your site, but your visitors won't, and they'll usually expect it to be obvious.

Decide what topics your site will cover, and how you can split them up into different pages rather than one long page. Make sure your first page contains links to all the others, and that those links really do explain what visitors will find there. On arrival at any other page, visitors should be able to switch back to the homepage with a single click and (if possible) to all your other pages too.

Ugh, I hate it when they do that!

When you plan your own site, consider what you like and dislike about other sites you've visited. For example, most people hate to find large graphics on a page before they know what the site is even about. Other pet hates are repetitive music, large unnecessary background WAV files, links that don't tell you what they're linking to, and text that's exactly the wrong colour for the background.

Of course, if you're going to have a website, you want people to visit it. Consider why they'd visit your site and make sure you deliver what you promise. Popular sites are those that give something away (we all love freebies don't we?) – it may be software, useful information, or entertainment, but a couple of paragraphs about your hobbies and a picture of your cat is unlikely to leave people panting for more. If you want to take this seriously, add a 'What's New' page to keep regular visitors informed about the latest changes and additions, and make sure it contains the dates of those changes and links to the relevant pages.

Finally, bear in mind that most visitors to your page are using a screen resolution of 800×600 on a 15-inch monitor. Although some sites ask visitors to switch screen resolutions to view their pages, no one is likely to do that – they expect you to design a site that looks good at any screen size. Try adjusting your own resolution, and the size of your browser window, every so often to see your pages as others may see them.

Don't trust the download times!

If you use a program that tells you the download time (or 'weight') of a page as you build it, don't rely on it too much. Not everyone uses a 56Kbps modem, not everyone will have a good connection to your site, and a download time can't include the hugely variable connection times. Think in terms of at least doubling the figure.

Talk To Your Service Provider

Before you begin the creation process, check a few details with your service provider. First, of course, you want to know how much web space is available to you. (If your provider doesn't give you web space for free, don't pay yet – you may be able to find free space elsewhere, as you'll find out in the next section.) Here are three more things to find out:

▶ Ask if you can upload your files by FTP. A few ISPs have their own methods of handling this, but most will tell you the address to connect to using your FTP program. You'll log on using your normal username and password and start copying the files across.

▶ Find out if you can create your own directory structure. Most ISPs will let you upload whole directories, but a few insist that only files can be uploaded. If all your links refer to files in subdirectories and you later find out that everything has to be in the same directory, you'll have a lot of editing to do!

▶ The URL to your site will normally be **http://www.** *serviceprovider/~username* with all the files (and subdirectories) in this directory making up your site. When somebody arrives at this directory an index file should be displayed automatically, and this would usually be your first, welcoming page. In most cases this will be called **index.htm** or **index.html**, but check this with your service provider in case their system uses something different.

The Quest For Free Web Space

Believe it or not, there are companies out there that actually provide web space entirely free of charge – you don't have to pay, or buy anything else from them, you don't have to carry advertising (other than perhaps a small logo with their name on it), and you don't have to make any commitments. Just go there, check the details, and grab with both hands.

The only negative aspect to these 'free space' companies – and it's a small one – is that if the company deletes all your files, or their computers go down for six months, you're not in a strong position to complain about it. If that doesn't bother you, try some of these sites to find out more about free web space:

▶ GeoCities at **http://uk.geocities.com**

▶ Phrantic at **http://www.phrantic.com**

▶ EasySpace at **http://www.easyspace.com**

▶ Tripod at **http://www.tripod.com**

▶ FortuneCity at **http://www.fortunecity.com**

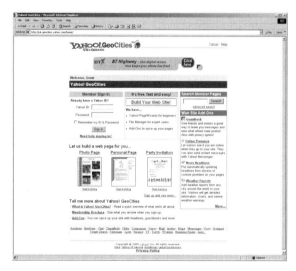

◀ GeoCities, one of the major providers of free space on the Web.

Of course it's under construction!

There's a trend on the Web to add 'Under Construction' graphics to indicate that a website isn't finished. Don't fall into that trap! The entire Web is under construction, and a good site should always be evolving. If, by 'Under Construction', you mean that the links don't work, either remove them or fix them!

You Need Buttons, Backgrounds, Bullets, Applets...

Armed with a good graphics program, there's not much you can't do, however limited your artistic talents. But why bother? You can find everything you need on the Web and download it for your own use. There are many sites handing out the many bits and pieces you might like to add to your pages, but let me unreservedly recommend (ahem) one of my own sites, WebSight, at **http://freespace.virgin.net/rob.young/WebSight** Here you'll find dozens of wallpaper backgrounds for your pages, graphical horizontal rule replacements, animated GIFs, Java applets and JavaScripts with easy download and setup instructions, and links to lots more useful stuff.

If that's not enough for you, head for the MSDN Downloads Area at **http://msdn.microsoft.com/downloads/default.asp** which will provide you with a bit of everything, including complete 'theme' sets of backgrounds, images and icons. For a little help on the art of page design itself, visit one of these:

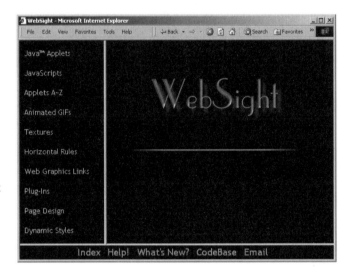

▶ Make WebSight your first stop for all those irresistable add-on goodies.

▶ Webmonkey at **http://hotwired.lycos.com/webmonkey**

▶ Creating Killer Sites at **http://www.killersites.com**

▶ Jeffrey Zeldman Presents… at **http://www.zeldman.com**

▶ Bare Bones Guide to HTML at **http://werbach.com/barebones**

▶ The Web Developer's Virtual Library at **http://www.stars.com**

Or, if you learn more easily by discovering how not to do it, visit Web Pages That Suck at **http://www.webpagesthatsuck.com**

You're Ready To Upload!

Or are you? Before you do so, load all your pages into your browser one by one and check them. Test all your internal links (links to other pages from your own site) by clicking them to make sure they work. If your HTML software has a built-in spellchecker, use it. If it doesn't, consider loading the documents into a word processor to spellcheck – you'll have to remember to save as plain text when you've finished, and put up with the spellchecker disagreeing with all of your HTML tags.

Now follow the instructions you were given by your service provider to upload the files to the web server. At the risk of being obvious (not everyone realises this straight off), every file that forms a part of your site must be uploaded – images, documents, ZIP files, sound files; if it's supposed to be a part of your website, it must be on the web server where everyone else can see it and not just on your own computer. As you upload, make sure you keep the directory structure the same. For instance, if all your graphics files are in a subdirectory called **images** (and your links to them look something like <IMG SRC="images/mypicture.gif">), you must have a directory on the web server called **images**, in the same relative location to your HTML documents, that contains the same graphics files.

Easy site upload with FTP

When you upload using an FTP program such as FTP Explorer, you don't have to transfer the files one by one. Once you've connected to your online directory, following the instructions given by your service provider, just select all the files and directories that make up your site in Windows Explorer and drag them into FTP Explorer's main window to transfer the lot in one go.

When your site is uploaded to the server, start your browser, type your URL into the address-bar and check each page to make sure that everything is as it should be (including all your links to other websites). If you need to change a file, make the change on your own system and then upload the file again – provided you don't change its name, it should replace the original. Depending upon your service provider's system, you should be able to see all your files and subdirectories in your FTP program and delete or rename them as needed.

▶ *For more details about uploading files, turn to Using A 'Real' FTP Program in Chapter 11.*

Hit The Publicity Trail

So you have a website, and it works. Now, you want people to come and visit it, so you need to let them know it exists. One method is to contact the authors of sites covering similar subjects and ask if they'd like to exchange links – you add a link to their sites in return for links to yours. The other, more useful way to publicise your site is to get it listed with as many search engines as you can. There are two ways to do this which should capture almost every search engine going.

Feed The Robots

The first thing to do is to adjust your homepage in such a way that the search engines using roving robot-programs will find your site and describe it correctly. First, make sure that the title of your page (which appears between the <TITLE></TITLE> tags) is as meaningful as possible. Second, add the <META> tag to the header of your page. This tag has two attributes: NAME= (which can be "keywords" or "description") and CONTENT=. Let's say your site is about camels:

```
<!DOCTYPE HTML PUBLIC "-//W3C//DTD HTML 4.0//EN">

<HTML>
<HEAD>

<TITLE>The Ultimate Camel Reference</TITLE>
<META NAME="keywords" CONTENT="camels, dromedaries,
quadrupeds">
<META NAME="description" CONTENT="The ultimate database
of camel information, plus our fabulous Spot The Hump
competition!">

</HEAD>

<BODY>

</BODY>
</HTML>
```

In the `keywords` tag, list the words that people might type into a search engine to find sites like yours. In the `description` tag, type a short paragraph that explains what your page is about, to whet the appetite of intrepid Web-surfers. Most search engines will display this description below the link to your site. It also helps if the first paragraph of text on your page sounds reasonably descriptive and appetising: some search engines will quote from this instead of using your meta description.

What happens if I don't add a META tag?

GOOD QUESTION! Either a large bundle of search engines won't be able to add your site to their database, or they'll index it wrongly. For example, if you leave out the description, the index will probably consist of the first few lines from your page which may contain no useful information at all.

Submit To The Directories

Some search engines and directories don't use robots, so you'll need to submit details of your site to them manually. One way to do this is to visit each search site, one by one, and look for a link marked **Add Your Site** or something similar, and then follow the instructions.

A better method is to visit a service that can submit your details to many search sites at once. There are hundreds of different search sites, and these services will want money from you to submit to the whole lot, but their free services cover several dozen of the major search engines and directories. Choose one of these services and nip along to fill in the details:

▶ Add Me! at **http://www.addme.com**

▶ Submit It! at **http://www.submit-it.com**

▶ WebPromote at **http://www.webpromote.com**

You might even choose to visit all three – keep a note of the search engines your details were submitted to using the first service, and then see if the remaining services cover any others. Take your time filling in the information, and make sure it's correct. When the form appears on the screen, you might want to disconnect from the Internet while you fill it in so that you don't feel rushed.

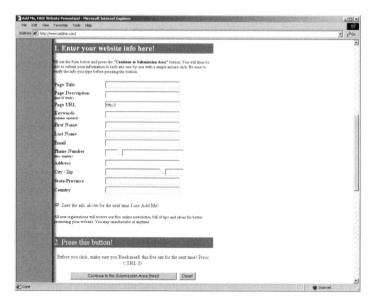

▶ Enter your details at Add Me! to register your site with the major search engines.

Gauge Audience Reaction

The only way to get true feedback about your site is to include email links on your pages, as we covered in Chapter 23, and to encourage visitors to tell you what they liked, what they didn't, and what they were hoping to see. A similar option is to add a **guestbook** to your site by visiting **http://www. guestworld.com** Visitors can open your personal guestbook to read other surfers' comments and add their own.

Another interesting device is to place a counter on your page that tells you (roughly) how many visits (or 'hits') your site has received. You might even want to put a counter on every page to get a rough idea of which links most visitors find tempting from your homepage. One of the most informative and reliable counter services can be found at TheCounter (**http://www. thecounter.com**). Fill in the simple details, choose a password if you don't want anyone else seeing your page statistics, and the service will then display some HTML code. Swipe it with the mouse, copy it to the clipboard, and then paste it into one of your pages. You'll need to repeat this for each counter you want.

Ask your ISP about counters

Some service providers have their own special program (called a CGI program) running on their web server that you can use to put counters on your pages. This is likely to give you a more realistic count than one of the 'free counter' services.

The highest compliment anyone can pay to your site is to say it's cool. If you think you've got a cool site, why not submit it to be judged by one of the site-review organisations on the Web? If you're successful, you'll be able to display a sort of 'I've got a cool site' logo, and you should get many more visitors tramping around your pages as a result. Here are some of those organisations' sites (well worth a visit, even if you don't yet have a cool site):

Judging Site	URL
Webby Awards	http://www.webbyawards.com
The Médaille d'Or	http://www.arachnid.co.uk/award
World Best Websites	http://www.worldbestwebsites.com
Too Cool!	http://toocool.com

And if you're not yet cool enough? Perhaps that's something to celebrate, but if you really want to be cool examine as many sites as you can that are sufficiently cool to win awards for it and try to discover what makes them that way. You'll also find tips, tricks and effects to increase your 'cool quotient' on the free CD-ROM in the back of this book.

APPENDICES

▶ **IN THESE APPENDICES . . .**

GETTING CONNECTED WITH WINDOWS 95/98

Windows 95 and 98 both include support for Internet connections that Windows 3.x didn't, making it easier to set up and a lot cleaner to use. There are three tasks to take care of: first you'll need to install the **TCP/IP** protocols that let your computer talk in 'Internet language'; second you'll install the **Dial-Up Adapter** that lets your computer make calls through your modem; and finally you'll create a **Dial-Up Networking connection** that you can double-click when you want to go online.

Installing TCP/IP

1 Open Control Panel and double-click the **Network** icon.

2 Click the **Add...** button.

3 In the left pane of the next dialog choose **Microsoft**, and in the right pane choose **TCP/IP**.

4 Click **OK**. You'll be prompted to restart your computer, but you might prefer to delay doing that until you've finished all the installations.

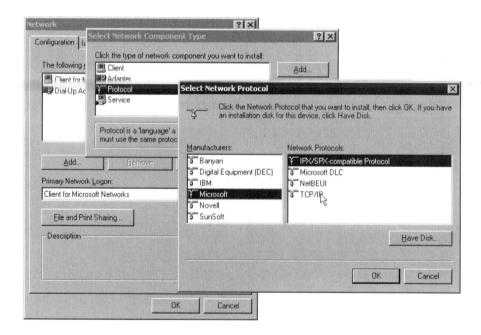

▶ The sequence of dialogs you'll see when installing the TCP/IP protocols.

Installing The Dial-Up Adapter

1 Check to see if you have **Dial-Up Networking** installed already. Double-click the **My Computer** icon and look for a folder-like icon labelled Dial-Up Networking. If it's there, skip straight to step 5. If you don't have that icon, you'll need to install it as follows (making sure you've got your Windows installation disks at the ready).
2 Open Control Panel and double-click **Add/Remove Programs**.
3 Click the **Windows Setup** tab, then select **Communications** and click the **Details...** button.
4 Check the box beside **Dial-Up Networking**, click **OK**, then click **OK** again to install it.
5 With Dial-Up Networking installed, go back to Control Panel, double-click **Network**, and then double-click on **Dial-Up Adapter**.
6 Click the tab marked **Bindings** and make sure there's a checkmark in the box beside **TCP/IP**. (If there isn't, click the box until the checkmark appears.) Click **OK**.

Creating A Dial-Up Networking Connection

1 Open My Computer and double-click the **Dial-Up Networking** icon.
2 Double-click the **Make New Connection** icon.
3 On the first page enter a name for your connection (any name you like). Click **Next**, and type the area code and phone number you were given to dial in to your provider's computer. Select the **United Kingdom** entry from the dropdown list of country codes. Click **Next**, then click **Finish**.
4 Now right-click this new connection's icon and select **Properties**. If you're dialling a local number to your service provider, remove the checkmark beside **Use country code and area code**. (If you were given an 0345 or 0845 number, which is charged at local rate, you'll need to leave this box checked.)
5 Click the **Server Type** button or tabbed page. Select **PPP: Windows 95, Windows NT 3.5, Internet** from the dropdown list, and make sure the only boxes that are checked on this page are **Enable software compression** and **TCP/IP**, as shown in the next screenshot.
6 Next, click the **TCP/IP Settings...** button and grab the list of details your service provider gave you.

7   If your service provider gave you your own IP address (which is very unlikely), select the **Specify an IP address** button and then enter the address in the box beneath. Otherwise make sure **Server assigned IP address** is selected.

8   Make sure **Specify name server addresses** is selected, and type the DNS address you were given into the **Primary DNS** box. If you were also given an alternative DNS address, type this into the **Secondary DNS** box.

9   Click **OK**, and **OK** again, and your connection is ready to roll!

▶ Following steps 7 and 8, this is how those dialogs should look once you've entered your settings into them.

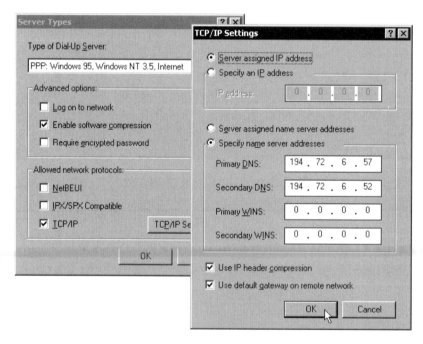

Using Your Connection

To start your connection, open your Dial-Up Networking folder and double-click the icon you just created. A dialog will appear, like the one shown in the next screenshot, into which you'll need to enter your username and the logon password you were given. To save you doing this every time, check the box marked **Save password**, then click **OK**.

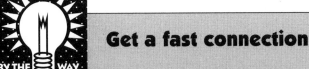

Get a fast connection

To get to that connection icon more quickly, drag it on to your desktop or Start menu to create a shortcut within easy reach. By editing the shortcut's properties, you could even add a shortcut key for ultra-quick access when you need it.

This box will be replaced by a smaller one that will keep you informed about what's happening with messages like **Dialling** and **Verifying username and password**. Soon you should see the magic word **Connected**. If so, you can now turn to Part Two of this book, start one of your client programs, and get well and truly Netted!

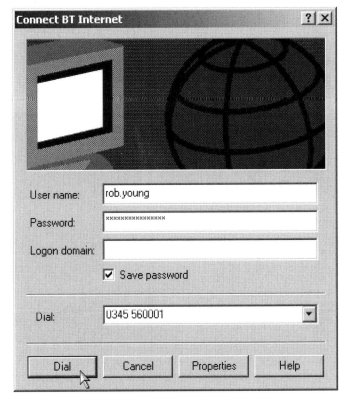

◀ Double-click your new connection, enter your user name and password, and click the Dial button.

When you've finished surfing and you're ready to log off, you need to click the **Disconnect** button. Where you find this will depend on your version of Windows. If the connection dialog minimised to a button on the Taskbar when you connected successfully, click that Taskbar button and you'll see the Disconnect button and the length of time you've been online. If the dialog vanished entirely when you connected, double-click the little icon in the tray that shows two tiny green computers: as well as the Disconnect button, you'll see your total online time together with the amount of data sent and received so far.

Automatic Dial-Up on Demand

The first time you run Internet Explorer it should display the Connection Wizard, a small program that prompts you for details about how you want to connect to the Internet. Armed with this information, Explorer can dial up automatically when you select an Internet shortcut or type a URL into its address bar, saving you the need to find and start your DUN connection manually.

If the wizard doesn't appear, and you like the 'wizardly' approach to entering details, you can start it yourself by clicking the appropriate entry in the **Internet Tools** folder on the Start menu. Alternatively, open Control Panel, double-click **Internet** and choose the **Connections** tab followed by the **Setup** button. After clicking the **Next** button in the wizard, make sure the option button labelled **I connect through a phone line and modem** is selected, then step through the remaining pages selecting the modem to use, the phone number to dial, and your user name and password, and finally choose a friendly name for this connection.

▶ *Turn to Appendix G for more about adding, removing and choosing connections, and dealing with email accounts.*

B

GETTING CONNECTED WITH WINDOWS 3.1

Although later versions of Windows have built-in support for Internet connections, Windows 3.x isn't at all difficult to configure. When you subscribed to your service provider you probably received a disk that includes a program called **Trumpet Winsock**. If you didn't, phone up and ask for it!

There are two steps to connecting: the first task is to install Trumpet Winsock and to edit your AUTOEXEC.BAT file so that Windows knows where to find this program. The second is to configure the program itself using the list of technical details you were given. (If you get into difficulties, Trumpet includes plenty of useful documentation to help you on your way.)

Installing Trumpet Winsock

1 Create a directory on your hard disk called C:\TRUMPET.
2 Copy all the Trumpet Winsock files from your ISP's disk into this directory (unzipping them if they were supplied in a ZIP archive).
3 Create a new program item in Program Manager with the command line **C:\TRUMPET\TCPMAN.EXE** so that you can start this program easily when you're ready to connect.
4 Now you need to edit your AUTOEXEC.BAT file using System Editor or Notepad to add this new directory to your path statement. After you've done so, it might look like this:

    SET PATH=C:\;C:\DOS;C:\WINDOWS;C:\TRUMPET;

5 Shut down Windows and reboot your computer to force Windows to read this newly edited AUTOEXEC.BAT file.

What is a Winsock anyway?

Winsock stands for Windows Sockets, and it's the software that Windows needs to be able to talk 'Internet language', using the TCP/IP protocols we met earlier. It doesn't do anything exciting, but it's the vital link that lets all your Internet programs talk to your ISP's computer.

Configuring Trumpet Winsock

1 Start Trumpet Winsock by double-clicking TCPMAN.EXE in your new TRUMPET directory (or by double-clicking its Program Manager icon if you created one).

2 As the program opens you'll see a dialog containing several fields into which you'll need to enter the details you were given by your ISP. (This dialog only appears the first time you run the program, and these settings will be saved the first time you close it.)

3 Type the **IP address**, **Netmask**, **Name server** (DNS) and **Default Gateway** IP addresses and the **Domain Suffix** into the correct fields (remembering to type the dots between each number). If you were given two DNS addresses, type both into the **Name server** field leaving a single space between them.

4 Check the **Internet SLIP** or **Internal PPP** box according to the type of connection you were given by your ISP, and make sure that the port setting matches the port to which your modem is connected and its correct speed is entered.

5 Click **OK** and you'll see the main Trumpet window – you're now ready to dial up and connect.

6 Open the **Dialer** menu and click **Login**. In the three dialogs that appear one at a time, enter the phone number you were given to dial in, your username and your password.

7 If all goes according to plan, Trumpet will connect to your ISP and you'll see a message like **CONNECT 38400** appear (it's the word 'Connect' that matters – the speed will depend upon your own modem). Press the ESC key on your keyboard, and you're ready to start one of your Internet programs, turn back to Part Two and start surfing!

If instead you see a message like **Script Aborted**, you have two options:

▶ Go back to the **Dialer** menu and choose **Manual Login**. Type **ATDT** followed by the phone number of your ISP's computer. As Trumpet tries to connect you, prompts will appear on the screen such as **Username:** and **Password:**. Type these details as you're prompted for them, pressing Enter after each. When you see the **CONNECT** message press ESC and you're officially online.

▶ Contact your ISP's support line to ask for a login script – the chances are that they'll have been asked for this many times before. Failing that, try editing the file LOGIN.CMD in your TRUMPET directory, according to the details included in Trumpet's own documentation.

USING NETSCAPE NAVIGATOR

In the sections of this book that deal with the World Wide Web and browsers, I've assumed that you're using Microsoft's Internet Explorer. If you're not, you're probably using the other contender for the crown, Netscape Navigator. Most of the facilities available in Explorer are also available in Navigator, and many of them can be accessed by similar toolbar buttons, menu options, or keystrokes, so you'll probably find it easy to steer Navigator around the Web from reading the earlier chapters. Nevertheless, to prevent confusion, the following table lists the main browser features that are found in different places or have different names to the Explorer counterparts.

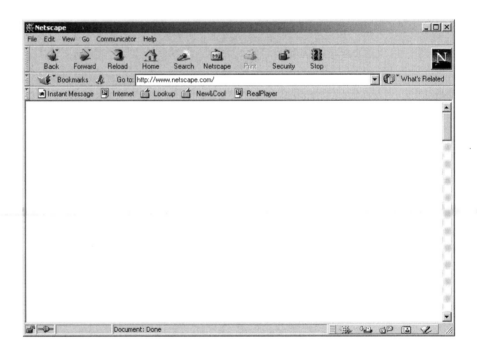

▶ Netscape
Navigator.

To do this...	...select this Netscape option
Reload the current page	Click the **Reload** button, or press Ctrl+R.
View the document's HTML source	Go to **View** I **Page Source**.
Open a second browser window	Press Ctrl+N, or select **File** I **New Navigator Window**. The new window will display your home page.
View the History list	Press Ctrl+H, or select **Communicator** I **Tools** I **History**.
Save a link to a site to visit again	Select **Bookmarks** I **Add Bookmark**, or press Ctrl+D. Bookmarks are the equivalent of Explorer's 'Favorites'.
Organise your bookmarks	Press Ctrl+B, or select **Bookmarks** I **Edit Bookmarks**.
Visit a bookmarked site	Select **Bookmarks** and click the site to visit on the menu.
Switch off automatic display of images	Open the **View** menu and click on **Show Images**.
Switch off Navigator's toolbar	Click on **View** I **Show** I **Navigation Toolbar**.
Switch off the address bar	Click on **View** I **Show** I **Location Toolbar**.
Switch off the lower button bar	Click on **View** I **Show** I **Personal Toolbar**.
View a list of installed plug-ins	Go to **Help** I **About Plug-ins**.
Open the default search engine site	Click the **Search** button on the main toolbar.
Choose a different Home page	Go to **Edit** I **Preferences...** and choose **Navigator** in the left panel. You can set different pages to be shown when Navigator is starting and when you click the Home button.
Edit settings for plug-ins and viewers	Go to **Edit** I **Preferences...** and click **Applications** in the left panel.
Turn on/off support for active content	Go to **Communicator** I **Tools** I **Security Info** and select from a list of content types to choose settings for each.
Change the size of the cache	Go to **Edit** I **Preferences...**, click on **Advanced** followed by **Cache** and type a new figure into the **Disk Cache** box.
Empty the cache directory	Go to **Edit** I **Preferences...**, click on **Advanced** and then **Cache**, and click the **Clear Disk Cache** button.
Find cool sites to visit	Click the **New & Cool** button on the lower button bar and choose **What's New** or **What's Cool**.

JARGONBUSTER
SUPER REFERENCE

Arriving on the Internet is a bit like arriving in a foreign country – suddenly everyone around you seems to be talking a different language. This is the part of the book that helps you to find out what they're going on about, or even to learn to speak like a native yourself. Yes, it's all the technical stuff, but we'll keep it as painless as possible.

Keep a look out for words and phrases in italic text – they indicate a related entry. The figures you'll find in square brackets (such as [252]) at the end of some of the definitions are the page numbers on which you'll find the subject covered in more depth.

access provider A general term for a company that lets you connect to the *Internet* by dialling in to their computer in return for money. This may be an *Internet Service Provider* or an *online service*.

ADSL (Asymmetric Digital Subscriber Line) A high-speed permanent connection to the *Internet* similar to a *leased line*, with a variety of speeds available. Downloads speeds are considerably greater than upload speeds, which is what that word 'asymmetric' is all about.

ActiveX A multimedia programming system developed by Microsoft for use on the *World Wide Web*. [207, 329]

alias A nifty short name for something whose real name is much longer. For example, your *email* software will usually let you refer to yourself as Joe Bloggs instead of joe_bloggs@somewhere.co.uk.

animated GIF A type of animation created by loading two or more *GIF* images into an animation program, setting an order and delay times, and re-saving as a single file. [356]

anonymous FTP A method of getting access to files on an *FTP* site without needing special permission or a *logon* name. Instead you enter **anonymous** as your logon name, and your *email address* as your password. [165]

anonymous remailers Services that will forward your *email* messages or newsgroup *articles* after stripping out your personal details, so that no one can tell who sent them. [223]

Archie A system that lets you track down files on *FTP* sites by entering the name of the file (or part of it) into a program that can search through indexes of files on these computers. [178]

archive A single file which usually contains several (or many) other files to make for quicker and easier *downloading*. Most archives also compress these files into a smaller space than they'd ordinarily take up, speeding up downloads still further. [193]

article For no particularly good reason, the name for a message sent to a *newsgroup*. [129]

ASCII Pronounced 'ass-key', and often referred to as **plain text**. This is a text system that allows ordinary numbers and letters, punctuation marks such as spaces, tabs and carriage returns, plus a few special characters, but no formatting or font information. ASCII text can be recognised by almost any type of computer and read in any word processor.

attachments Files included with a message to be sent by *email* or to a *newsgroup*. Messages that contain attachments are indicated by a paper-clip icon in most software. [107]

attributes In *HTML*, these are additions to *tags* that let you specify or change what the tag should do. For example, `<HR>` creates a rule across the page. Adding the `WIDTH=` and `ALIGN=` attributes lets you create a short rule placed on the left side of the page. [346]

bandwidth A general term for the amount of information that can be transferred over an *Internet* connection. Often used in terms of 'wasting bandwidth' by, for example, sending the same *article* to 30 different *newsgroups* when it was only relevant to one.

BBS (Bulletin Board System) A computer that provides an *email* service and file archives (and perhaps more), which members can connect to via *modem*. Some online services such as CompuServe started life as BBSs before becoming connected to the *Internet*.

binaries or binary files The term for a file that contains anything but plain *ASCII* text (such as a program, movie, or formatted document). Also appears in *newsgroup* names to indicate that non-text files can be attached to *articles* in the group.

bookmarks The Netscape Navigator name for *Favorites*.

bounced email *email* messages that come back to you instead of being delivered, usually because you typed the *email address* wrongly.

browser The vital piece of *Internet* software, ostensibly designed for viewing pages from the *World Wide Web*, but capable of handling almost all of your Internet activities. The two most popular browsers are Microsoft's Internet Explorer, and Netscape's Navigator. [47]

cache A folder on your own system into which your *browser* stores all the files it *downloads* from the *World Wide Web* in case you want to view those pages again – it can then load them quickly from this folder instead of downloading them all over again. [70]

chat A type of conversation that takes place by typing messages back and forth instead of speaking (other than to swear at the chat software). A popular chat system is *IRC*, but *online services* have their own chat rooms, and other software allows one-to-one chatting by 'dialling-up' an *email address* rather like using a telephone. See also *talk*. [144]

client The name for something (usually a software program) that makes use of a service. For example, your *email* program is a client that makes use of the email service. The opposite term is *server*. [11]

compressed files see *archive*.

containers The name for the type of *tags* used in *HTML* that must have a closing tag (such as <B>...</B> for bold text). The text to which the tags are being applied is contained within them.

cookies Small text files that some *websites* store on your computer so that they know who you are next time you visit. [209]

cyberspace A word coined by William Gibson in his novel 'Necromancer'. It's used as a very generalised term for the Internet and everything that comes with it.

Dial-Up Networking The *TCP/IP stack* built into Microsoft Windows 95, Windows NT 4.0, and later operating systems, that makes setting up an *Internet* connection a relatively pain-free task.

DNS see *Domain Name System*.

domain name The name given to a computer on the *Internet* that's (vaguely) recognisable to human beings, such as **www.royalnetwork.com** Every computer on the Net has its own unique name.[8]

Domain Name System (DNS) Also defined as Domain Name Server. This system translates the friendly *domain names* that we humans like to work with into *IP addresses* that computers like to work with. [9]

dot address Another name for *IP address*.

downloading The act of copying files (of any type) to your own computer from some other computer. The opposite term is *uploading*.

Dynamic HTML A formal name for the combination of ordinary *HTML* and scripting in languages such as *JavaScript* that can be used to create feature-rich interactive *web pages*.

e-commerce A 'catch-all' term relating to financial transactions that take place on the Net, along with the software, hardware and *protocols* that are involved.

email or **e-mail** Short for 'electronic mail', a system that lets you send text messages over a *network* from one computer to another. [96]

email address An address consisting of your *username* and the *host* name of your service provider's computer, in the form **username@host**. Because this host name is unique, and you're the only subscriber with that username, the email is as personal to you as your phone number. [97]

emoticons Little pictures (usually faces) made out of typed characters and viewed sideways-on, such as :-) meaning Happy. [112]

encryption The term for altering data or text to turn it into meaningless gobbledegook. Only someone with the correct decoding information (or 'key') can read and use it. [211]

FAQ (Frequently Asked Questions) A list of questions and answers on a particular subject. These are frequently placed in *newsgroups* so that the group doesn't become bogged down with new users asking the same questions all the time. You'll also find FAQs on websites, and almost anywhere else in the computing world.

FTP (File Transfer Protocol) One of the many *protocols* used to copy files from one computer to another on the Internet. Also used in terms like 'an FTP site' (a site that lets you grab files from it using this protocol), and as a verb, as in 'You can ftp to this site'. [162]

Finger A command (or a software program that sends the command) which returns information about someone whose *email address* you entered. Also used as a verb, so this is one instance in which you can 'finger' someone and get away with it. [181]

flame A negative or abusive response to a *newsgroup article* or an *email* message. [138]

follow-up A reply to an *email* or *newsgroup* message that contains the same subject line (prefixed with RE) and continues the same *thread*.

freeware Software that you don't have to pay for. [188]

Favorites A menu in Microsoft's Internet Explorer *browser* (and a corresponding folder on your hard disk) containing shortcuts to sites that you visit regularly. You can revisit a site easily by clicking its name on the menu, and add new sites to the menu with a couple of clicks. [52]

gateway A program or device that acts as a kind of translator between two *networks* that wouldn't otherwise be able to communicate with each other.

GIF One of the two major graphics formats used on the *Internet* (along with *JPEG*). GIF images can be saved with between 2 and 256 colours, so they contain less information than the 16-million-colour JPEG format, and therefore make smaller files. They're suitable for anything but photographs and the most lifelike art. See also *animated GIF*. [351]

Gopher A menu-based system for storing, searching for, and retrieving documents, which was the precursor to the *World Wide Web*. [174]

history list A list of recently visited sites stored by your *browser* so that you can see where you've been, get back there easily, or find out what someone else has been using your browser for. [53]

homepage Two definitions for this one: 1. The page displayed in your *browser* when you first run it, or when you click the Home button. 2. The first page (or main contents page) of a *website*.

host A computer connected directly (and usually permanently) to the *Internet* that allows other computers to connect to it (like your service provider's computer). This also leads to the expression 'host name' which means the same as *domain name*.

HTML see *Hypertext Markup Language*.

HTTP (HyperText Transfer Protocol) The *protocol* used to transfer web pages around the *Internet*, along with the images and other ingredients that go with them.

hypertext A system of clickable text used on the *World Wide Web*, as well as in older Windows help files and CD-ROM-based encyclopaedias. A hypertext *link* can be inserted wherever a cross-reference to another part of the document (or an entirely different document) is needed. [49]

Hypertext Markup Language (HTML) A fairly simple system of textual codes that can be added to an ASCII text file to turn it into a web page. [332]

IAP see *Internet service provider*.

image map A single image divided into several 'hot' areas and placed on a *web page*. Each area will take you to a different page or file when clicked.

Instant Messenger A software program that allows the user to see which of his friends are online and to exchange short conversational messages with any of them in real time. IM software is free, with programs available from AltaVista, Yahoo, AOL, Microsoft and others. [159]

Internet Often shortened to just 'the Net'. The Internet is a gigantic *network* of computers, all linked together and able to exchange information. No one owns or controls it, and anyone can connect to it. Without the capital 'I', an internet is a more general term for networks connected to each other.

Internet access provider (IAP) see *Internet service provider.*

Internet Protocol (IP) see *TCP/IP.*

Internet telephony see *talk.*

IP address (Internet Protocol Address) Every computer on the *Internet* has its own unique address, which can appear in two forms: the friendlier *domain name*, or as an IP address that computers themselves use. This consists of four numbers separated by dots, such as 148.159.6.26. Also known as a 'dot address'. [8]

IRC (Internet Relay Chat) An *Internet* service that provides one of the most popular *chat* systems which can be accessed using many different IRC programs. Chat rooms in IRC are referred to as 'channels'. [147]

ISDN An abbreviation for Integrated Services Digital Network. An ISDN line allows faster access to the *Internet* than current modems allow, and can simultaneously handle voice and data. [22]

Internet service provider (ISP) A company that allows anyone to connect to the *Internet* by dialling in to their *host* computer. All they ask in return is that you give them money (although recently some have started taking their money from different sources and providing this service for free). Also sometimes referred to as an Internet access provider, or IAP. [19]

Java A software-programming language developed by Sun Microsystems Inc. The language is often used to write small programs called 'applets' that can be inserted in a web page.

JavaScript A similar language to *Java*, except that it's written in plain text and can be inserted 'as is' into an *HTML* document to place effects or small programs on a web page.

JPEG Along with *GIF*, this is one of the two most-used formats for images on the Net. This format saves information for 16.7 million colours, making it ideal for photographs but creating unnecessarily large files for most forms of artwork.

leased line A line leased from the telephone company that provides a permanent, dedicated connection to an *Internet Service Provider*. Leased lines are lightning fast and cost a small fortune. (Also known as a 'T1 connection'.) [23]

link As a noun, a link is a piece of clickable *hypertext*, identifiable by being underlined and a different colour from the ordinary text around it. As a verb, to link to a site or page means the same as to open or *download* it.

log off A synonym for 'disconnect' – logging off means telling the computer you're connected to that you've finished for this session.

log on/logon Either of these can be used as a noun or a verb. When you log on to a service or computer you are identifying yourself, usually by entering a *username* and password. This act may be referred to as 'a logon', or 'logging on'. Your username may be termed a 'logon name'.

lurking A cute term for observing something without taking an active role. This may refer to visiting *chat* rooms and just following conversations rather than chatting, or reading *newsgroups* without *posting* any *articles* yourself.

mailing list This can mean two things: 1. A list of *email addresses* to which you can send the same message without making endless copies of it, all with different addresses inserted. 2. A discussion group similar to *newsgroups*, but all the messages sent to the group are forwarded to its members by email. [139]

mail server A computer (or program) dedicated to transferring *email* messages around the *Internet*. This might be referred to as an *SMTP* server or a *POP3* server.

MIME (Multipurpose Internet Mail Extensions) A method of organising different types of file by assigning each its own 'MIME type'. Most of the *Internet* software you use can recognise these types and determine what to do with a file it receives (or ask you how you want to treat it). MIME is used to handle *attachments* in *email* and *newsgroup* messages, as well as files found on web pages.

mirror site An exact copy of a site located on a different computer. Many popular sites have one or more mirrors around the world so that users can connect to the site nearest to them, thus easing the load on the main computer.

modem An acronym formed from the words 'modulator' and 'demodulator'. A modem converts data back and forth between the format recognised by computers and the format needed to send it down telephone lines. [16]

MP3 An abbreviation of MPEG Third Layer, a madly popular sound format that uses 10:1 compression with little loss in quality (provided your processor is fast enough to decompress the file while playing it). [311]

MPEG Along with *QuickTime*, one of the two most popular formats for movie files on the *Internet*, requiring an MPEG player and (ideally) special hardware for playback. [314]

MUD (Multi-User Dungeon) A type of text-based adventure game that might be played by a single user, or by multiple users adopting characters and 'chatting' by typing messages. [178]

Netiquette An amalgamation of the words 'Internet' and 'etiquette' that refers to good behaviour on the Net. Netiquette essentially boils down to two rules: avoid offensive comments and actions, and don't waste Internet resources (or *bandwidth*). [116, 137]

network Two or more computers that are connected to each other (or connected via telephone lines and *modems*) and can pass information back and forth.

newbie A colloquial name for someone new to the *Internet*, or to a particular area of it, and perhaps prone to a bit of fumbling around. Although a slightly derogatory term, it's not meant to be offensive – you might describe yourself as a newbie when appealing for help.

newsgroups A discussion group with a particular topic in which users leave messages for others to read and reply to. There are over 50 000 such groups, and many more *mailing lists* which follow similar methods. Newsgroups are sometimes referred to as *Usenet* groups. [124]

newsreader The software program you use to access *newsgroups*, and to read, send, and reply to *articles*.

news server A computer (or program) dedicated to transferring the contents of *newsgroups* around the Net, and to and from your computer. This might be referred to as an *NNTP* server.

NNTP (Network News Transfer Protocol) One of many *protocols* used on the Net to transfer information around. This particular protocol handles messages from *newsgroups*.

offline A synonym for 'not connected'. In Net terms, being offline is generally a good thing (unless you're trying and failing to get *online*): the ability to compose messages offline and send them all in a bunch later, or view *downloaded* files offline, can save you money in connection charges.

online A synonym for 'connected'. Anything connected to your computer and ready for action can be said to be online. In *Internet* terms, it means that you've successfully dialled in to your service provider's computer and are now connected to the Net. The opposite term is *offline*.

online service A members-only service that allows users to join discussion groups (or 'forums'), exchange *email* messages with other members, download files, and a fair bit more besides. Most popular online services (such as America Online and CompuServe) are now connected to the *Internet* as well. [18, 34]

packet The name for a unit of data being sent across the Net. A system called 'packet switching' breaks a file up into packets, marks each with the addresses of the sending and receiving computers, and sends each packet off individually. These packets may arrive at your computer via different routes and in the wrong order, but your computer uses the extra information they contain to piece the file back together.

PDA (Personal Digital Assistant) A miniature electronic device that functions as a contacts list, appointment manager and memo taker, and may also be able to send and receive *email* messages and access *WAP* services.

PGP (Pretty Good Privacy) A popular, but complicated, system of *encryption*. [211]

PING (Packet InterNet Groper) The name of a command (or a program that sends a command) that tests a connection between two computers. It does this by sending a tiny amount of data to a specified computer and noting how long it takes to reply. (The reply, incidentally, is called a PONG.) [182]

plug-in An add-on program for a *browser* that can play or display a particular type of file in the browser's own window. [309]

PoP (Point of Presence) An unnecessarily technical name for a phone number you can dial to connect to your service provider's computer. Many service providers have PoPs all over the country; others cater just for the major cities or a single small area.

POP3 (Post Office Protocol) One of two *protocols* (along with *SMTP*) used to transfer *email* messages around the Net. POP is used for receiving email, and lets you collect your messages from any computer you happen to be using. The '3' refers to the latest version of the protocol. [99]

portal A new name for what is essentially a *search engine*. A portal aims to be your starting point for a spot of surfing, providing links, additional information such as news headlines, weather and TV schedules, as well as search facilities.

posting When you send an email message, the word 'sending' is quite good enough. When you send a message to a *newsgroup*, it isn't. Instead, for no adequately explained reason, the word 'posting' is used.

PPP (Point to Point Protocol) A *protocol* used to connect computers to the Internet via a telephone line and a modem. It's similar to *SLIP*, but more recent and easier to set up.

protocol A type of 'language' that two computers agree to speak when they need to communicate and don't speak each other's native language. In other words, a sort of Esperanto for computers, but networking and *Internet* connections use a great many different protocols to do different things.

Public key encryption The most-used method of *encryption*, where two pieces of text are used as 'keys'. One is a public key which anyone can use to encrypt something for you; the other is your private key, used to decrypt such material when it arrives. [211]

QuickTime Along with *MPEG*, this is one of the most popular movie file formats on the Net, developed by Apple. To view these files you'll need the QuickTime Viewer. There is also a virtual reality version (QuickTime VR) which is gaining in popularity. [314]

RealAudio The most popular format for *streaming* audio on the Net, requiring the RealAudio Player (included with Internet Explorer) for playback. [310]

refresh (or **reload**) Forcing the *browser* to *download* a web page again by clicking a toolbar button labelled Refresh (in Internet Explorer) or Reload (in Netscape Navigator). You might do this to make sure you're looking at the latest version of a page, or as an attempt to get things moving again if the page began to download and everything ground to a halt.

rot13 (rotated 13) A simple method used to *encrypt email* and *newsgroup* messages so that you won't accidentally read something that might offend you. [133]

search engine A website that maintains an index of other web pages and sites, allowing you to search for pages on a particular subject by entering keywords. Because these engines gather their information in different ways, you can get markedly varying results from using different search sites. [78]

server A computer or program that provides a service to a *client*. For example, your email client (the program that lets you work with *email* messages) connects to your service provider's mail server when you decide to send or receive your email.

service provider A general term for a company that gives you access to the *Internet* by letting you dial in to their computer. This may be an *Internet service provider* or an *online service*.

shareware A system for selling software that lets you try before you buy. If you like the program, you pay for it. If you don't, you stop using it and delete it from your system. [188]

signature A short piece of text you can create that gets appended to your *email* and *newsgroup* messages when you send them. This might give contact information (perhaps your name, email address, company name etc.), a neat little phrase or quote, or perhaps an elaborate piece of *ASCII* art (rather like an *emoticon*, but bigger).

SLIP (Serial Line Internet Protocol) A similar *protocol* to *PPP*, but older and best avoided (especially if you use Windows 95, Windows NT 4.0, or later).

smiley see *emoticon*.

SME An abbreviation for Small to Medium-sized Enterprise, the kind of venture that was called a 'small business' until someone realised there was no memorable abbreviation for that.

SMTP (Simple Mail Transfer Protocol) Along with *POP3*, one of the two *protocols* that are used to transfer *email* messages around the Net. SMTP can be used to both send and receive messages, but POP3 has more flexibility for receiving. When POP3 is being used, SMTP simply handles the sending of messages. [99]

SoHo An acronym for Small office, Home office. Not a building as you might expect, but used in the context 'a SoHo user' to refer to a type of computer user.

source The name for the *HTML* document that forms a web page, containing all the *tags* that determine what your *browser* should display, and how. You can look at the source for a web page in Internet Explorer by clicking the View menu and selecting Source.

spamming A Net jargon term for sending the same message to multiple *newsgroups* or *email* recipients regardless of their interest (or lack of it). Most spamming consists of unsolicited advertisements. Apart from the personal aggravation it causes, spamming is also a massive waste of *bandwidth*. [138]

streaming Some of the latest formats for video and audio on the Net allow the file to play while it's being *downloaded*, rather than forcing you to wait for the entire file to download first.

tags The name for the HTML codes added to a plain ASCII document which turn it into a web page with full formatting and links to other files and pages. [332]

talk A talk program lets you speak to someone elsewhere in the world using your *modem* and *Internet* connection instead of your telephone. You need a soundcard and microphone, and the other person must be using the same program you are. Also known as Voice Over the Net (VON). The term 'talk' is also used to describe the kind of typed *chat* that takes place between two people rather than a group in a chat room. [153]

TCP/IP (Transmission Control Protocol/Internet Protocol) Two vital *protocols* that work together to handle communications between your computer and the rest of the *Internet*.

TCP/IP stack For a computer to connect to the *Internet*, it must have a TCP/IP stack, which consists of TCP/IP software, *packet* driver software, and sockets software. Windows 95 and later Windows operating systems come with their own TCP/IP stack called *Dial-Up Networking*. In Windows 3x, the TCP/IP stack has to be installed separately: one of the best stacks is Trumpet Winsock (see also *Winsock*).

Telnet A program that allows *Internet* users to connect to a distant computer and control it through their own computer. Nowadays the main use of Telnet is in playing games like *MUDs*. [176]

thread An ongoing topic of conversation in a *newsgroup* or *mailing list*. When someone *posts* a message with a new subject line they're starting a new thread. Any replies to this message (and replies to replies, and so on) will have the same subject line and continue the thread. [131]

thumbnail image A small version of a larger image displayed on a *web page*. A thumbnail is often used to let the visitor preview a picture and decide whether to click it to view the full-sized version.

TLAs (Three Letter Acronyms) Not necessarily acronyms, and not necessarily three letters either, but TLAs are a type of shorthand for common phrases used in conversation and messages on the Net, such as BTW for 'By the way'. [113]

Transmission Control Protocol (TCP) see *TCP/IP*.

uploading The term for copying files from your own computer to a distant computer, usually by using *FTP*. The opposite term is *downloading*.

URL (Uniform Resource Locator) (Pronounced 'earl'.) The unique 'address' of a file on the *Internet* consisting of a *protocol* (such as http://), a computer name (such as www.computer.co.uk) and a path to the file on that computer (such as /public/files/program.zip).

Usenet A large network that distributes many of the Net's *newsgroups*. [124]

username A unique name you're assigned by a service that enables you to *log on* to it and identify yourself, demonstrating that you're entitled to access it. When you set up your *Internet* service account, your username will usually form part of your *email address* too. [28]

UUencode/UUdecode To send computer files in *email* or *newsgroup* messages, they have to be converted to plain *ASCII* text first. UUencoding is a system for converting files this way; uudecoding converts the text back into a file at the other end. Special software may be needed to do this, but many email and newsgroup programs have built-in automatic UUencode/UUdecode facilities. [108]

VBScript A scripting language developed by Microsoft, similar to *JavaScript*.

Veronica An acronym for 'Very Easy Rodent-Oriented Net-wide Index to Computerized Archives'. Veronica is a facility built into *Gopher* that allows searching for files on gopher sites.

viewer A program used to view, play or display files that you find on the Net. Unlike a *plug-in*, a viewer will open the file in its own separate window. Because it's a stand-alone program, you can also use it *offline* to view files already on your own system. [309]

virus A small program created by a warped mind that can use various methods to attach itself to programs. When the program is run, so is the virus. A virus might do no more harm to your system than making it go beep occasionally, or it might trash all your data and even make your computer unusable. The main risk of 'catching' a virus comes from using programs on a floppy disk of unknown origin or *downloaded* from the *Internet* without first running them through virus-checker software. [212]

Voice Over the Net (VON) see *talk.*

VRML (Virtual Reality Modelling Language) A language used to build three-dimensional models and 'worlds' that you can view using special software. [317]

WAIS (Wide Area Information Server) A little-used service for searching databases of information on the Net.

WAP (Wireless Application Protocol) Special web-like pages written in a language called *WML* (similar to the Web's own *HTML*) can be downloaded into the new breed of WAP-enabled mobile phones, pagers and *PDAs*, and read while on the move. These devices have four- or eight-line displays for text and simple graphics. [226]

Web see *World Wide Web.*

web page A single document (usually having the extension .htm or .html) forming a tiny part of the *World Wide Web*, often containing text, images, and *links* to other pages and files on the Web. To view web pages you need a *browser*. [45]

web server A computer or program dedicated to storing *web pages* and transmitting them to your computer to be viewed in your *browser*.

website A collection of related *web pages* and files, usually created by, or belonging to, a single individual or company, and located on the same *web server*.

web space Usually refers to space on a *web server* provided to *Internet* users so that they can create and publish their own *websites*. This space may be provided free, or for a monthly charge. [364]

Whois A command (or a program which can send the command) that can find someone's email address and other information about them based on the name you enter. [183]

Winsock An abbreviation of Windows Sockets, the sockets software program for Windows operating systems called Winsock.dll that forms the basis of a *TCP/IP stack*.

WML (Wireless Markup Language) A text-based language used to write pages of (mainly textual) information that can be viewed on *WAP*-enabled devices. WML is based on *XML* and could be thought of as a very cut-down version of the Web's own *HTML*.

World Wide Web A vast collection of documents and files stored on *web servers*. The documents are known as *web pages* and are created using a language called *HTML*. All these pages and files are linked together using a system of *hypertext*. [42]

XML (eXtensible Markup Language) A language very similar to *HTML* (used to write web pages) but with the benefit that users can extend the language with their own custom additions. Future versions of HTML are likely to be more XML-oriented.

HTML TAG GLOSSARY

The following is a quick-reference guide to the most useful HTML tags (including those covered in Chapters 23 and 24) together with their attributes. You'll find examples of these and more on the CD-ROM if you'd like to see what they look like in use (and, perhaps, just copy the code instead of trying to understand it!)

The list below has been set out as follows:

▶ For HTML elements that must have a closing tag, both the opening and closing tags are included, separated by an ellipsis (…) which is where your own text will go.

▶ Where information must be placed between double quotes, they have been included.

▶ As usual, any text in **_bold italics_** will be substituted with your own settings.

▶ Where only fixed alternatives are available (as in the case of alignment options) they are separated by pipe symbols, such as **left | right | center**.

Comments

```
<!--...-->
```
Turns all the text between these elements into a comment ignored by browsers.

Document Structure

```
<HTML>...</HTML>
```
Encloses the whole document, containing the <HEAD> and <BODY> sections.

```
<HEAD>...</HEAD>
```
The header portion of the document, containing the <TITLE> and, optionally, the <META> elements.

`<BODY>...</BODY>`

Encloses the body portion of the document, including all text to be displayed and tags used for formatting, links, images, etc. Optional attributes are:

`BGCOLOR=`*`colour`*	Colour of the page background.
`TEXT=`*`colour`*	Default colour of the page's text.
`LINK=`*`colour`*	Colour of hypertext links.
`VLINK=colour`	Colour of visited links.
`ALINK=`*`colour`*	Colour of active (just-clicked) links.
`BACKGROUND=`*`"file"`*	Image file to be tiled as page wallpaper.

`<BASE>`

Specifies a URL from which all relative links in a document will be resolved, or a default frame or window name into which all links will be opened. One or both of these attributes must be used:

`HREF=`*`"url"`*	The base URL to resolve links.
`TARGET=`*`"frame"`*	The default frame or window name.

`<META>`

Provides information about the document itself, such as providing descriptions and keywords for use by search engines, or author and expiry details. Either or both of the first two attributes may be used; the CONTENT attribute must be present.

`HTTP-EQUIV=`*`http header`*	Recognised HTTP header such as **Expires**.
`NAME=`*`meta name`*	Name of META information, such as **Author**.
`CONTENT=`*`value`*	The value to be associated with the given name.

Title & Headings

`<TITLE>...</TITLE>`

Encloses the title of the document. This must be included in the header.

`<H1>...</H1>`

Encloses text to be formatted as a heading. `<H1>` defines the largest possible heading, `<H2>` is slightly smaller, and so on down to `<H6>`, the smallest. Any of these can take the optional attribute:

ALIGN=center | left | right   Aligns the heading on the page. The default is **left**.

Character Formatting

`<FONT>...</FONT>`

Specifies or alters the type and style of font to be used for the enclosed text. Takes one or more of these attributes:

FACE="*font1, font2, ...*"   Name of font to be used, plus alternatives.

SIZE=1 | 2 | 3 | 4 | 5 | 6 | 7   Size of the font to use. The default size is 3.

COLOR=*colour*   Colour in which the text should be displayed.

`<B>...</B>`

Formats the enclosed text in bold type.

`<I>...</I>`

Formats the enclosed text in italic type.

`<U>...</U>`

Underlines the enclosed text.

`<S>...</S>`

Strikes through (crosses out) the enclosed text.

`<EM>...</EM>`

Emphasises the enclosed text; most browsers will format this as italic type.

`<STRONG>...</STRONG>`
Strong emphasis of the enclosed text; most browsers will format this as bold type.

`<TT>...</TT>`
Formats the enclosed text using a typewriter-style font.

`<BIG>...</BIG>`
Makes the enclosed text one size larger.

`<SMALL>...</SMALL>`
Makes the enclosed text one size smaller.

`<SUP>...</SUP>`
Formats the enclosed text as superscript.

`<SUB>...</SUB>`
Formats the enclosed text as subscript.

`<BLOCKQUOTE>...</BLOCKQUOTE>`
Formats the enclosed text as a quotation, usually by indenting it left and right.

`<PRE>...</PRE>`
Displays the enclosed text exactly as typed, observing carriage returns, styles, spaces, etc.

Paragraphs & Layout

`<P>`
Indicates the start of a new paragraph, inserting a blank line before the text that follows this tag, and aligning it with the left margin by default.

`<P ALIGN=center | left | right>...</P>`
Works in the same way as `<P>` by itself, but aligns the enclosed text centrally or with the left or right margins.

`<BR>`

Inserts a line break at the point where the tag appears. You can use this repeatedly to insert blank lines as well. Optionally takes the following attribute:

**`CLEAR=left	right	all`**	The following text will be placed at the next point where there is a clear position at the left or right margin, or a clear position at both margins.

`<NOBR>...</NOBR>`

Prevents the enclosed text from breaking at the right margin.

`<WBR>`

Marks a point where the text may be wrapped to the next line if a break is necessary in a line. Usually used within <NOBR> tags.

`<HR>`

Places a horizontal rule across the width of the page with a blank line above and below it. Optional attributes are:

`WIDTH=number(%)`	Width of the line in pixels or as a percentage of page width.
`SIZE=number`	Height of the line in pixels. The default is 2.
`COLOR=colour`	Colour of the line (automatically made solid).
`NOSHADE`	Removes 3D shading to make a solid line.
**`ALIGN=center	left	right`**	Sets alignment of the line. The default is **center**.

`<CENTER>...</CENTER>`

Places all the enclosed text, images and other content centrally on the page.

Lists

`<LI>`
Creates a list entry when used with `<UL>`, `<OL>` or `<DIR>`. Automatically places the entry on a new line. `<LI>` can also be used by itself to place a bullet at the start of a new line.

`<UL>...</UL>`
Creates an unordered (or bulleted) list, using entries placed after `<LI>` tags.

`<OL>...</OL>`
Creates an ordered (numbered) list, using entries placed after `<LI>` tags, and taking the following optional attributes:

`START=number`	The number from which the list should count.
`TYPE=1	A	a	I	i`	The numbering system to use: numerical | capital letters | small letters | roman numerals | small roman numerals. The default is numerical.

`<DIR>...</DIR>`
Creates a directory list of entries by indenting the `<LI>` entries that follow.

`<DL>...</DL>`
Creates a definition list, using `<DT>` and `<DD>` to create the list entries within the `<DL>` tags.

`<DT>`
Creates an entry in a definition list. The entry is automatically placed on a new line and aligned with the left margin.

`<DD>`
Creates a definition for a `<DT>` entry. The text following the `<DD>` tag is automatically placed on a new line and indented.

Images & Multimedia

`<IMG>`

Inserts an image at that point on the web page. The `SRC=` attribute is required, the others are optional.

`SRC="filename"`	The URL, or name and location, of the image file.
`ALIGN=top	middle	bottom	left	right`	Alignment of the image. The default is left.
`WIDTH=number`	The width of the image.
`HEIGHT=number`	The height of the image.
`VSPACE=number`	The space in pixels to leave clear above and below.
`HSPACE=number`	The space in pixels to leave clear to either side.
`ALT="text"`	Alternative text to be displayed.
`BORDER=number`	0 means no border. Higher numbers give thicker borders.
`USEMAP=map name`	Indicates that this is an image map, and gives the name of the map to be used.

`<MAP>`

Used with client-side image maps to specify the name of the map, and to plot the co-ordinates of areas of the image and assign URLs to them. Takes the attribute:

`NAME=map name`	Specifies the name of the map.

`<SCRIPT>`...`</SCRIPT>`

Inserts a script into an HTML document, usually in the header. Needs the attribute:

`LANGUAGE=JavaScript	VBScript`	The name of the scripting language used.

`<MARQUEE>`...`</MARQUEE>`

Places a scrolling marquee on the web page using the text enclosed within these tags. The text will be the colour last specified (either in the `<BODY>` tag or by enclosing the entire marquee code within `<FONT>` tags.) The available attributes are:

`WIDTH=number(%)`	Width of the marquee in pixels or as a percentage of page width.
`HEIGHT=number`	The height of the marquee.
`VSPACE=number`	The space in pixels to leave clear above and below.
`HSPACE=number`	The space in pixels to leave clear to either side.
`ALIGN=top | middle | bottom`	Aligns the marquee with any text on the same line.
`BGCOLOR=colour`	The colour of the marquee's background.
`DIRECTION=left | right`	The direction in which the text should move. The default is **left**.
`BEHAVIOR=scroll | slide | alternate`	Determines how the text should move. The default is scroll.
`LOOP=number | infinite`	The number of times the marquee should repeat, or an endless repetition.
`SCROLLAMOUNT=number`	How many pixels the text should scroll at a time.
`SCROLLDELAY=number`	Length of pause between each movement of the text.

`<APPLET>`...`</APPLET>`

Inserts a Java applet on the web page, taking these attributes:

`CODE="class file"`	The name of the Java class to be run.
`CODEBASE=location`	The location of the class file if not in the same directory as the HTML document.

`WIDTH=number`	The required width of the applet.
`HEIGHT=number`	The required height of the applet.
`VSPACE=number`	The space in pixels to leave clear above and below.
`HSPACE=number`	The space in pixels to leave clear to either side.
`ALIGN=center | left | right | middle | texttop | textbottom | textmiddle | baseline`	The alignment of the applet.
`ALT="text"`	Alternative text to be displayed if the browser doesn't support Java applets.
`NAME=name`	Assigns a name to the applet.

`<PARAM>`

A tag used with Java applets to specify optional settings that might have been built into the applet by its author. Takes the following two attributes:

| `NAME=name` | The specified parameter name. |
| `VALUE="value"` | The chosen value for that parameter. |

Links

`<A>...</A>`

Creates a link to the web document or file named in the `HREF=` attribute, or creates an anchor which can be linked to by using the `NAME=` attribute.

`HREF="url | name"`	Formats the enclosed text as a link to the URL or named anchor. The value may also be **"mailto:*emailaddress*"**.
`TARGET="frame"`	Specifies the name of a frame or window in which the linked document should be opened.
`NAME="name"`	Creates an anchor at the point where the enclosed text occurs that can be linked to by adding **#*name*** to the end of the `HREF=` value.

Tables

`<TABLE>...</TABLE>`

Formats the enclosed text (including the rest of the tags in this category) as a table. The following optional attributes can be added:

`ALIGN=center | left | right`	Sets the alignment of the table. The default is **left**.
`BORDER=number`	Thickness of border. The default is no border.
`WIDTH=number(%)`	Width of the table in pixels or as a percentage of page width.
`CELLPADDING=number`	Space between the sides of a cell and its contents, in pixels.
`CELLSPACING=number`	Space between the table's border and its cells, in pixels.
`BGCOLOR=colour`	Background colour of the table (recognised only by Internet Explorer).
`BACKGROUND="file"`	Image file to be used as a table's background (Explorer only).
`BORDERCOLOR=colour`	The colour of the table border (Explorer only).

`<TR>...</TR>`

Short for 'table row'. The enclosed text and `<TD>` tags will form a new row of cells in a table. (The closing `</TR>` tag can be left out with no harmful effects.) This tag can take the ALIGN, BGCOLOR, BACKGROUND and BORDERCOLOR attributes exactly as used by the `<TABLE>` tag, plus the following:

`VALIGN=top | middle | bottom | baseline`	Sets the vertical alignment of all text in this row.
`CHAR="character"`	Sets a particular character that will be aligned according to the ALIGN= setting.
`CHAROFF="number%"`	Sets a percentage offset for the first alignment character.

<TD>...</TD>

Short for 'table data'. This tag creates a new cell in the current row and encloses the text (or other content) to be placed in that cell, although the closing tag may be left out. <TD> can take the ALIGN, BGCOLOR, BACKGROUND, BORDERCOLOR, VALIGN, CHAR and CHAROFF attributes mentioned above, as well as the following:

COLSPAN=*number*	The number of columns that this cell will span.
ROWSPAN=*number*	The number of rows that this cell will span.
NOWRAP	Prevents the text from wrapping in a cell.

<CAPTION>...</CAPTION>

Can be used within the <TABLE> element to create a caption above the table using the enclosed text. The available attribute is:

ALIGN=top | bottom | left right	Sets the alignment of the caption.

HTML COLOUR NAMES

Colours in HTML come in two flavours: *named colours* and *hex numbers representing colours*. The hex system is explained in greater detail on the CD-ROM, but in brief, any colour you want to use is made up of varying proportions of red, green and blue. Each of these three colours can have a value of anything from 0 to 255, which gives a total of 16.7 million possible shades available.

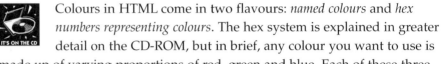

However, there are still some browsers that can't display all these colours. To ensure that your pages look the way they're supposed to on almost any system, it's preferable to stick with the 140 colours listed below. The corresponding hex numbers are given here too, and you can enter either into your HTML documents – the tag <FONT COLOR=FF0000> means just the same as <FONT COLOR=RED>. For want of a better system, the colours are simply presented in alphabetical order by name. You'll also find a colour chart with swatches on the free CD-ROM accompanying this book.

Name	Hex	Name	Hex
AliceBlue	F0F8FF	AntiqueWhite	FAEBD7
Aqua	00FFFF	Aquamarine	7FFFD4
Azure	F0FFFF	Beige	F5F5DC
Bisque	FFE4C4	Black	000000
BlanchedAlmond	FFFBCD	Blue	0000FF
BlueViolet	8A2BE2	Brown	A52A2A
Burlywood	DEB887	CadetBlue	5F9EA0
Chartreuse	7FFF00	Chocolate	D2691E
Coral	FF7F50	CornflowerBlue	6495ED
Cornsilk	FFF8DC	Crimson	DC143C
Cyan	00FFFF	DarkBlue	00008B
DarkCyan	008B8B	DarkGoldenrod	B8860B
DarkGray	A9A9A9	DarkGreen	006400
DarkKhaki	BDB76B	DarkMagenta	8B008B
DarkOliveGreen	556B2F	DarkOrange	FF8C00
DarkOrchid	9932CC	DarkRed	8B0000
DarkSalmon	E9967A	DarkSeaGreen	8FBC8F
DarkSlateBlue	483D8B	DarkSlateGray	2F4F4F
DarkTurquoise	00CED1	DarkViolet	9400D3
DeepPink	FF1493	DeepSkyBlue	00BFBF

Name	Hex
DimGray	696969
Firebrick	B22222
ForestGreen	228B22
Gainsboro	DCDCDC
Gold	FFD700
Gray	808080
GreenYellow	ADFF2F
HotPink	FF69B4
Indigo	4B0082
Khaki	F0E68C
LavenderBlush	FFF0F5
LemonChiffon	FFFACD
LightCoral	F08080
LightGoldenrodYellow	FAFAD2
LightGreen	90EE90
LightSalmon	FFA07A
LightSkyBlue	87CEFA
LightSteelBlue	B0C4DE
Lime	00FF00
Linen	FAF0E6
Maroon	800000
MediumBlue	0000CD
MediumPurple	9370DB
MediumSlateBlue	7B68EE
MediumTurquoise	48D1CC
MidnightBlue	191970
MistyRose	FFE4E1
NavajoWhite	FFDEAD
OldLace	FDF5E6
OliveDrab	6B8E23
OrangeRed	FF4500
PaleGoldenrod	EEE8AA
PaleTurquoise	AFEEEE
PapayaWhip	FFEFD5
Peru	CD853F
Plum	DDA0DD

Name	Hex
DodgerBlue	1E90FF
FloralWhite	FFFAF0
Fuchsia	FF00FF
GhostWhite	F8F8FF
Goldenrod	DAA520
Green	008000
Honeydew	F0FFF0
IndianRed	CD5C5C
Ivory	FFFFF0
Lavender	E6E6FA
LawnGreen	7CFC00
LightBlue	ADD8E6
LightCyan	E0FFFF
LightGray	D3D3D3
LightPink	FFB6C1
LightSeaGreen	20B2AA
LightSlateGray	778899
LightYellow	FFFFE0
LimeGreen	32CD32
Magenta	FF00FF
MediumAquamarine	66CDAA
MediumOrchid	BA55D3
MediumSeaGreen	3CB371
MediumSpringGreen	00FA9A
MediumVioletRed	C71585
MintCream	F5FFFA
Moccasin	FFE4B5
Navy	000080
Olive	808000
Orange	FFA500
Orchid	DA70D6
PaleGreen	98FB98
PaleVioletRed	DB7093
PeachPuff	FFDAB9
Pink	FFC0CB
PowderBlue	B0E0E6

Name	Hex		Name	Hex
Purple	800080		Red	FF0000
RosyBrown	BC8F8F		RoyalBlue	4169E1
SaddleBrown	8B4513		Salmon	FA8072
SandyBrown	F4A460		SeaGreen	2E8B57
Seashell	FFF5EE		Sienna	A0522D
Silver	C0C0C0		SkyBlue	87CEEB
SlateBlue	6A5ACD		SlateGray	708090
Snow	FFFAFA		SpringGreen	00FF7F
SteelBlue	4682B4		Tan	D2B48C
Teal	008080		Thistle	D8BFD8
Tomato	FF6347		Turquoise	40E0D0
Violet	EE82EE		Wheat	F5DEB3
White	FFFFFF		WhiteSmoke	F5F5F5
Yellow	FFFF00		YellowGreen	9ACD32

ACCOUNTS & CONNECTIONS

It's no surprise that the vast majority of the online world is using Internet Explorer to browse the Web and Outlook Express to handle email – after all, the majority of the online world uses Windows, and these programs stare back at you from the Windows desktop, begging to be used. Most ISPs' setup CD-ROMs make a great job of configuring these programs to dial up, surf the Web, and handle email without causing you any grief, but once in a while you'll hit a question or a quandary. Here are answers to some of the most-asked questions about dial-up connections, ISPs and email accounts.

How can I get rid of an unwanted service provider I installed and changed my mind about?

One of the problems of the 'free ISPs' that abound today is that it's easy to add another connection to your computer, which then adds another email account to Outlook Express and makes itself the default Internet account on your system, but it's not obvious how you remove all this stuff if you don't like it. Here's how to give that unwanted account the boot.

1 In Internet Explorer, go to **Tools | Internet Options | Connections.**
   Click the name of the ISP you don't want, and click the **Remove** button.
   Then click the one you want to use by default and click the **Set Default**
   button. Click **OK**.

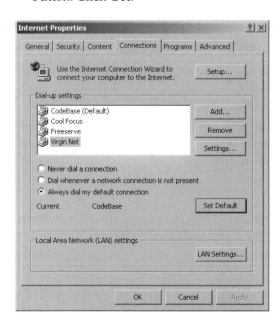

▶ From the
Internet Options
page you can
select any dial-up
account and
delete it or set it
as the default.

2   Start Outlook Express and go to **Tools | Accounts**. In a similar way, remove the unwanted ISP from the list of accounts and set one of the remaining accounts as the default. Click the **Close** button.

3   Open **My Computer,** followed by **Dial-Up Networking**, and delete the icon for the ISP you don't want.

This should work for most ISPs, but a few add customisations to your system or use their own dial-up programs, and this method won't necessarily be successful with those. You may be able to remove them by choosing **Add/Remove Programs** from Control Panel, selecting your ISP's name from the list (if it appears there) and clicking the **Add/Remove** button.

Outlook Express is still trying to send my email through my old service provider (which I thought I'd deleted), so my messages aren't being sent.

Start Outlook Express and go to **Tools | Accounts | Mail**. In the list of accounts, click the ISP you don't want to use and click the **Remove** button (if you really do want to delete it, otherwise ignore this step). Next, click the name of the ISP you *do* want to use and click the **Set as Default** button. Finally click **OK**. Using that second step, you can set any email account as your default without having to delete other accounts.

I have two email accounts. How can I choose which one to send a message from when writing it?

Some users have two service providers set up on their computers, and use one account for personal email to friends and the other for business email. This sets the name the recipient will see as the sender of the message, and the address they'll reply to. In Outlook Express, though, one account is always your default account, and when you click the **New Message** button, that's the account the message will be sent from.

Actually, that ain't necessarily so. The **From** field of the message window is a dropdown list: just click the arrow button at its extreme right and you can choose any other account you want to use to send the message. When you reply to an incoming email, the From address will automatically be the account the incoming email message was sent to, but you can change this in exactly the same way.

▶ Choose the account to use when you compose a new email message.

I've just bought a new computer. How can I copy my existing Internet connection onto it?

It's always worth making a note of the dial-up phone number, usernames and passwords used to connect to your service provider so that you can recreate a connection if you need to. That may be because you buy a new computer (in which case you could look up the details on the old computer) or it might be because your computer developed problems. If it's the second of those, the details might be gone for good, so now's a good time to write them down somewhere safe!

With those details to hand follow these steps to set up the connection.

1 In **My Computer**, **Dial-Up Networking**, double-click the **Make New Connection** icon and follow the simple steps to enter the dial-up phone number and a friendly name for the connection. This creates a new icon in the Dial-Up Networking folder. Double-click that icon, enter your connection username and password, and allow it to dial up so that you can check it connects successfully. Then you can disconnect. (You'll find a more complete version of this step in Appendix A.)

2   Start Internet Explorer, go to **Tools | Internet Options | Connections**, and make sure this new connection is shown there. If you want it to be your default connection, select it and click the **Set Default** button. Finally, click **OK**.

3   Start Outlook Express and go to **Tools | Accounts | Mail**, click **Add**, and click the **Mail** option. Work through the dialog that appears to enter your name, email address, username and password, along with the names of the mail servers (your ISP can tell you those if you don't know them).

I have two email accounts. Can I retrieve my mail from both at once, instead of having to close the connection and redial for the second?

It should be possible, provided both are POP3 email accounts. Start Outlook Express, go to **Tools | Accounts** and click the **Mail** tab. In the list of accounts, one will be marked as the default and you're already receiving mail from that one properly. Select the other account, click **Properties** and check the box marked **Include this account when receiving mail**. Next time you send and receive mail you'll find out if it works. If Outlook Express can't contact the second mail server it'll tell you so, and you may want to go back to the Accounts page and remove the checkmark again to stop Outlook Express displaying an error message each time you collect mail.

◀ Choose **Request Read Receipt** when you write a new message and you should receive a note when the recipient reads it.

How can I check if a message has been received by the person I sent it to or is still waiting to be collected from the server?

While you're writing the message in Outlook Express, go to the **Tools** menu in the message window and choose **Request Read Receipt**. When the recipient opens the message, a short automatic email confirmation should be sent to you. Whether it really will depend on the settings the recipient has chosen (in Outlook Express, these are in Tools | Options | Receipts). Users can turn off this feature completely, or choose to be asked if a receipt should be sent, giving them the chance to say 'No'.

I'm trying to send a photo by email, but it's taking a long time to send it. What can I do?

It would also take just as long to receive it at the other end, so you wouldn't be popular! Scanned photos often end up in TIFF format, one of the many types of image file computers can work with, and these can be huge files. For Internet use, you need to convert the photo to JPEG format, which compresses the file without losing too much quality. Almost any graphics program will be able to do this (try Paint Shop Pro from **http://www.jasc.com**
 if your own graphics program doesn't seem to). Open the image file in that program, choose **Save As** from the File menu, and open the list labelled 'Save as type' in the Save dialog. Look for an option marked JPEG or JPG, select it, and click the **Save** button. You'll then have a second image file in the much smaller JPEG format that you can attach to the email message and send.

DIRECTORY

1: UK Internet Service Providers

Use the list below to find an ISP with the services you're looking for and a local POP, then give them a ring and check some of the details mentioned in Chapter 2. All ISPs noted here offer full UK coverage and the basic services of email, World Wide Web, FTP, IRC and newsgroup access. Extra details are included under *Notes*.

Bear in mind that this isn't an exhaustive list, and these details change regularly – for example, many web space allocations have recently risen from under 5Mb to 25Mb or more – so it doesn't hurt to ask if the details don't exactly match what you're looking for. Most ISPs have special packages for business users and a choice of home-user accounts. If you already have Internet access, an increasing number of free and subscription ISPs will let you sign up online.

Company:	Abel Internet
Telephone:	0131 445 5555
email:	info@abel.net.uk
WWW Site:	www.abel.net.uk
POPs:	UK coverage
Notes:	ISDN, 10Mb web space, unlimited email addresses

Company:	BT Internet
Telephone:	0800 800001
email:	support@btinternet.com
WWW Site:	www.btinternet.com
Notes:	ISDN, unlimited web space & email addresses. Free weekend & evening calls via BT SurfTime

Company:	CableNet
Telephone:	01424 830900
email:	sales@cablenet.net
WWW Site:	www. cablenet.net

Company:	CityScape
Telephone:	01223 566950
email:	sales@cityscape.co.uk
WWW Site:	www.cityscape.co.uk
Notes:	ISDN, 6.5Mb web space, 24-hour support

Company: ClaraNET Ltd
Telephone: 0800 358 2828
email: sales@clara.net
WWW Site: www.clara.net
Notes: ISDN, various account offers, reduced call charges

Company: Demon Internet
Telephone: 020 8371 1234
email: sales@demon.net
WWW Site: www.demon.net
Notes: ISDN, 20Mb web space, unlimited email addresses, 24-hour support. BT SurfTime
              access possible

Company: Direct Connection
Telephone: 0800 072 0000
email: sales@dircon.net
WWW Site: www.dircon.net
Notes: ISDN, 20Mb web space, unlimited email addresses

Company: Dorset Internet
Telephone: 01202 659991
email: sales@lds.co.uk
WWW Site: www.lds.co.uk
Notes: ISDN, 25Mb web space, 2 email addresses, 24-hour support

Company: Enterprise
Telephone: 01624 677666
email: sales@enterprise.net
WWW Site: www.enterprise.net
Notes: ISDN, 25Mb web space, unlimited email addresses

Company: Force 9
Telephone: 0800 073 7800
email: sales@force9.net
WWW Site: www.force9.net
Notes: ISDN, unlimited web space & email addresses

Company: FreeInternetGroup – TFI
Telephone: 020 8636 7377
email: marketing@thefreeinternet.net
WWW Site: www.thefreeinternet.net
Notes: Sign-up online, 0800 internet access 24/7, no call charges, keep your existing telecom provider, no monthly subscription fees

Company: Frontier Internet Services
Telephone: 020 7536 9090
email: info@ftech.net
WWW Site: www.ftech.net
Notes: ISDN, 25Mb web space, unlimited email addresses

Company: Global Internet
Telephone: 0870 909 8043
email: info@globalnet.co.uk
WWW Site: www.globalnet.co.uk
Notes: ISDN, 50Mb web space, unlimited email addresses

Company: Internet Central
Telephone: 01270 611000
email: sales@netcentral.co.uk
WWW Site: www.netcentral.co.uk
Notes: ISDN, 2Mb web space, 5 email addresses

Company: NetDirect Internet
Telephone: 020 7731 3311
email: info@netdirect.net.uk
WWW Site: www.home.netdirect.net.uk
Notes: ISDN, 25Mb web space, unlimited email addresses

Company: Nildram
Telephone: 0800 072 0400
email: sales@nildram.co.uk
WWW Site: www.nildram.co.uk
Notes: ISDN, 25Mb web space, unlimited email addresses

Company: Primex Information Services
Telephone: 01908 643597
email: info@alpha.primex.co.uk
WWW Site: www.primex.co.uk
Notes: ISDN, 25Mb web space, unlimited email addresses

Company: U-NET Limited
Telephone: 0845 330 8000
email: sales@u-net.net
WWW Site: www.u-net.net
Notes: ISDN, 25Mb web space, unlimited email addresses, 24-hour support

Company: UUNET
Telephone: 0500 474739
email: sales@uk.uu.net
WWW Site: www.uk.uu.net
Notes: ISDN, 50Mb web space, 5 email addresses

Company: Wave Rider Internet
Telephone: 0121 603 3888
email: info@waverider.co.uk
WWW Site: www.waverider.co.uk
Notes: ISDN, 50Mb web space, 6 email addresses

Company: Zetnet Services
Telephone: 01595 696667
email: info@zetnet.co.uk
WWW Site: www.zetnet.co.uk
Notes: ISDN, 25Mb web space, unlimited email addresses

Company: Zoo Internet
Telephone: 020 8961 7000
email: support@zoo.co.uk
WWW Site: www.zoo.co.uk
Notes: ISDN, 5Mb web space, 2 email addresses

Company:	BTClick.com
Telephone:	–
email:	–
WWW:	www.btclick.com
Notes:	Download software from website. Uses talk21 Web-based email

Company:	Cable & Wireless Internet
Telephone:	0800 0923001
email:	–
WWW:	www.cwcom.net
Notes:	Phone for software or download. 20Mb web space, 5 email addresses. Cheap call time offers available

2: UK Free Service Providers

What *is* free? As I mentioned earlier in the book, free may mean that you only pay for your connection calls, or it may mean that you don't even pay for those. If you're not paying for the calls, it's likely that you'll pay either a single fixed fee to sign up to the service, or a monthly fee of a few pounds for unlimited online time.

Remember that the details below may change as more and more companies adjust their ideas of what 'free' means to match ours. During the next year more service providers will join the BT SurfTime scheme (or an equivalent) to allow unlimited Internet call time for a fixed price: this could easily include many of the service providers in the list above as well.

Company:	Free-Online
Telephone:	0870 7060504
email:	sales@free-online.net
WWW:	www.free-online.net
Notes:	Unlimited web space & email addresses, free support

Company:	Freeserve
Telephone:	–
email:	info@freeserve.com
WWW:	www.freeserve.com
Notes:	Free disk from Dixons or PC World, or signup online. 15Mb web space, unlimited email addresses. Unlimited free evening and weekend access calls via BT SurfTime

Company: ic24
Telephone: 020 7643 3215
email: ic24@mgn.co.uk
WWW: www.ic24.net
Notes: Phone for software or download. 10Mb web space, 5 email addresses. Limited free
               access call time at weekends

Company: NTL ntlworld
Telephone: 0800 052 1815
email: –
WWW: www.ntl.co.uk
Notes: Single startup fee, unlimited free access

Company: Virgin Net
Telephone: 0500 558800
email: advice@virgin.net
WWW: www.virgin.net
Notes: Signup online. 10Mb web space, 5 email addresses. Free evening and weekend
               access calls via BT SurfTime

3: UK Online Services

The following is a list of online services available in the UK. Online services are being put under pressure by the deals offered by some of the 'free' service providers in the lists above. Although you'll probably have to pay *something* as a monthly charge, the combination of subscription and call charges may be a lot less now than it was a year ago. Remember that the quality and quantity of members-only content will vary considerably between services: try to find out exactly what you'll be getting for your money (if you have to pay for it).

Company: America Online (AOL)
Telephone: 0800 279 1234
email: queryuk@aol.com
WWW: www.aol.com
Notes: 10Mb web space, 7 email addresses, single monthly fee with fixed rate 1p per minute
               connection calls

Company: CIX
Telephone: 0845 355 5050
email: sales@cix.co.uk
WWW: www.cix.co.uk
Notes: 5Mb web space, unlimited email addresses

Company: CompuServe (CSi)
Telephone: 0870 6000 800
email: UKCSSVC@cs.com
WWW: www.compuserve.co.uk
Notes: 10mb web space, 7 email addresses, phone for software or download

Company: LineOne
Telephone: 0800 111 210
email: support@lineone.net
WWW Site: www.lineone.net
Notes: 5 email addresses, web space, sign up online

Company: MSN FreeWeb
Telephone: 0346 002000
email: —
WWW Site: msn.co.uk
Notes: Service provided via BT Click, Web-based email via Hotmail

Company: SurfLink
Telephone: 0800 053 0609
email: info@surflink.co.uk
WWW Site: www.surflink.co.uk
Notes: 2Mb web space, 5 email addresses, Web-based email

Company: UK Online
Telephone: 0800 053 0609
email: support@ukonline.net
WWW Site: www.ukonline.co.uk
Notes: Unlimited web space, sign up online or phone for software

4: UK Cyber Cafés

3W Cafe
4 Market Place, Bracknell, Berkshire RG12 1DT
Tel: 01344 862445
email: dave@3w.co.uk
www site: www.3w.co.uk

Beiderbeckes Internet Café/Restaurant
30/32 Bondgate, Darlington, County Durham
Tel: 01325 282675
email: wired@beiderbeckes.co.uk
www site: www.users.dircon.co.uk/~beider3

Cable CyberBar
Molineux Stadium, Waterloo Road, Wolverhampton WV1 4QR
Tel: 01902 651111
email: info@mbcis.co.uk
www site: www.mbcis.co.uk

Café Internet
22/24 Buckingham Palace Road, Victoria, London SW1W 0QP
Tel: 020 7233 5786
email : cafe@cafeinternet.co.uk
www site: www.cafeinternet.co.uk

CafeNet
2/3 Phoenix Court, Guildford, Surrey GU1 3EG
Tel: 01483 451945
email: internet@cafenet.co.uk
www site: www.cafenet.co.uk/

Cyberia Café
39 Whitfield Street, London W1P 5RE
Tel: 020 7681 4200
email: cyberia@easynet.co.uk
www site: www.cyberiacafe.net

Cyberia Café
73 New Broadway, Ealing W5 3AL
Tel: 020 8840 3131
email: ealing@cyberiacafe.net
www site: www.ealing.cyberiacafe.net

CyberZone
1 Dingwall Road, Croydon, Surrey CR0 2NA
Tel: 020 8681 6500
email: zone1@cyberzone.co.uk
www site: www.cyberzone.co.uk

Electric Frog
42-44 Cockburn Street, Edinburgh
Tel: 0131 226 1505
email: admin@electricfrog.co.uk
www site: www.electricfrog.co.uk

Get Surfed!
4-6 Peterborough Road, Harrow, Middlesex HA1 2BQ
Tel: 020 8426 4446
email: info@getsurfed.co.uk
www site: www.getsurfed.co.uk

Intercafé
Debenhams, Oxford Street, London
Tel: 020 7631 0063
email: managers@intercafe.co.uk
www site: www.intercafe.co.uk

NetPlay Café
8 Fletchers Walk, Paradise Circus, Birmingham B3 3HJ
Tel: 0121 248 2228
email: info@netplaycafe.co.uk
www site: www.netplaycafe.co.uk

Netscafé
9 Bennington Street, Cheltenham, Gloucestershire
Tel: 01242 232121
email: info@netscafe.co.uk
www site: www.netscafe.co.uk

Revelations
27 Shaftesbury Square, Belfast BT2 7AB
www site: www.revelations.co.uk

Window on the World Cyber Bar
Kirklees Media Centre, 7 Northumberland Street, Huddersfield, West Yorkshire HD1 1R1
email: WoW_Cafe@architechs.com
www site: www.architechs.com/mediacentre/wow_cafe

5: UK Software Companies

Company	Telephone	WWW Site
Adaptec	–	www.adaptec.com
Adobe Systems	020 8606 4008	www.adobe.co.uk
Allaire	01638 569600	www.allaire.com
Apple	020 8308 8614	www.apple.com
Asymetrix/Click2Learn	020 7517 4200	www.asymetrix.com
Attica Cybernetics	01865 791346	www.attica.com
Autodesk	01483 303322	www.autodesk.co.uk
Berkeley Systems	–	www.berksys.com
Borland	01734 320022	www.borland.com
Broderbund	01753 620909	www.broderbund.com
Brooklyn North Software Works	0500 284177	www.brooknorth.com
Claris/Filemaker	0800 422322	www.claris.com
Corel	0800 581028	www.corel.com
Delrina	020 8207 7033	www.delrina.com
Digital Workshop	01295 254590	www.digitalworkshop.co.uk
Dorling Kindersley	020 7753 3488	www.dk.com
Dr Solomons	01296 318733	www.drsolomon.co.uk
Electronic Arts	01753 549442	www.ea.com
Gold Disk	01753 832383	www.golddisk.com
Health Perfect	020 8200 8897	www.healthperfect.co.uk
IBM	023 9249 2249	www.software.ibm.com
Interplay	01235 821666	www.interplay.com
Intuit	01932 578500	www.intuit.co.uk
JASC, Inc	–	www.jasc.com
Lotus Development	01784 445808	www.lotus.com
Macromedia	020 8358 5858	www.macromedia.com
McAfee	01753 827500	www.mcafee.com

Company	Telephone	WWW Site
MetaCreations	020 8358 5858	www.metacreations.com
MGI Software	020 7365 0034	www.mgisoft.com
Micrografx	0191 5100 203	www.micrografx.com
Microsoft	0345 002000	www.microsoft.com
Mindscape	01444 246333	www.mindscape.com
NetObjects	01638 569600	www.netobjects.com
Nico Mac Computing, Inc	–	www.winzip.com
Ocean	0161 839 0999	www.infogrames.co.uk
Oki	01753 819819	www.oki.co.uk
Pegasus Software	01536 495000	www.pegasus.co.uk
Psygnosis	0151 282 3000	www.psygnosis.co.uk
Quark Systems	01483 451818	www.quark.com
Quarterdeck UK	01245 494940	www.symantec.com
RealNetworks	020 7629 4020	www.real.com
Sage	0191 255 3000	www.sage.com
Serif	0800 376070	www.serif.com
SoftKey	020 8789 2000	www.softkey.com
SoftQuad	020 8387 4110	www.sq.com
Starfish Software	020 8875 4455	www.starfish.com
Steinberg	020 8970 1924	www.steinberg-us.com
Symantec	020 7616 5600	www.symantec.com
Visio	0800 132047	www.visio.com
Wang UK	020 8568 9200	www.wang.com

6: UK Hardware Companies

Company	Telephone	WWW Site
Agfa	020 8231 4416	www.agfa.co.uk
AMD	01256 603121	www.amd.com
Award	–	www.phoenix.com
Aztech	0118981 0118	www.aztech.co.uk
Brother UK	0161 931 2354	www.brother.com
Canon	0990 143723	www.europe.canon.com
Casio	020 8450 9131	www.casio.com
Cirrus Logic	–	www.cirrus.com

Company	Telephone	WWW Site
Compaq	0845 270 4065	www.compaq.com
Creative Labs	01245 265265	www.creaf.com
Data Becker	01420 22707	www.data-becker.co.uk
Dell	0870 152 4699	www.dell.co.uk
Diamond Multimedia	01189 444400	www.diamondmm.com
Epson UK	01442 261144	www.epson.co.uk
Fujitsu	0870 128 2829	www.fujitsu.co.uk
Gravis	01296 397444	www.gravis.com
Hauppauge	020 7378 0202	www.hauppauge.com
Hayes	01276 704400	www.hayes.com
Hercules	01635 294300	www.hercules.com
Hewlett-Packard	0990 474747	www.hp.com
Hitachi	020 8848 8787	www.hitachi.com
IBM	0870 601 1036	www.ibm.com
Iiyama	01438 314417	www.iiyama.com
Imation	01344 402200	www.imation.com
Iomega	0800 973194	www.iomega-europe.com
JVC	020 8208 7654	www.jvc.com
Kodak	01442 261122	www.kodak.co.uk
IMC (Umax)	01344 872800	www.imcnet.com
Intel	01793 404900	www.intel.com
Lexmark	01628 480640	www.lexmark.com
Logitech	020 8308 6581	www.logitech.com
Matrox	01753 665500	www.matrox.com
Maxtor	01483 747356	www.maxtor.com
Microsoft	0870 601 0100	www.microsoft.com
Mitsumi	01276 29029	www.mitsumi.com
NEC Computer Products	020 8993 8111	www.nec.com
Nikon	0800 230220	www.nikon.com
Nokia	0990 003110	www.nokia.com
Oki	01753 819819	www.oki.co.uk
Olivetti	0990 111145	www.olivetti.com
Pace	0990 561001	www.pacecom.co.uk
Packard Bell	01628 508 200	www.packardbell-europe.com
Panasonic	0990 357357	www.panasonic.co.uk
Phoenix Technologies	–	www.phoenix.com

Company	Telephone	WWW Site
Pioneer	01753 789789	www.pioneer-eur.com
Plextor	–	www.plextor.com
Primax	01235 535524	www.primax.net
Psion	01908 261686	www.psiondacom.com
Samsung	020 8391 0168	www.samsung.com
Seagate	0800 783 5177	www.seagate.com
Sharp	0990 274277	www.sharp-uk.co.uk
Sony UK	0990 111999	www.sony.com
Syquest	0118 538 5857	www.syquest.com
Taxan	01344 484646	www.taxan.co.uk
Toshiba	01932 828828	www.toshiba.co.uk
Trust Peripherals	01376 502050	www.trust.com
Umax	01344 871344	www.imcnet.com
US Robotics	0800 225252	www.usr.com
Viewsonic	01293 643900	www.viewsonic.com
Visioneer	01908 260422	www.visioneer.com
Western Digital UK	01372 360055	www.wdc.com
Xerox	01429 855060	www.xerox.com
Xircom	01256 332552	www.xircom.com

7: UK Retailers

Company	Telephone	Products/WWW Site
AJP	020 8208 9744	Notebook PCs www.ajp.co.uk
Byte Direct	0500 888910	PCs/Peripherals/Software
Carrera	020 8307 2800	PCs/Notebook PCs www.carrera.co.uk
Choice Systems	020 8993 9003	PCs/Notebook PCs www.choicesystems.co.uk
Compaq	0845 270 4065	PCs/Notebook PCs/Peripherals www.compaq.com
Currys	01442 888000	PCs/Peripherals
Dabs Direct	0800 138 5120	PCs/Peripherals/Software/Consumables www.dabs.com

Company	Telephone	Products/WWW Site
Dan Technology	020 8830 1100	PCs www.dan.co.uk
Dell	0870 152 4674	PCs www.dell.co.uk
Dixons	01442 888000	PCs, Peripherals/Software/Consumables www.dixons.co.uk
Elonex	0800 542 2935	PCs, Notebook PCs www.elonex.co.uk
Evesham	0800 496 0800	PCs/Notebook PCs www.evesham.com
Gateway 2000	0800 142000	PCs, Notebook PCs www.gateway.com/uk
Grey Matter	01364 654200	Software www.greymatter.co.uk
Insight	0800 073 0730	PCs/Peripherals/Software/Components www.insight.com/uk
Javelin Computers	01254 505505	PCs/Peripherals/Components www.javelincomputers.co.uk
Mesh Computers	020 8208 4701	PCs www.meshplc.co.uk
MX2	01481 253526	Consumables www.mx2.com
NEC Direct	0870 010 6321	PCs/Notebook PCs www.necdirect-europe.com
PC World	0990 464464	PCs/Peripherals/Software/Consumables www.pcworld.co.uk
Pico Direct	0870 729 6111	Notebook PCs/Notebook peripherals www.picodirect.co.uk
Palmtops Direct	01491 822604	Handheld PCs www.palmtops.co.uk
Panrix	0113 2444 958	PCs www.panrix.co.uk
Qual Technology	01737 855800	PCs/Notebook PCs/Peripherals www.qual.co.uk

Company	Telephone	Products/WWW Site
Simply	020 8498 2100	PCs/Peripherals/Software www.simply.co.uk
Software Warehouse	0800 0355 355	PCs/Software/Peripherals/Consumables www.software-warehouse.co.uk
Tech Direct	020 8286 2222	PCs/Printers/Peripherals/Consumables www.techdirect.co.uk
The Link	01442 888000	PCs/Peripherals
Technomatic	0800 248000	PCs/Peripherals/Software/Components www.technomatic.co.uk
Time Computer Systems	0800 316 2317	PCs www.timecomputers.co.uk
Tiny Direct	0800 731 7283	PCs www.tiny.com
Viglen	0990 486 486	PCs, Notebook PCs www.viglen.co.uk
Virgin Megastore	020 7631 1234	Software www.virgin.co.uk
Watford Electronics	0800 035 5555	PCs/Software/Peripherals/Components www.watford.co.uk

8: UK Internet Services

Company	WWW Site	email	Telephone
Domain Name Registration			
DomainsNet	www.domainsnet.co.uk	support@domainsnet.com	020 7549 5341
Net Names	www.netnames.co.uk		0800 269049
Nic Names	www.nicknames.co.uk	sales@ nicknames.co.uk	0800 298 2333
Simply Names	www.simplynames.co.uk	domains@simplynames.co.uk	01684 893020
Supanames	www.supanames.co.uk		0870 741 0939
The Name	www.thename.co.uk	sales@thename.co.uk	0800 091 4242
UK Reg	www.ukreg.com	sales@ukreg.com	

Website Design			
Absolute Internet	www.absoluteinternet.com	info@ absoluteinternet.com	0800 074 6837
Digital Portfolios	www.digitalportfolios.com	webguru@digitalportfolios.com	020 7372 8584

Company	WWW Site	email	Telephone
Dreamteam Design	www.dreamteam.co.uk	info@dreamteam.co.uk	01273 204206
Imaginet	www.imaginet.co.uk	sales@imaginet.co.uk	0800 052 7194
Internet Assist	www.i-a.co.uk	info@i-a.co.uk	0800 731 2784
Moonfish	www.moonfish.co.uk	fish.market@moonfish.co.uk	0870 070 4321
Webform	www.webformdesign.co.uk	enquiries@webformdesign.co.uk	01777 860508
WWW Solutions	www.wwwsolutions.co.uk	info@wwwsolutions.co.uk	0800 783 5255

Website Hosting

Company	WWW Site	email	Telephone
CompuWeb Communications Services	www.cwcs.co.uk	info@cwcs.co.uk	0870 703 1000
DataGate	www.datagate.co.uk	sales@datagate.co.uk	020 8573 3263
The Dream Studio	www.dreamstudio.co.uk	info@dreamstudio.co.uk	01474 532023
Ebusi.net	www.ebusi.net	sales@ebusi.net	020 8748 4840
Positive Internet Company Ltd	www.positive-internet.com	good@positive-internet.com	0800 316 1006
FireByWire Ltd	www.firebywire.com	info@firebywire.com	020 7643 2241
Ghoulnet Internet Services	www.ghoulnet.com	sales@ghoulnet.com	0800 074 7581
InterHost	www.interhost.co.uk	sales@interhost.co.uk	020 8880 4613
London Web Communications	www.londonweb.net	sales@londonweb.net	0800 096 8306
Shared Knowledge	www.sharedknowledge.net	works@sharedknowledge.net	01707 885800
Skymarket	www.skymarket.co.uk	sales@skymarket.co.uk	0800 915 9159
Web Tapestry	www.webtapestry.net	info@webtapestry.net	0800 015 1718
WinBiz	www.winbiz.co.uk	sales@winzib.co.uk	0800 027 0340

Merchant Services

Company	WWW Site	email	Telephone
Barclays Merchant Services	www.bms.barclays.com		0800 616161
NetBanx	www.netbanx.com	sales@netbanx.com	01223 847175
SecureTrading	www.securetrading.com	sales@securetrading.com	0800 0289151
WorldPay	www.worldpay.com	sales@uk.worldpay.com	01223 715151

9: UK General Services

Data Transfer, Conversion, Duplication

AL Downloading Services	020 8994 5471	www.aldownloading.co.uk
Media Direct	0800 000441	

Data Recovery (Disk failure, corruption, viruses)

DataQuest International	07071 880025	www.welcome.to/dataquest-international
OnTrack Data Recovery	0800 10121314	www.ontrack.co.uk
Vogon International	0800 581263	www.vogon-international.com

PC Rental

MC Rentals	01952 603534	
Hire-Ring	020 8838 5495	
Skylake Rentals	0800 373118	
Team Management PC Hire	020 7702 9242	www.pchire.com

PC Security/Anti-theft

Microcosm	0117 983 0084
Secure PC	020 7610 6611

PC Memory

AW Memory	01382 807000	
Crucial Technology	0800 013 0330	www.crucial.com/uk
Memory Express	0870 900 9500	
Offtek	0800 698 4100	www.offtek.co.uk
UKMemory.com	01948 663666	www.ukmemory.com

Printer Consumables

Big Rom	0800 074 4283	
Cartridge Club	0800 328 5072	
Cartridge Express	08000 267023	www.consumables.net
CompuJet	0800 026 7435	
InkSpot	020 8953 9192	www.inkspot.co.uk
Inky Fingers	0870 241 0229	www.inkjetuk.com
Jetica	01603 748002	
Manx Print Care	0800 0566610	www.mcb.net/jettmanx
Squire International	0800 698 7474	www.squire.co.uk
Themis	0800 376 8980	

Blank Disks/Storage

Owl Associates	01543 250377	
Product Trade & Services	0800 136502	
Squire International	0800 698 7474	www.squire.co.uk

INDEX

ACKNOWLEDGEMENTS

Although only one name finds its way onto the front cover, it takes the efforts of a huge team of people to turn my scribbles into a finished book. My warmest thanks go to everyone involved for doing what they do so well, and in particular:

Clare Christian, my commissioning editor, who starts everything rolling, and then keeps it rolling until the book arrives on the shelves.

Sally Carter and Kathryn Ekstrom, the production editors: my scribbles go in, a book comes out. How does that happen?

Rachel Hackworth and the whole marketing team, without whom the rest of us would be a waste of space!

Tracey Smith at Pantek Arts for lending us her superb design and editorial skills.

WHAT'S ON
THE CD-ROMs?

Licensing Agreement

This book comes with a CD software package. By opening this package, you are agreeing to be bound by the following:

The software contained on this CD is, in many cases, copyrighted, and all rights are reserved by the individual licensing agreements associated with each piece of software contained on the CD. THIS SOFTWARE IS PROVIDED FREE OF CHARGE, AS IS, AND WITHOUT WARRANTY OF ANY KIND, EITHER EXPRESSED OR IMPLIED, INCLUDING, BUT NOT LIMITED TO, THE IMPLIED WARRANTIES OF MERCHANTABILITY AND FITNESS FOR A PARTICULAR PURPOSE. Neither the book publisher nor its dealers and its distributors assumes any liability for any alleged or actual damages arising for the use of this software.

What's On The CD-ROMs?

The first thing you need to look at is the WHSmith.co.uk CD-ROM, giving you fast and easy access to the outstanding WHSmith Internet service. Turn to the back of the book for details about how to use the WHSmith.co.uk CD-ROM to get online and start surfing.

Next, take a look at all the goodies packed onto the UK Internet Starter Kit CD-ROM to help you get the most from this book and your Internet connection.

The UK Internet Starter Kit CD-ROM

Chapter-by-Chapter
Every chapter in the book has its own section on the CD containing instant links to all the great websites mentioned in that chapter, along with one-click installation of the recommended software. Keep this section on your screen as you read each chapter so that you can explore all these great sites and services as you read about them.

Software Directory

You've probably noticed the *It's On The CD!* icons scattered throughout the book, indicating that the software program you're reading about can be installed straight from the CD-ROM. You can install all those programs from the Chapter-by-Chapter section, but there's a lot more software on the CD than I've mentioned in the book – multimedia plug-ins and viewers, graphics and HTML utilities, indispensable 'gadgets & gizmos', and much more. The Software Directory section provides descriptions, screenshots, web page links and easy one-click installation of *every* software title included on the CD.

HTML Reference

The superb WHSmith.co.uk service gives you free disk space to create your own website. But where do you start? Start with Chapters 23–25 in this book, and then go to the HTML Reference section, where you'll find a mass of examples and explanations sorted into categories such as Images & Multimedia, Links, Colours, and Tips & Tricks. Whether you want to learn more about HTML or just see some ideas in action and copy the examples into your own pages, the answers are all at your fingertips.

Web Directory

Along with the hundreds of sites given in the book, and the clickable links to them all in the Chapter-by-Chapter section of the CD-ROM, I've included well over 1000 more in the Web Directory section. Sites are sorted into 24 categories such as Music, Travel, Computing, Humour and Web Authoring. Just pick a category, click a link, and enjoy!

How Do I Get To All This Stuff?

Just insert the CD into your CD-ROM drive and the Autorun program should start automatically after a few seconds. If it doesn't, choose Run from the Start menu, type **d:\autorun** (replacing 'd' with the drive letter of your CD-ROM drive if necessary) and press Enter.

First, click on **View ReadMe File** to read essential information about using the CD, installing the accompanying software titles, and easy instructions for setting up Microsoft® Internet Explorer. When you're ready to continue, click **Start!** in the Autorun program. This will open the index page of the CD in your web browser. In true Web point-and-click style, you can browse through all the great CD-ROM sections mentioned above.

Now you've read all about the **Internet**, you'll want to get **online**.
It's **free** to get **online** with

WHSmith.co.uk

The WHSmith.co.uk difference

▶ **Free** Internet access

Unlimited access with no setup charge or monthly fee – you only pay for the cost of local phone calls.

▶ **Free** email accounts

Unlimited email addresses, so each member of the family can have their own private mailbox.

▶ **Free** Cyber Patrol

Usual price £39.95. This is great for families as it automatically screens out unsuitable material from the net.

▶ **Free** Web site kit

Enables you to create and publish your very own Web site.

▶ Online **shopping** with WHSmith

Our Internet shops are completely secure and offer an amazing range of books, CDs, films, games, magazines and stationery.

▶ The **Education Zone**

Free access to the *Hutchinson Family Encyclopedia* (including a National Curriculum guide) and a wealth of other in-depth information for students, parents and teachers alike.

▶ **Entertainment** online

Latest news and reviews for books, films, albums and games, and a great place to share your own opinions with others.

▶ The best of the **net**

The latest news 24 hours a day, plus our selection of the most useful and entertaining services and sites on the Internet.

WHSmith.co.uk system requirements

Check here to find out what computer hardware and memory you need to use the WHSmith Internet software

▶ **Computer/processor**
486DX/66 MHz or higher processor

▶ **Operating system**
Windows 95/98 or Windows NT 4.0

▶ **Memory**
16MB Ram for Windows 95/98
or 24MB RAM for Windows NT 4.0

▶ **Disk space required for installation**
100MB for full installation

▶ **Other**
CD-ROM Drive, Modem & Telephone or ISDN Adapter and Digital Line

How to get online

To install the WHSmith.co.uk software your computer must have a CD-ROM drive, a modem and at least 100MB of free disk space.

1   Insert the WHSmith.co.uk CD, at the back of this book, into your CD-ROM drive. Click the orange ellipse next to '**Install Internet Explorer 5**'.

2   Click '**I accept the agreement**' – you must accept the licence agreement before installing the WHSmith.co.uk software. Click the '**Next>**' button.

3   Select '**Install now – Typical set of components**' then click the '**Next>**' button.

4   Click the '**Finish**' button on the '**Restart computer**' screen.

5   Once your computer restarts, please read our customer contract. Click '**Finish Installation**'.

You are now ready to access the internet.
Simply click the '**WHSmithOnline powered by BTClick**' icon on your desktop. To register for email, Cyber Patrol and Web space, click on the relevant link on the menu bar.

Need help?

At first the Internet can be a confusing place. **WHSmith.co.uk** helps guide you through to make sure you get the most out of the Internet. Our helplines are open daily from 8 a.m. to 11 p.m.

If you have problems with Internet access call
0870 240 0910
(charged at the national rate)

For problems with talk21 call
0906 302 2233
(charged at 50p per minute)

New customer offer

Save £5 !

As a first-time customer of WHSmith.co.uk you'll save £5 when you purchase online.

▶ **Shopping couldn't be easier**

All you have to do is spend £30.00 (excluding postage and packaging) to qualify for this offer.

WHSmith.co.uk